THE GOLDEN THREAD

WHERE TO FIND PURPOSE IN THE STAGES OF YOUR LIFE

THE GOLDEN THREAD

WHERE TO FIND PURPOSE IN THE STAGES OF YOUR LIFE

Holly Woods, PhD

NEW DEGREE PRESS

THE GOLDEN THREAD

Where to Find Purpose in the Stages of Your Life

ISBN		
	978-1-64137-502-3	*Paperback*
	978-1-64137-503-0	*Kindle Ebook*
	978-1-64137-504-7	*Ebook*

EARLY PRAISE FOR
THE GOLDEN THREAD
BY HOLLY WOODS

———

We are living in extraordinary times of darkness and light as we navigate the shifts into kosmic awakening. Holly Woods has crafted an important and outstanding contribution to the map of this journey. As Holly combines the emerging research on consciousness and finding purpose in our lives, she includes stories of clients and a deep dive into her own life journey, bringing a richness of real-life experience. Holly's rare and radical transparency courageously reflects her deep commitment to finding the deepest meaning and purpose in our lives. My deepest hope is that we all will have this kind of willingness. It will change our lives and our world.

MARJ BRITT, ED.D., AUTHOR, YOUR SOUL'S INVISIBLE
CODES, FOUNDER CALLED BY LOVE INSTITUTE

The Golden Thread is a deeply insightful and enjoyable read about purpose as a GPS throughout all stages of our lives. Can't recommend it enough!

CHIP CONLEY, NY TIMES BESTSELLING

AUTHOR, CEO OF JOIE DE VIVRE HOSPITALITY,

FOUNDER MODERN ELDER ACADEMY

If you want a straightforward analysis of the science and psychological adventure of discovering purpose, this book has it all. Holly Woods takes us on a heartfelt journey in a humorous, brutally honest and authentic display of her decades of knowledge in the field. If you truly want to find your purpose, read this book. If you are not sure if you want to find your purpose, then you absolutely must read this book. It will make you think deeply about your own golden thread and change your life.

EMANUEL KUNTZELMAN, FOUNDER GREENHEART

INTERNATIONAL AND GLOBAL PURPOSE MOVEMENT,

EDITOR PURPOSE RISING AND PURPOSE TO THE PEOPLE.

How does life purpose evolve as we grow older? Is the experience of Dante's "Dark Wood" unique on each life journey? The continuities and discontinuities of our lives are connected in mysterious ways that become ever more complex. Much depends on discovering, aligning, and responding to this Golden Thread. Holly's writing exquisitely holds the creative tension between discovery and guidance, clarity and mystery, personal and universal. It guides by enabling the reader with maps, signs, and inspiration to stay true to the Golden Thread that illumines the way to our unique destiny.

AFTAB OMER PH.D., PRESIDENT, MERIDIAN UNIVERSITY

Holly Woods dives deep into purpose to show us how elemental purpose is in shaping our critical personal and business decisions and results. She reflects on her own life's journey and others' stories to explore the stages of purpose, how to clarify our purpose, and where that journey can take us. I highly recommend this book for business and organizational leaders and those who want to evolve their business and brands to be more authentic, impactful, and sustainable.

LAURIE PILLINGS RINKER, BRAND AND BUSINESS STRATEGIST, AND PRINCIPAL OF BRANDS THAT DELIVER™.

The Golden Thread comes at the perfect time, shining light on our shadowy times. In an accessible way, Holly Woods gifts us with inspiring stories reflecting her vast life-lived experiences, shares her intellectual genius in synthesizing a massive amount of purpose work, and reveals a practical path for activating our own purpose. There are so many reasons I encourage you to read The Golden Thread right now, including seeing how your purpose develops over your lifetime, finding resources, being inspired by others' purpose journeys.

Holly, thank you for this massive missive.

SUSAN LUCCI, FOUNDER & CIRCLE FACILITATOR AT 2BIG4WORDS, AND CONTRIBUTING AUTHOR, PURPOSE RISING AND CO-AUTHOR THE PURPOSE FIELD GUIDE

This is a passionate book, appropriately enough, about finding your purpose and passion, written by a woman who has clearly found both. Supported by moving stories and hard data, Holly Woods demonstrates how each of us can find our calling and so live fuller, more satisfying, and more contributory lives.

ROGER WALSH MD, PHD, PROFESSOR, UNIVERSITY

OF CALIFORNIA, AUTHOR OF ESSENTIAL

SPIRITUALITY: THE SEVEN CENTRAL PRACTICES

Holly Woods offers a clear narrative of what purpose is, how we can find it, and what stops us from fully expressing it. The Golden Thread speaks to the war between the lie of separation and the truth of wholeness and connection to the Source of all that is. As we move through life, our sense of purpose becomes the golden thread that guides us home to the truth, even while changing its expression over time. Holly shows us clearly that while purpose and woundings dance together to shape the direction of our lives, purpose leads the dance. Filled with case studies of individuals who have found and are living their purpose, she shows us how others have found their purpose and lived the various expressions of it. I can affirm that it's worth the work to uncover yours. The Golden Thread can help you find it.

JOHANNA LYMAN, FOUNDER AND CEO, NEXTGEN ORGS,

BOARD PRESIDENT, CONSCIOUS CAPITALISM

OF THE SAN FRANCISCO BAY AREA

Holly Woods' incredibly refreshing and deep exploration of the real meaning of purpose and its lifelong influence on each of us has made a significant contribution to the field. All those who help others improve their lives will find much here to expand and inform their practices. I especially recommend The Golden Thread to all who truly want to understand the nature of their own deep inner purpose and its influence on their lives."

DON MCCREA, PHD, FAMILY & SMALL BUSINESS EXIT COACH, FOUNDER YOUR BUSINESS LEGACY

The Golden Thread is truly golden in helping us to find and follow our purpose, as it shape-shifts throughout our development. Holly's book is a blessing to put feet on the ground for some critical thought during these tumultuous times when so many of us are, as Robert Kegan says, "in over our heads."

VIV HAWKINS, INTEGRAL COACH & SPIRITUAL DIRECTOR, FOUNDER OF LIFECALLS

In The Golden Thread," Holly Woods takes readers on a journey of self-discovery, helping them reimagine their lives with more purpose, meaning and joy. It's a powerful antidote for these chaotic times.

WENDY MARX, AUTHOR OF THRIVING AT 50 PLUS.

This book is dedicated to
my daughters,
Lindsey and Laurel,
who are my
Reason for Being.

ACKNOWLEDGMENTS

———

Each person who enters my life comes with a gift to share, either obvious in its contribution or not so much. I now recognize that the opportunities to love and evolve exist simultaneously.

I acknowledge a lifetime of friends, family, colleagues, and others I hold dear, who have held my heart in surprising success or more somber difficult moments. Most notably, I cherish my daughters Lindsey and Laurel, my father Glen, his wife Karen, and my sister Vicky.

I've been graced with a handful of wonderful friends who've watched me struggle and grow into each next phase, who shake their heads at my traumas and breathe sighs of relief at my persistence. When you're a nomad like me, enduring friendships are challenging, and yet a handful have been Rocks of Gibraltar. I will be forever grateful to Chris Morris, Donna Duffy, Jeanne Briggs, Nancy Robbins, Agathe Daae-Qvale, Jeffrey Smith, Barry Auchettl, Carista Luminare, Quiana Grace Frost, Carol Benson, Amanda Cruise, Katherine Lee, Don McCrea, and Katy Bray, who all had my back and nudged me to live up to my full potential. And I'm blessed by a long list of souls with whom I've traversed rugged mountains, paddled stormy waters, or communed in the field each week on the open dance floor of life.

I've been blessed with many amazing mentors and colleagues, some of whom I interviewed here. I'd also like to thank Desda Zuckerman, Stephen Busby, Jessica Dibb, Terry Patten, Karin Carrington, Michael Wolff, Susan Frederick, Laura Divine, and Joanne Hunt, and others with whom I have navigated the rocky roads.

I'd like to thank Professor Eric Koester of the Creator Institute, and the many creative souls at New Degree Press. Special thanks to my beta-reader community, whose feedback was invaluable.

And I am humbled by the army of Beings who have graced my life with their guidance and care, and with whom I traveled this great distance.

> *"May the positive forces,*
> *whatever be their name,*
> *render me worthy of accessing*
> *the mysteries of Synchronicity.*
> *Here I am; I am ready.*
> *Here I am;*
> *I breathe and participate*
> *in the wave of the moment*
> *of Synchronicity.*
> *So be it."*

OBERTO AIRAUDI, THE BOOK OF SYNCHRONICITY

HOW TO READ
THIS BOOK

This book has many parts and one purpose.

Just like you.

Some parts of the book may appeal to you more than others. I'd suggest that you review the Table of Contents and decide what you may want to derive from the book. What are the reasons you picked up this book to read in the first place?

Then, start with what inspires you.

The **Introduction** is obviously an overview of the book, where you'll read the stories and curiosities that inspired the book and come to understand why the questions must be asked and answered.

Chapter 1 explains the hypotheses about the Golden Thread that will be explored in chapters 3 through 6.

Chapter 2 gives an overview of a few philosophies, frameworks, and practices behind finding purpose; the current science that demonstrates the importance of purpose in our lives; and why you should set out to find your Golden Thread.

Chapters 3 provides an overview of the frameworks that help to show where purpose lives in the stages of your life.

Chapters 4 to 6 provide detail about the early, middle, and late stages of your life, as well as individual stories about how the Golden Thread shows up distinctly with the nuanced expression of purpose over time.

Chapter 7 attempts to make meaning out of what's been discussed and guide you to derive your own meaning as well.

Chapter 8 describes what I believe are the most significant actions we should be taking—each of us and all of us. I hope you'll concur after reading all that comes before, and that you may find additional inspiration for your own life.

Chapter 9 shares why your purpose is foundational in your own life and suggests four important principles for your own purposeful path.

Most chapters start with an introduction and end with a conclusion that help you gain the most significant ideas presented in the chapter.

Many chapters conclude with my "Notes from the Field," having observed as a scientist and practitioner how the Golden

Thread manifests in people's lives. You may have additional notes to add.

You'll also find a "Self-Reflection" section at the end of each chapter. You may choose to use these guiding questions as inspiration for uncovering the Golden Thread in your own life.

Lastly, if you find the ideas and guidance here inspirational, go make use of it. Share it with others. In addition to links to and resources from my own work in chapter 9, you'll find a link to resources from other practitioners or companies that may better suit you. For all our sakes, please find your Golden Thread and weave it into your life.

CONTENTS

INTRODUCTION

The room was packed. I hadn't expected that.

In fact, when I entered to prepare, I put away at least half the chairs because I expected no one would come to hear.

But I was wrong.

As the session was about to start, people kept trickling in. In fact, they were tripping over each other trying to get a chair. A couple of men helped to pull back out the clunky chairs I had stacked. People walking in late stood at the sides of the room or hastily pulled out another chair, clanging the chair legs against each other as they tried to quietly sit down.

I took a deep breath. Now I was nervous. Before, I was just going to have a conversation with a circle of friends about my hunches and observations from my work with clients. But now, this gathering was going to be a real presentation, and I would have to use those damn slides I put together at midnight the night before. I'd procrastinated until the last minute, when I finally realized I didn't have any way out of this presentation and would really have to show up and share what I knew with the world.

I took another deep breath, wiped my sweaty palms, and started.

This book was inspired by that room full of colleagues at the Global Purpose Summit in 2018, and by a number of my mentors, some of whom I interviewed for this book. Many were excited about my insights and the patterns I was seeing in my clients, and they kept pestering me to share what I know, so they could do their own work better.

But like most of us, I wasn't prepared to share "all of me" in the world until that day, when my friends and colleagues insisted that I be more of myself. I'd postponed writing about my work and wisdom about purpose until the call could no longer be ignored.

Like many other times in my life, I was called into what I "can't not do," which you'll see is underneath the "thread" that pulls us into a more truthful expression of ourselves. And thus, this book was born.

I hope this book will inspire all of us to see what we "can't not do," so we can all live more purposeful lives.

WHY IN THE WORLD DOES PURPOSE MATTER?

There is no passion to be found in playing small—in settling for a life that is less than the one you are capable of living.

—NELSON MANDELA

Recently, a remarkable number of people of all ages across the planet have become concerned with purpose as an indicator of having lived a successful life—more than wealth, a prestigious career, or positions of notoriety (NetImpact, 2012). Even in the corporate sector, purpose is being reported as among the top three indicators of a successful career (Levit & Licina, 2011).

And for good reason. Even though the field of "purpose science" is fairly young, purpose seems to have a positive effect on two primary areas of significance in our lives: health and well-being, and success (financial and otherwise). See Chapter Two for a more thorough review of the scientific literature about purpose.

But, as a teaser, purpose affects personal income and wealth, financial performance of a business, employee performance and engagement, leadership, job satisfaction, and corporate/business strategy. In the health arena, purpose affects lifespan (longevity), acute and chronic health conditions, mental health and well-being, self-care and screening, emotional regulation, learning, memory and cognition, sex and love, along with much more that you'll read about later in this book.

Knowing your purpose—and living it—positively affects every facet of your life, leading more and more people to want it.

Yet, despite this significant surge in the drive to live purposefully, the field of purpose, the data, and my own experience suggest that most people aren't able, ready, or willing to do the seeking. And even if most people are ready and willing, they don't know how to find it or know it to accomplish these significant outcomes.

While more and more people are craving an awareness of their purpose, meaningful lives of greater contribution, and a feeling of fulfillment and satisfaction in the course of their daily lives, most don't know how to get there.

SO WHAT'S THE PROBLEM? WHY CAN'T PEOPLE FIND (AND LIVE) THEIR PURPOSE?

The best things in life make you sweaty.

—EDGAR ALLEN POE

Most psychologists agree that almost no one is born knowing their purpose, but that most often purpose needs to be found, created, or learned (Baumeister & Vohs, 2006; Frankl, 2006; Maddi, 1970; Park, Park, & Peterson, 2010). The vast majority of individuals must, therefore, embark on some sort of search or developmental process.

My own life experience, along with that of other practitioners and scholars of purpose (Keyes 2011), suggests the search for purpose can be daunting, stress-inducing, and a temporarily isolating endeavor, especially without guidance or support. Victor Frankl, an Austrian neurologist and psychiatrist and later a Holocaust survivor, wrote *Man's Search for Meaning* (1946), in which he observed that the search process often leads to inner tension, frustration, and distress.

This condition of psychosocial distress related to seeking purpose is termed "Purpose Anxiety," or the "negative emotions experienced in direct relation to the search for purpose— experienced either while struggling to find or struggling to enact one's purpose in life" (Rainey, 2014).

Yet, actually finding and living a purposeful life is well worth the discomfort because of the abundance of positive life outcomes associated with doing so.

But that's not all. The process of searching for purpose is a transformative growth experience, creating an organic evolution of consciousness or human development. And, as this book will illustrate, the search for purpose is also key to the discovery of your true identity, and thus, the path to finding your way home to yourself.

In this book, I'll share through stories that the search for purpose not only allows you to claim and deliver the greatest contributions you came to make, but also liberates the wounding of your childhood and adulthood so you can become the whole, complete and fulfilled human you were born to become. And purpose is right there with you, all along, if you know how to look for it.

HOW MY PURPOSE LED ME HERE

Failure is simply the opportunity to begin again, this time more intelligently.

—HENRY FORD

Success is not a good teacher; failure makes you humble.

—SHAH RUKH KHAN

If failure makes one more intelligent and humble, I'm especially qualified to write this book. Almost every step of this lifetime has sent me down a path in seemingly the *wrong* direction to live a purposeful life, which gave me deep compassion and great insight by figuring out how all these "wrong turns" were indeed useful.

Perhaps it would be easier to tell you what traumas, tragedy, or heartache I *haven't* experienced, rather than those I have. I ultimately figured out that each tragedy (if used well enough) offers us two gifts: first, a glimpse into the "shadow" side of our identity, and secondly, the "gift" of recalibrating our focus so that we can be more intentional and directed toward our purpose.

One of the things that got me through my trauma-filled life was the consistent "voices" I heard in early childhood that told me I had something important to do with my life. I was shy about having voices and mystical experiences as a child, so I kept it to myself. And then the voices left until later in life, as they returned when I'd begun to heal the trauma and become embodied again.

I learned early in childhood to stand up to the abusive nature of my mother, who had an undiagnosed mental illness. I vividly recall standing in the kitchen, age four, with my little fist raised, staring angrily at my mom, who was about to hit me.

I yelled, "You can't hit me anymore," trembling with fear for the likely repercussions that would come from standing up to her.

She gasped and stopped mid-strike. Her hesitation and wide eyes indicated she obviously hadn't expected that from such a small being. She stood there for a moment, unsure of her next action, then slowly turned back to the sink. Not another word was uttered.

Not only did I succeed in stopping my mother's slaps and swats from then on, but I learned that I could defend my younger sister under similar circumstances. While other forms of abuse continued, I experienced some recognition that I had a power to wield even while small.

I became a formidable truth-teller at an early age, which yielded great power and authority. It also wreaked significant havoc on future careers and relationships. I didn't know then that "truth-telling" would be a major part of my identity and my purpose. It has become the psychic scalpel I use to help my clients uncover and claim their purposeful lives.

My mother's deep unrest also invited me as a child to nurture her, the parent. I remember seeing my mother sitting on our couch one sweltering summer afternoon in our Houston-area home. We'd had a traumatic morning—my two sisters, my mother, and me—involving much yelling, screaming, and crying. My mother was reading the paper with a glass of iced tea.

I sat down next to her.

"I love you," I told her, hoping to be welcomed into her arms.

She smiled, acknowledging my words, pulling me into her side. We embraced, holding each other's cracked hearts and licking our wounds together, both as fragile and strong as the bond we created.

Loving unconditionally, powerfully, compassionately, was a hallmark of my childhood and later adulthood, when I came to see that one of the expressions of my purpose was to "shine love onto shadow." I've used this capacity as a mother, practitioner, and in relationships.

As I floated through relationships and marriages, attempting to fill the bottomless pit that was my need to be seen and heard, each relationship offered me a glimpse of myself that I was unable to grasp until later. Because of my doctoral work and research in human development, as well as decades of therapy and other modalities recovering from my own depression and suicidal tendencies of several decades, I was hyper-alert to the issues that occurred in a relationship. Often, my need to be heard created a firestorm related to the "truths" I shared in trying to liberate us from the suffering. Which in fact, I did, but often at the expense of the love and compassion that had initially prompted the lesson.

At one point in my last marriage, I nearly died, hopeless and drowning in the culture of neglect and denial related to substance abuse in the ski resort town where we lived in central Colorado. My marriage and one of my stepsons had succumbed to the disastrous consequences of alcoholism. I spiraled ever downward, silenced by the rage and bullying of my husband and by my own suicidal despair. I was only buoyed by the need to parent my own two children, knowing I had to hang on for their sake.

During this time, I saw an internist who was treating a few of my immuno-suppressed systems. After reviewing my medical chart and the latest lab results for the twelve chronic conditions that I'd developed during this time, he came and stood in front of me. He looked me squarely in the face.

"You're just going to have to live with these issues. There's nothing I can do." He took a breath and waited for my response.

I looked at him, taking in the kindness in his eyes and the pain he was experiencing at having to share this news.

"There's nothing you can do?" I reviewed the handwritten list of conditions that I'd brought to my exam that day. Maybe

I'd been hoping he had a miracle up his sleeve for at least some of the diagnoses on my list. I waited for an unlikely response, praying I was somehow mistaken about what I'd heard. I wanted to live. Really, I did.

"No." He waited another moment, attempting to cradle the hopelessness of the situation. "But I can recommend a good pain clinic in Denver that will help make it easier for you."

I was sitting on the raised table in the exam room, the patient gown exposing my heart and soul—broken open. The kind doctor I'd known for a few years was compassionate and caring but had no idea what choices he was making me face.

I could quit. Call it good. I'd tried mightily and seemed unable to find an end to the relentless challenges this life-time was bringing me. Or I could stand up and fight for what I knew was my birthright. To live a noble life, to find the reason I had come back to this fucked-up life after all, to figure out what I'd signed up for and why I'd had to endure all this suffering.

I'd already found my way into deep spiritual practice and began hearing the callings for a more intentional path a few years prior, so I knew a way out had to exist. I vowed that day that I would neither kill myself nor live in constant pain. I swore that I would not live a life of quiet desperation. One in which I was a victim to circumstances. One in which I would never be who I was meant to be.

As Michael Meade describes of the choices he was forced to make in his own life in a similar scenario, "In the sudden grip of both life and death, I had to tell a story, I had to become what was seeded within me. In doing that, I began the process of coming to know myself" (Meade, 2010, *Fate and Destiny*). I'm glad to have chosen, rather than allowing the circumstances of my life to choose for me.

Purpose anxiety was never something I experienced, mostly because I'd had to fight so hard to stay alive that I was fighting for my purpose as a means of truly living.

My own transformational (and nomadic) life has kept me on the veritable evolutionary edge of existence in this lifetime. Each calling to the next career, relationship, or fertile ground on the planet I call home has offered me another opportunity to "sharpen the saw" of my craft, refine the gift, integrate the fractured parts to become a whole human, and embody the purpose that I came to live.

I've learned that the more I accept and honor each of the seeming "mistakes" I've made in life, along with the circumstances which I fell "victim" to, the more easily I can see the shadow and thus the gift of the experience. The more easily I can be called into my next evolutionary leap, as the swirling invitation to "fight entropy" unfolds before me (Swanson).

In fact, I now see the circumstances of my childhood as a cause of my effort to amplify my gifts to survive the context of my family. My mother periodically exclaimed to my two sisters and me that she wished "I'd never had you." And while those words were painful to hear from a parent, I realized that this experience was one of many in my life that forced me to choose to survive so I could truly become myself.

My childhood context also pushed me to figure out how to use my gifts wisely, so I wouldn't repeat the experience with my own children. I changed my doctoral focus to human development when I was pregnant with my first child because I realized I didn't know what the hell I was going to do as a parent, and I sure wasn't going to repeat what I'd been through.

Each of the debacles I found myself in growing up and in adulthood forced me to figure out how to survive it, giving me this creative capacity to expand myself and the circumstances so I could live through it. Over time, my curiosity grew and I began to see how the circumstances were benefiting me. With each of the traumas, I was gaining a "gift." And thus, my journey became a deep inquiry into how to find and live my one authentic life, using everything I experienced as fodder. Living On Purpose.

It takes courage to grow up and become who you really are.

—E. E. CUMMINGS

WHY I DO WHAT I DO IN THE WORLD, AND HOW IT AFFECTS YOU

I call myself a purpose activator. I am a "bridge" between the spiritual and physical realms, among other things. The job is not one for sissies; it requires guiding people into their soul calling or essential nature. It's cutting-edge and courageous work, trying to engage, inspire, and encourage people to reach their highest potential, and then providing support to them as they build lives, careers, or businesses around that.

But because of my psychic capacity and expanded consciousness, I can help my clients see what they can't, including their optimal products, gaps in their systems and infrastructure, and their own blind spots.

I'm also a business and organizational consultant and master coach and mentor, working with inspired leaders, visionaries, innovators, and changemakers whose purpose-driven dreams, visions, organizations, and businesses are changing the world, and who want to accelerate their impact, influence, and inspiration. I help them navigate the personal and business challenges of building or scaling their meaningful product and infrastructures into more profitable business.

In my more than thirty-five years of helping hundreds of clients live into their true potential and purpose, I've discovered principles to guide people in living their purpose (more on this in chapter 9). These principles make up the *Purpose to Impact Roadmap*™, the foundation for my work with individuals, groups, and businesses or organizations.

You can download the *Purpose to Impact Roadmap*™:

http://bit.ly/PurposeImpactRoadmap

Explore and learn more about my coaching/mentoring and consulting work, in addition to gaining access to courses, group programs, workshops and speaking opportunities:

http://hollywoodscoaching.com

This proven model guides people to:

- **Align** with their true purpose so they can create Clarity about who they are, Confidence to create aligned lives, products and systems, and uncover and commit to their Contribution for more impact.
- Create an **Agile** approach to life and work, designing careers and products or services that respond to strategic markets while they create systems aligned with purpose. This agile alignment with Purpose and Possibility will create more Profit through strategic decisions and aligned infrastructure to grow or scale their businesses.
- **Amplify** their careers or businesses to have more Impact, Influence, and Inspiration through structures that support their career transitions or business systems to rock the world with their purpose-driven products and offers.

It calls on all the facets of my own purpose to accomplish these tasks on my clients' behalf (see chapter 9.)

I'm a scientist and student of human evolution. I began studying human development as an undergrad, earned my doctorate in human and organizational development, and have worked in the human development/human potential arena for thirty-five years. I am a Certified Integral Master Coach® and have studied and regularly use the Stages of Consciousness framework in my own practice. Most significantly, in raising four children, I had the chance to examine the complexities and nuances of child and youth development firsthand in several unique and fascinating beings.

I'm a social and spiritual activist, because I'm helping to create a better world full of evolved humans, taking us to our next stage of humanity. My visionary and psychic capacities—as well as my polymath orientation—come in handy when contemplating my own and the world's next steps.

Those of us who are true purpose practitioners are not so visible or even credible, as compared to activists attempting to remedy the imbalance of social injustice or inequity. Most social activists are lauded as courageous and heroic because the issues are so blatant and concrete, unlike inspiring and aligning people with their purposeful lives.

Helping people uncover their Soul Purpose and live it is like finding a needle in a haystack, pulling teeth, and playing a game of hide-and-seek all at the same time. Most of us have learned to hide our true nature so completely, to protect our false identity and to avoid the shame of our wounding, that we'll do almost anything to prevent being "found out." And the irony is that we want to find our way home, to the place of unconditional love and true power. And despite being required to help people navigate their own manipulations, I believe I'm among the most blessed people on the planet, to get to see people's souls and call them to their life's work.

I'm intensely curious about how we'll navigate the increasingly complex and challenging world we find ourselves in and craft solutions to help us travel there with more grace than fear. The Stages of Consciousness discussed in this book, developed by Terri O'Fallon and her team (chapters 3-6), have guided me in my own journey and inform my work, along with other models and many modalities.

But as you can see from my story above, I didn't come to my purpose straightaway. I've had to find my way into each next expression of purpose by hook or crook. You'll read many case studies throughout the book (including mine) related to how people came into their own Golden Thread in different stages of life.

I've come to know some of the facets of my purpose as these:

I Speak Powerful Truths to Shine Love onto Shadow to Liberate Soul's Potential and Reunite Love and Power.

Refining each facet of my purpose has created trial, tribulation, and terror since my childhood, and I continue to polish it to this day. As for most of us, claiming my purpose and the wisdom that accompanies it took decades because:

- I clearly didn't know what my purpose was; my wounding kept me hiding and my purpose cloaked. I lived a painful (yet functional) "default" life for years. Needless to say, I suffered a lot.
- Even when I was living some version of my purpose, it was raw and vulnerable and messy, and I didn't express it well. No one (including me) could tell that it had anything to do with my purpose.
- I kept looking for a version of purpose that would have Angels delivering it with a certificate or have bells and whistles attached to it to let me know it was there. I had no clue that it looked different in different stages of life, or that it would come wrapped as the illuminated *and* shadowy parts of myself.

I believe coming to grips with "finding ourselves," making our greatest contribution, despite and because of our shadows and struggles, and sharing it with the world should just not take so long.

And, more recently, an updated purpose statement is related to taking us all to the next stage of humanity.

The purpose of this book and my work in the world is to help us liberate our souls to have a life of love and power—to express our purpose in the world in such powerful ways that we, and the planet, will never be the same.

And thus, the thesis of this book (detailed in chapter 1):

- Purpose is "findable," if you know where and how to look and are willing to listen closely.
- There's a "thread" that runs through our lives, albeit varying by the phase of life, that gives us remarkable and significant clues to make our "search" easier.
- Seeking (and uncovering) purpose also resolves significant aspects of the challenges, distractions, and wounding that keep you stuck and suffering. It's just part of the package.

Most people would definitely choose to live on purpose, if they thought such a feat was attainable. My client work over the last thirty-plus years and my own life have demonstrated this truth. And, of course, every new paradigm must face the resistance of the former worldview, and I still encounter others' resistance to believing that we all have a nuanced, one-of-a-kind Soul Purpose. Engaging people on this journey before they're ready is not easy.

And yet, because I'm Living On Purpose, and I came to help you find yours, I would rather die than stop doing that.

So I'll keep trying to inspire and engage us all to live our purpose. And that's the point. When you've uncovered your purpose, "come home" to yourself, and begin living it, there's no way in hell you "couldn't not do it." It infuses every cell of your being with the dynamic energy of inspiration, and ultimately synchronicity, to do what you're meant to do.

And this phenomenon matters to you, because you can benefit from the cutting-edge work that I and many others are bringing to the planet so that we can live our highest truth and make our greatest contribution. We need your gift now, while you still have a chance to share it (see chapter 8).

OPRAH'S STORY: PURPOSE TO POWER

Oprah Winfrey is one of the greatest living examples of someone who listens and follows the whispers of her purpose. She *lives* at her evolutionary edge.

Most know of Oprah's story, with its meager Mississippi origins of living with her grandmother and later shuttling between her mother in Milwaukee and father in Tennessee. But less commonly known is that Oprah began "play-acting" in front of farm animals and giving speeches at church in very early childhood (Encyclopedia of World Biography). Every chance she got, she would demonstrate her love for teaching, including helping her cousins spell the Biblical names, Shadrach, Meshach, and Abednego, correctly (Winfrey, 2019). Oprah notes, "I firmly believe it is no coincidence that I ended up sharing wisdom with millions in what became the world's largest classroom" (Winfrey, 2019).

After having begun her life in extreme poverty, as a victim of sexual abuse, and with a number of false starts early in her career as a reporter, Oprah ultimately found her way into broadcast media that allowed her to represent her true voice. She's the first to admit that "both . . . miraculous and disastrous outcomes . . . can occur depending on how you respond to life's whispers." She suggests that "it's a quiet nudge from deep within saying, *Hmmm, something feels off. A small voice that tells you, This is no longer your place of belonging*" (Winfrey, 2019).

Oprah's own evolutionary path has been an example for billions around the planet. But rather than imagine that she's lucky, or that fate dealt her a good hand, we should recognize that she's not unique in having a purpose. Her primary uniqueness is in that she listens (still), as she describes it, to the "pit in your stomach, or the pause before you speak . . . the shiver, the goosebumps that raise the hairs on the back of your neck." She compels us to "get still enough to identify what makes [us] unique and connect to hope, possibility and fulfillment in all areas of [our] life" (Winfrey, 2019).

WHAT IS THE GOLDEN THREAD & WHY DOES IT MATTER?

Inside each one of us there is a mostly hidden, mostly golden, mostly eternal image or aspect of being, similar to the gold that is buried in the earth. We are the earthlings, the children of the earth, and therefore we are a replica, in a sense, of the earth itself. One of the ideas that is important is: As above, so below. As outside, so within.

—MICHAEL MEADE

While my own life story is the foundation for the patterns that emerged and are articulated here, I needed twenty years of time-tested experiments with my clients, validated by their own stories, to uncover the deep powerful truth about what I now call the "Golden Thread."

The Golden Thread is the "through-line" in your life's tapestry.

As Meade (2010) describes it:

"The soul is threaded through with a plotline from the beginning that aims at a destiny that might be possible to find before the end."

The Golden Thread was there at birth, and possibly in many other lives. It represents the longing and expression of your unique Soul Purpose.

In addition,

You are the only one with this unique Golden Thread of Purpose. There is no other "thread" like yours.

And while a thread running through your life may not be a unique idea (nor is it fully accepted yet by most), the fact that it's *findable* and that it provides you adequate information about your unique nuanced expression such that you can *figure out how to live it* is remarkable!

And because I've spent close to forty years as a scientist and transformational practitioner dissecting the patterns of my own and others' suffering to get whole and healthy—and along the way developed intuitive and psychic capacities to see beyond the material—I gained tremendous capacity to see these Golden Threads.

My goal in this first book of a trilogy is twofold. First, I want to help you realize that every single part of your life has been purposeful. All the mistakes, all the wrong turns, the lack of good choices or discernment, failures, even the seeming accidents. It all "fits" into your purpose. There are really no "mistakes."

I'm not suggesting the existence of a "grand plan" (though there may be), but rather that everything in life is an opportunity to learn something useful about yourself so you can move forward with more ease—if you choose to use it.

And my second goal is to help you look back and begin to examine the events of your life so you can find the first hints of your Golden Thread—to know that each developmental stage of your life was purposeful, and to now become more focused, discerning, intentional, and aligned with the most authentic version of you.

Living On Purpose is about becoming more of who you are, and less of who you are not.

In this book, I'll share stories and details about how that Golden Thread occurs in different stages of our lives, which I believe is why we can't see it easily. But it's always there. And we're always on purpose, more or less, either in our gift or our shadow, which are two sides of the same coin of purpose.

I'll share with you through stories, including my own, how I came to see this Golden Thread that exists for us all, its effect on your life, and how you can make use of it to live your fullest expression and make your greatest contribution. By Living On Purpose, you can have greater impact in your life and in the lives of many others.

IF PURPOSE CALLS YOU: A UNIQUE VIEW

When you hear, a mile away and still out of sight, the churn of the water as it begins to swirl and roil, fretting around the sharp rocks—when you hear that unmistakable pounding—when you feel the mist on your mouth and sense ahead the embattlement, the long falls plunging and steaming—then row, row for your life toward it.

—MARY OLIVER, WEST WIND #2

You will love this book if you:

- Have been searching for you own purpose and wondering why you can't find it. Perhaps you know that it's right in front of you and you just can't see it. You'll gain some clues about where to find it in your life, both from the stories of your past and your current experience.
- Want to be inspired by people successfully living their purpose so you can see purpose in action.
- Support someone in your life or work who is attempting to have a life of more meaning, fulfillment, and purpose (and who wants to contribute more fully in this time of crisis). Dig in: I offer lots to digest about how to support others in finding their purpose.
- Are an academic or practitioner who wants to understand how signifiers of purpose run through our lives and vary in expression by the developmental tasks in each stage of life.
- And, especially, if you want to contribute your greatest gifts in this time of crisis on the planet—this book is for you.

The Golden Thread is a nonfiction book that speaks to visionaries or entrepreneurs who want to execute their ideas, veteran professionals who want to find more meaning in their careers, seekers who have been looking for years without success and want to embody their spirituality, and parents who want to help their children find their purpose earlier than they did. It's for those seeking to uncover the origins of how their lives have been truly aligned with their Soul Purpose, and to provide support to those who may have lost hope of a life with meaning.

A "WHY" THAT MATTERS: WHAT WE NEED NOW

This book will dispel any notion that your life doesn't matter. I'll show you how your own nuanced one-of-a-kind purpose is right there in front of you, waiting to be discovered, so you can listen to its whispers and let it guide you like a GPS to a more fulfilling and impactful life.

Most people think or believe that:

- Purpose is a job or career, or a passion, and that you usually figure it out as an adult, if at all.
- Childhood wounding is bad and prevents you from living a good life.
- We are "defined" at an early age, which becomes the identity our lives get stuck with.

But—based on my thirty-plus years of research and activating thousands of clients to "find themselves," and then to live powerful, aligned lives guided by their deep Soul Purpose, I've come to witness that:

- Purpose is the seed that guides us throughout our lives. Passions and curiosities are indicators of purpose, and jobs and careers are expressions of purpose, but they are not inherently our purpose. In this book, I'll demonstrate how purpose shows up in different parts of our lives through our unique expression.
- Our childhood wounding is an indicator of purpose, which we can use to uncover our purpose as we explore and heal that wound. In this book, I'll show why we're required to do this "growing up" and accomplish the

developmental tasks at different stages of life, to fully express our purpose.

- Our Soul Purpose is evident at very early stages in life, as our soul pulls us in the direction of our longings. In this book, I'll demonstrate how we sabotage that pull and limit our own evolution and purposeful expression.

In fact, the greatest reason to Live On Purpose is not just for your own fulfillment or satisfaction, but because you are the only one who can share what is represented by your one Golden Thread (which may have many expressions in a lifetime).

I invite you into this story about the Golden Thread, not for intellectual, spiritual, health, financial, or even moralistic reasons—though certainly enough data justify finding your purpose for any of those reasons, some of which I've already shared. Mostly, I invite you in for pragmatic reasons. Living On Purpose is the most effective way to have a life of well-being, health, joy, worthwhile relationships, meaning, and accomplishment (Seligman 2011).

And, lastly, the most significant reason to Live On Purpose is because you and your Golden Thread are needed now more than ever. If a solution to the world's most complex, compounded, multidimensional challenges exists, this is it. Every one of us living up to our greatest expression, our highest potential.

It is never too late, and there is still time.

And because you still have time, I offer an invitation to you, the reader. At the end of many chapters of this book, you'll see the "Self-Reflection" questions. After you've read the chapter, I invite you to stop and explore what's true for you. What did you learn about yourself that could aid in your own exploration of purpose? What do you see in your life that contextually shaped who you have become? Who do you imagine yourself becoming, in light of all this?

And most of all: what inspires you?

What is yours to do, here and now, that could impact your own life, and the world?

REFERENCES

Baumeister, R.F. & Vohs, K.D. (2001). The pursuit of meaningfulness in life. In Snyder, C.R. and Lopez, S.J. (Eds), Handbook of positive psychology, 608-618. New York: Oxford University Press.

Dispenza, J. (2019). Becoming Supernatural: How Common People are Doing the Uncommon. How common people are doing the uncommon. Carlsbad, CA: Hay House.

Encyclopedia of World Biography. Oprah Winfrey biography, accessed September 5, 2019, https://www.notablebiographies.com/We-Z/Winfrey-Oprah.html).

Frankl, V.E. (2006). Man's Search for Meaning. Boston: Beacon Press.

Keyes, C.L.M. (2011). Authentic purpose: The spiritual infrastructure of life. Journal of Management, Spirituality & Religion, 8 (4): 281–297.

Levit, A. and Licina, S. (2011). "How the Recession Shaped Millennial and Hiring Manager Attitudes about Millennials' Future Careers." Commissioned by the Career Advisory Board: DeVry University. Accessed on October 10, 2019 http://www.careeradvisoryboard.org/public/uploads/2011/10/Future-of-Millennial-Careers-Report.pdf.

Maddi, S.R. (1970). The Search for Meaning, in M. Page (Ed), The search for meaning. Nebraska symposium on motivation, 137-186. Lincoln, NE: University of Nebraska Press.

Maslow, A. (1947). A theory of human motivation. Psychological Review 50(4): 370-396.

Meade, M. (2010). Fate and destiny: The two agreements of the soul. Housatonic, MA: Greenfire Press.

Net Impact. (2012). Talent report: What workers want in 2012. Accessed on October 11, 2019 www.netimpact.org/whatworkerswant.

Park, N., Park, M., and Peterson, C. (2010). When is the search for meaning related to life satisfaction?" Applied Psychology: Health and Well-Being, 2(1):1-13.

Rainey, L. (2014). The search for purpose in life: An exploration of Purpose, the search process, and purpose anxiety. Master's thesis Philadelphia: University of Pennsylvania. http://repository.upenn.edu/mapp_capstone/60.

Seligman, M.E.P. (2011). Flourish: A visionary new understanding of Happiness and well-being. Miami: Atria Paperback.

Swanson, C. The torsion field and the aura. Subtle Energies & Energy Medicine 19(3): 43. http://journals.sfu.ca/seemj/index.php/seemj/article/view/425.

Winfrey, O. (2019).The path made clear: Discovering your life's direction and purpose. New York: Flatiron Books.

CHAPTER 1

THE KEY HYPOTHESES OF PURPOSE

Be a lamp, or a lifeboat, or a ladder.
Help someone's soul heal. Walk out
of your house like a shepherd.

—RUMI

LIES, MORE LIES, AND SELF-DISCOVERY

Most of us are afraid to uncover our purpose.

Sure, we talk about wanting to find meaning and fulfill-ment. And yet, somehow, deep inside, we know that if we do "find" our purpose, it will severely betray the stories we've told about ourselves for a lifetime. But rather than betraying our insignificant moments or erring ways, our purpose will betray us as more than, better than, more whole and unerring than, more fulfilled and perfect than anything we could ever have imagined.

Then what?

What if we are always already on purpose, and the "thing we came to do" is right in front of us? And, mostly, we are afraid to listen, afraid that "finding" our purpose will betray the constrained identity or small self we pretend to be. The identity that lets us off the hook from pushing ourselves to be our fullest expression.

In this chapter, you're going to hear the stories of:

- Brandon, a self-described jock whose reparations from dishonoring women helped him discover his own need for self-dignity and connection, which led to his purpose in honoring the gender balance between men and women,
- Carol, who discovered that she really could "do what she loved" in retirement and make it work the second time around, and
- Agathe, whose fascination with strangers led her to launch two European startups with a mission to integrate immigrants into important industrial sectors,
- among others.

UNVEILING THE TRUTHS ABOUT PURPOSE

Enough of the lies, already. Here are some compelling truths I've garnered from a lifetime of seeking my own purpose and working with hundreds of clients over thirty-plus years:

- Our soul compels us toward its fullest expression. It is always pulling, calling us toward the illuminated version of us—who we really are.
- The wounding, limiting beliefs and "lack" that we experience early in life create "shadows" that cloak the true version of ourselves. Those wounded sub-psychic "parts" that fractured from our wholeness cause us to "shut down" to who we really are. When we constrict in this way, we no longer hear our soul calling us (and if you were lucky enough to escape childhood without overt trauma, you'll likely have some shared collective trauma or social expectations serving as your anchor; we all have work to do).
- Purpose shows up throughout our lifetime, in every stage. We could see it in plain daylight if we knew what to look for. The shadowed version of our purpose looks exactly the opposite of what we'd expect of our purpose. Our "shadow" is our soul's way of working out the kinks of our wounding.
- Purpose is expressed in every aspect of our lives: job/career, vocation and avocation, relationships, and lifestyle. We are often unaware of how purpose affects our choices.
- Knowing more about our "through-line" or the Golden Thread of our soul's calling, our purpose, would:
  - Resolve our dissatisfaction or "unresolved" feelings about our lives and help us to feel more "on purpose" and settled, knowing that it all works out.
  - Refine our nuanced understanding of who we are, leading to a more focused direction in our current life.
  - Help us navigate the next stages of our lives.

What if all that were true?

My job, in this book, is to demonstrate how each of these beliefs about purpose is indeed true, and that living "as if" you too can find purpose will support you in finding your way home to your purposeful life.

KNOWING WHERE TO GO NEXT IS OFTEN ABOUT ASKING THE RIGHT QUESTIONS

Three key questions that I've asked for a decade have led me to practice, observe, and refine my own methods with clients over time. My hope is that the exploration of these three questions, posited as hypotheses that we will explore in this book, will help us gain some understanding about where, how, and why purpose shows up in our lives as it does.

THE THREE KEY HYPOTHESES ABOUT PURPOSE

HYPOTHESIS ONE: PURPOSE IS OUR GPS.
We're always on purpose.
Our soul is always pulling us in the direction of a fuller expression of our authentic nature. We just don't recognize it or can't see it.

In fact, in any lifetime, we can see an unlimited number of "expressions" of purpose. These expressions are *more* than just a career, job, project, or relationship (though all of these *can* be expressions of purpose). The number of expressions of purpose is only limited by our availability to hear the "calling" to live into our next expression. As we hear the call, we garner the needed capabilities or resources to move into that expression with ease. If you're in alignment, these resources show up in synchrony.

If this hypothesis is true,
Purpose sets us up to experience a "pull" or a longing, which generates reactions that might look like enthusiasm, passion, energy, creativity or creative expression, love, or excitement. All of these expressions can help us figure out whether an invitation or a decision is in alignment with our organic nature. It also may show up as fear, trepidation, anxiety, or another shadow force, if we're fighting against our wounding to be more of ourselves. In my work with clients, I help them build capacity to listen to these "pulls" from our soul that show up as emotional, somatic, energetic, intuitive, and psychic imprints.

Being/Living On Purpose is an evolutionary journey or "movement," not a stopping place. It is not something to be attained, but to be lived. In hindsight, we can see a "through-line" or thread running through our lives that directs us toward greater and greater expression and contribution. Part of why elders in our contemporary world are more likely to find or live their purposeful expression is because they've "let go" of societal expectations to be someone else, often after they've already lived those expectations at great expense.

CASE STUDY: CAROL
[This case study is based on a client whose name and other identifying features are omitted.]

You'd never imagine that a fiercely independent woman like Carol would've needed to go into nature as a child to get out of the way of her big brother's bullying. Carol's repression, triggered by her brother, was a launchpad for her first business and would lead to the unfolding of events over the next several decades. She would routinely "get into woods, creeks, meadows. . . . Nature became my retreat and haven. A safe place" for her to nourish herself. In fact, her natural inclination to use nature as nourishment ultimately led to her current role working for a large social movement to promote a path to soil health and food independence.

Carol explains that she's "always listened for input from life. Life is always talking to me." She describes herself as having "always been a bit of a nerd around soil science." As Carol shared her story about her first career, she recalls that "when it came time to figure out what I wanted to do for a living, I just couldn't. . . . I didn't want to be a part of the whole business thing that was going on. I wanted to stay in the woods. I loved animals and plants."

Yet, Carol didn't have a direct path to do what came naturally. She nearly gave up on the idea of being close to the earth. While her desire was to be a farmer, this dream was squashed early on in her Midwestern culture ("boys are better and girls are limited"), so she accepted that as reality and pushed it away. Carol was, however, one of those people who listened to the "do what you love and the money will follow" mantra of the late '80s.

She started a home-based vegetable-growing business. She would go to the farmers' market every Saturday to sell her produce, and on other days to restaurants. The business grew quite big, and she was selling produce she would grow in the field, doing what she loved. But her revenue was barely enough to cover her costs, even though she had a chance to be near her children in their early years. Carol recalls with disappointment that she "never paid myself more than $1/hr, even though I got to raise my children and do something I enjoyed."

Ultimately, as her kids grew and wanted expensive sneakers, she knew she needed another income. She took a job working for a retail company doing office and computer work, and simultaneously went back to school during the evenings and weekends. Carol sighs when she says, "I have no idea how I did it. I went from a high school diploma to a master's degree while working full time and raising kids and growing a business."

Carol claims that "it didn't work out for me." And in her mind, it didn't. She started a business doing what she loved "but realized I was never going make enough money to support my life. I wasn't headed for being financially viable and eventually I had to admit defeat. It was really hard. I got practical, which I'm good at doing."

In the midst of what she'd considered a failed business, Carol went back to school—ultimately earning a master's in business—and then followed the lead to work as a director at a renowned university. While she acknowledges that she had satisfaction during the time that she worked as a director, her lament of the experience is that she "sold my time for money." She knows that it was "good work that was done well, but it wasn't enough for me in the end."

Often, we see failure when in fact the spring flowers are poking their way through the snow. She realized only later that the vegetable business helped her learn how to grow things and also how to run a business, developing new systems each time her business would scale. And her long and successful career in administration at the university taught her the ins and outs of running a bigger business.

I met Carol when we were in a spiritual community, where we became co-conspirators in our evolutionary journeys. At the time, Carol was still a director at a university and was nurturing her own desire to make a bigger difference through a few smaller endeavors that pulled her forward in her purpose.

My work with Carol as a client didn't start until she had left the university and began searching for more meaning and a way to express herself purposefully. She describes that time as a "sense of amazement and emotional release. I can't believe I really did it [left a stable job]. Along with being ready to retire, I wanted a sense of greater purpose that was 'hand in glove' with that." She felt great relief in leaving the constraints of her job, and adds with enthusiasm, "I still have a lot to offer."

But Carol didn't escape scot-free from her "day job" at the university. She'd developed some autoimmune issues and found through her own study of the causes that they were related to the stress of her relentless work. Because of her need to care for herself and find more meaning, Carol explains that she looked at typical models of:

"What retirement is supposed to look like, how to do it. . . . There were many interferences with finding a simpler way. . . . When I started my 'retirement' plan, I simply didn't know what I was doing and I was fine with that. I wanted to see what happened next."

She could sense the societal expectations about what she should be doing and knew that was not her own path.

Carol participated in a Purpose Masterclass I taught, designed to help people align with and amplify their purpose. As a relatively new retiree from her university job, she was volunteering in various nonprofits, "looking for herself" as people often do when "seeking" their purpose outside of themselves.

As we uncovered the roots of Carol's purpose in the Masterclass and cleared away the distractions and limiting beliefs about who she was to help her navigate her next step, she began to re-explore how nature fit into her soul's schema. Her internet searches led her to regenerative agriculture as a topic she was interested in and ultimately to internet videos by a scientist studying soil science and the human biome. Carol describes that the "crazy point in our planetary situation where nature is suffering, related to that first connection I found as a little kid" caused her to think that if the planet is going to survive the next hundred years:

"Nature needs me now with all the capacities and everything I've pulled together over my life, especially with the revolution in agriculture that needs to happen. Farmers' kids are getting so sick, it has to change. It's unbelievable what we have collectively done to the soils—since early history we've been

soiling our nest. The fertile crescent is now complete desert. No vegetation can exist there. There's nowhere else to go. It's time. This is it."

Carol also realized that all the research she'd done about health issues, to find answers to her own autoimmune disorders, was the coming together of threads already in her life. When she read the work of this scientist, she felt his angle on the agricultural revolution was what needed to occur. Carol described that she "could see how it all tied into my mental smarts and ease of figuring things out, my health issues, the early nature interests, my own startup business experience, and a love of the people who live close to the land."

Because Carol had worked through the constraints of her childhood beliefs of "not being good enough" during the Masterclass, she decided she wanted to take on a role in sustainable farming. She boldly wrote to the scientist's company to see how she could support them. She surmised, "Here I am with all these offices and program management talents" to assist them, and realized she was exactly in the right place at the right time to support a company that needed help to get its message out in the world.

Because of her courage, Carol's vast experience and aligned purpose are now benefiting an emerging resource to study and improve soil science technologies that connects with her childhood dream. Carol described that she'll often:

"Feel bursts of energy in relation to this- just wanting to do whatever I can, play my little part to fulfill some unique role, this unique combination of capacities and skills I can

contribute. I just don't want to be sitting on my hands while the planet goes up in flames. You know what I'm saying? This mobilizes me."

Carol's job requires her to mobilize and motivate large groups of people "to get this thing moving." She pauses and then laughs at the bigness of the question she's about to ask: "How do you help people have a revolution and be enough yourself?" In response to that question, she's just putting one foot in front of the other, helping to create a platform to help young people, mostly from corporate environments, so they too can make their biggest contributions.

As we came to the end of our interview, Carol noted, "I have a meeting at 11 a.m. I can't be late." Better later than never.

Every flower blooms in its own time.
—KEN PETTI

HYPOTHESIS TWO: OUR PURPOSE IS HIDDEN BY OUR WOUNDING

Childhood wounding causes us to become someone other than ourselves.

When our family scenario is healthy enough, we as children come to know ourselves by the things that delight us. Some of us love animals or nature, some are inspired by music or art, and others like to build things and take them apart. While the objects we "like" are usually not a representation of our purpose, the manner in which we explore the content and how or why it delights us is an indicator of our true inspiration.

The optimal "self-knowing" that arises in childhood is often our first experience of identifying with the natural expressions of purpose. These childhood expressions are an incomplete and simplified version, related to stage of development (see chapter 3), that draw us forward, just as a GPS shows us where to go. However, many of us don't experience the optimal scenario that would allow us to know ourselves, or to be able to "read" the GPS.

What happens instead of this optimal self-awareness is that we aren't given the attention, resources, or encouragement to grow up attending to the curiosities of our own interests. If we did get the resources we needed, we'd have greater self-expression and self-awareness. We'd grow up to be ourselves more fully in childhood and adolescence. Instead, our identity shapes around what others want us to be, which is an inconsistent or repressed version of who we really are.

Mahler et al. (2008) developed the Separation-Individuation Theory, which guided the field of child development in this regard. In childhood development lingo, the early childhood stage at which individuation occurs is the rapprochement stage (twelve to twenty-four months), around the time when infants turn into toddlers and become the infamous and defiant "terrible twos." The crucible of this stage for us as children is to become separate from our primary parent without feeling alone in the world or abandoned.

Often, the separation of child and parent doesn't go well. The parent may be oblivious to the child's growing need for an independent identity or not have individuated well themselves. Or perhaps the parent doesn't provide the support needed to encourage enthusiasm for the child's interests. Or the parent has a need for the child to stay attached so they can feel needed. Or myriad other reasons that set up an unhealthy attachment between child and parent or caregiver.

A child's desire for independence can be marred by either a "too much" attachment or a fear of abandonment, either in this early period of rapprochement, or in a later stage when individuation should happen (Kins, Byers, Soenens, 2012). When the child-parent attachment doesn't go well, the child's identity also doesn't fully form, and self-awareness is compromised. Successful completion of this stage of childhood development is essential to a stable sense of self and yet so often does not occur, compromising how children come to know themselves.

As you can imagine, eventually when a child doesn't develop an adequate level of self-awareness or self-identity, their authentic nature and deepest soul desires are suppressed. This suppression leads to overt expression of the childhood wound, rather than the authentic gifts of purpose. Hill, Burrow, and Sumner (2016), who studied young adults, found that:

"Emerging adults who report a higher sense of purpose tend to have more positive attachments to parental figures," and that these "emerging adults with a higher sense of purpose also reported fewer difficulties with the separation–individuation process, which in turn partially explained why purposeful emerging adults report a greater sense of personal mastery."

As the earliest type of childhood wounding plays out over the lifespan, it will look differently at each stage of life and hide our purposeful identity until we resolve the "self-knowing" wound. This process in fact encompasses the meat and potatoes of the "shadowed" part of our personality. We can't see that which we don't know about ourselves, and uncovering who we really are often becomes too painful after childhood because we've stuffed it down so far.

As we resolve our childhood (or later) wounding, our purpose becomes more evident, organically, and we become more fully expressed and able to contribute our unique, one-of-a-kind genius.

If this hypothesis is true,
Our life is the "school" that trains us to develop the skills we need to overcome the challenges of our childhood and live meaningful lives. But when we're in the midst of a serious trauma, we don't usually see that it's going to turn out alright. We see ourselves as victims, which further calcifies our identity that shaped around our childhood wounds.

Yet, life provides the transformational fodder for our human development. We can only evolve into more aware humans and grow purposefully, if we can see ourselves and our "circumstances" in a new light.

Most of us believe that the trauma, tragedy, and seemingly "unfortunate" circumstances of our lives just "happen" to us. However, from the 30,000-foot view, all those debacles, including our childhood wounding, have benefit. And while this reality may be hard to stomach, an extension of that thinking is to suggest that all traumas are just mirror (mere) expressions of ourselves, as even contemporary medical science suggests that we draw resonant energies and experiences to us to reflect our own energetic potential (Ross, 2019; Muehsam and Venture, 2014).

And a further extension is that the wounding is the "mirror" image (or flip side) of the purposeful gift itself. What we didn't accomplish in childhood (or some other developmental stage) is played out through our "inner children," which are repressed sub-psychic parts that fracture during our childhood and ultimately express in rebellious or diminished ways (Steele, 2017). These "parts" are often hidden to the individual—and thus, the "shadow" (Jacoby, 1942)—but seen quite markedly as part of the egoic personality by everyone around us. Resolution of these wounds requires careful assessment of the stage of development in which the wound was formed, and what type of suppressed split, projected, or introjected "part" is involved before integration of the fractured part can be accomplished fully.**

**Side note: Many healers, therapists, and practitioners often attempt to help their clients integrate these parts without an accurate assessment of the origin of the part. While modalities have been in existence for a while to access these parts (e.g., Voice Dialogue, among others), recent research has helped us understand the importance of determining the "stage" of development at which the fractured part occurred and providing a more nuanced resolution and integration of distinct forms of shadow (see chapters 3-6).*

CASE STUDY: BRANDON PEELE

At one point in his twenties, Brandon Peele realized, *Holy fuck, I'm an asshole*. With a deep apology, he shares that "I was profoundly ignorant about myself and everything else in the world. I'd constructed my life to become a sociopath." In that stage of life, he decided to move out west and start over, leaving behind the security of his successful career so he could begin the true work of becoming himself.

As we become sincerely committed to living a more honest life, we quickly realize the need to uncover the key aspects of ourselves that get in the way of our authenticity. Brandon Peele figured this necessity out in spades, after his epiphany, and performed an earnest job of resolving his ogre parts and sexist ways. Through deep personal work resolving childhood issues, he's spent the better part of two decades making amends for the travesty of his adolescent and young adult behaviors.

But Brandon's attempts to reconcile his own dignity and self-worth kept him from seeing the aspects of his childhood that were clues to his own essential nature. The shame of his youthful indiscretions caused him to over-identify with the aggressor, rather than the child whose feminine side had been repressed.

What Brandon hadn't done, because of his own remorse, was celebrate the parts of his younger self that had been attempting to honor gender equity. As a kid, he tried to grow up with dignity for himself and for others, including his female friends. When he finally realized that his toxic environment had rewarded him for abuse of women, his shame prevented him from seeing those facets of his personality that stood in the light. His story of who he'd become was marred by his fixation on the shadowed parts.

Most of us who work in the purpose field have come to know that you must be "blessed" by your own purpose before it can become fully expressed. Tim Kelley, founder of the True Purpose Institute, teaches that we must first learn to share our blessings (a facet of purpose) with ourselves (Kelley, 2013). In other words, if we aren't giving ourselves some version of our purpose, we can't fully contribute it in the world.

Brandon has done decades of personal development work—starting in grad school and later through the Mankind Project, a peer group men's support network, and numerous programs at Landmark Education, a personal growth organization. He shared that his updated version of his purpose was to "bless the dignity of the human soul" but that he was challenged in figuring out how to offer this beyond his one-on-one clients.

As we tapped into Brandon's expression of purpose as a child and teenager during our interview, we uncovered that he'd always had the capacity to identify with and honor others. As we spoke, it became clear that in some of his rebellious behaviors, especially around the disregard of women, he was trying to dignify himself in a childhood that had repressed his raw young self in gender-balanced ways.

Brandon admits that as a child and preteen, he "loved making friendship bracelets with the girls." He was passionate about "art, drawing, and building things. But my dad and bullies told me that art and femininity were for homosexuals." When his parents divorced, he strongly wanted girls as friends, especially those whose parents had divorced. He talked with girls for hours on the phone. Brandon imagines that he was "drinking in the feminine essence" at the time. As a means to cope with the repression, he took in friends who could help him mirror parts that had been denied.

But Brandon also loved games and sports. He enjoyed playing war, basketball, baseball, football. Indiana Jones was his favorite hero. As Brandon's feminine parts were rejected by some of his peers and parents (his only two fights were the result of being "called a fag by two sons of mobsters"), he became a wild child and was known for "lighting things on fire and thieving. And I would strip naked and dance around." Brandon was equally punished for these radical rebellions as he was for being "too feminine."

His father also "inseminated his worldview with wealth, success, and achievement, and manipulated him into a career in business" at an early age. Brandon recalls "busting ass" in his freshman year of high school to please his dad. He spent fifteen hours per week swimming, studying hard, and dating pretty girls. Upon showing his dad his straight-A report card—meant to also accommodate his parent's expectations of him—his dad questioned the one class he loved, a studio art course. Brandon excitedly told his dad he'd take Studio Art II next semester. His dad resoundingly denied that possibility, stripping Brandon of any real acknowledgment that his own desires and interests mattered. Brandon was emotionally shattered, which further repressed his own nascent self-identity.

Brandon's exposure to misogynistic views from his dad, the authors he read, and his male friends who pressed him to be sexual all created a pressure cooker for a boy whose true identity was repressed. From these myriad pressures, Brandon eventually succumbed and embodied overt sexism. When he crossed over the line of consent as a teen, he was abiding by the cultural beliefs that had been instilled in him by his dad, the culture, and his friends that "women are bad, dumb, too emotional to do anything useful." As Brandon now sees it, the seeds were planted at an early age for him to be a perpetrator.

This "reinforcement for being bad and wrong" basically led him to "fuck the rules" in everything that tried to keep him repressed. He spent most of his teens and twenties living out the fantastical macho image that had been projected onto him as acceptable, at the expense of the women in his life and of his own dignified identity.

Not until he was enrolled in a personal development program in business school did Brandon begin to inquire into his reckless patterns. During a class discussion about the morals of cheating on your spouse, Brandon's professor, Srikumar Rao, suggested, "Whatever you put out into the universe comes back to you one-thousand-fold" (Brandon recalls this moment with great reverence and a Hindi accent).

This event led to Brandon's "Holy fuck" awakening and conscious desire to reformulate his identity.

As Brandon later became aware of who he wanted to be—which wasn't the "oversexed bad boy"—he began to tap into the man who had the ability to be deeply vulnerable and dignified with both men and women.

Brandon has engaged his passion for purpose through multiple venues, as an author of *Planet on Purpose (2018)* and *The Purpose Field Guide (2018),* speaker, coach, organizational consultant, and co-founder of the Global Purpose Leaders group. He serves as part of the Leader body of the Mankind Project to help men become emotionally mature, powerful, compassionate, and purpose-driven to heal society's deepest wounds. Brandon also supports many women who are corporate refugees to reclaim their own repressed femininity through individual and group support.

Since the completion of this interview, Brandon has taken on the role of vice president of People Science of ion Learning. He is responsible for ion's enterprise purpose program, thought leadership, research, and West Coast client partnerships.

Your purpose in life is to find your purpose and give your whole heart and soul to it.

—BUDDHA

HYPOTHESIS THREE: OUR EXPRESSION OF PURPOSE VARIES BY DEVELOPMENTAL STAGE

Purpose remains "hidden" unless we can see it through the filters of our stages of life.

This happens for two reasons. First, our ability to see or experience our purpose can be supported or sabotaged by our early stages of individuation (discussed above). And second, during each phase of life, the developmental tasks needed for us to "ripen" into our next stage require us to expand our perspective or awareness, often called "worldview." As we develop into each next stage of life, we gain the capacity to "see" contexts more broadly—and to heal our wounding—giving us the chance to see our purpose even more clearly as well (see chapters 3-6 for more detail).

Thus, the "thread" of our purpose, which would be more readily seen if not for the wounding that occurs and hides it from us, is also more apparent if we are looking for the most likely expression in any given developmental phase.

If this hypothesis is true,
The threads of purpose will show up in some simple form at each developmental stage, successfully building in complexity and context as we become more nuanced, complex, and context-aware over our lifespans. Early expressions of purpose (up to adolescence, and adulthood in some cases) will look like a primary awareness of self and individual orientation, to explore self relative to others and stabilize principles and values. Further discussion of the stages of development or consciousness relative to purpose will be discussed in chapters 3-6.

The expression of our purpose will also shift from a "being" stage (passive, or contextually relevant conceptualization and articulation of one's own meaning and identity) to a "becoming" stage (or active, in which the understanding of self and meaning is practiced in the relevant contexts). So that we do not move from "being" early in life to "doing" later in life—the process is a constantly iterative cycle that includes and integrates former tasks of development into each subsequent stage.

I propose that our soul "longs" to express itself (as true self, or authentic nature) and goes to great effort to ensure that we complete our developmental tasks. It does so by offering us events or circumstances that "trigger" us to confront the wounding that keeps our purpose hidden. These "triggers" are merely mirrors of our own shadow. While in an earlier developmental stage, these mirrors will look like trauma or tragedy, they are also opportunities to do the deep work to liberate us from the constrained identity that buries our purpose.

As we develop, the victim orientation loosens and we begin or complete the individuation process and let go of the socially acceptable forms of ourselves. Then, in the relief of being more of who we are and less of who we are not, we can accept that all of life's opportunities create catalytic opportunities to inquire into advanced stages of consciousness about self and our place in the world.

CASE STUDY: AGATHE DAAE-QVALE

Who would imagine that a little girl in Norway, who vowed to include the loners and the "outsiders," would have to overcome her own forms of isolation and rejection to help resolve one of the most significant crises of our time?

In fact, Agathe Daae-Qvale, an intrepid consultant who brings her formidable technology skills to almost any industry (and has worked in the technology and energy production industries), is helping spawn a new economic sector in Europe destined to support the integration of immigrants into foreign cultures, or to bring the "outsiders" in, much like she did as a child.

Because of Agathe's experience as an immigrant herself, she saw the shift to nationalism in Norway (and many other countries around the world), resulting from the massive global migration of people out of war-torn countries or oppressive governments. Her interest in this topic occurred because of the influx of immigrants into the economy and culture of Norway (and around the globe).

In Norway, as increasingly in other cultures, people chose to believe that they should take care of "their own kind," rather than the immigrants, leading to a nationalistic fervor that excluded immigrants from existing societal and economic infrastructures. The inherent devaluing and marginalization of immigrants led to even greater economic disparity and disenfranchisement among the immigrants.

So what did Agathe's early interests look like that might have indicated her deep interest in creating safe containers to bring the "outsiders" in?

In addition to begging her mother to regularly set a table for twelve, Agathe had a deep sense of curiosity that led her to want to learn things from people who were different from her, and also those who had a curiosity to learn from her. When her parents sent her to bed early when they had visitors over, she tossed and turned, unable to sleep because of her curiosity about these new people. At sixteen, she was an exchange student in New Zealand, and her lust for travel never ceased: she's now been to dozens of countries. About half of her professional life has been spent working abroad.

Agathe felt she always had an interest in expanding her mind. She wanted to learn English because she would be able to speak to so many more people. Next came Spanish, and now she speaks five languages. So while many people love to travel, her interests were heightened because of her fascination with "going through life, opening doors, meeting people." She felt she was part of something greater as a result. She describes the most rewarding experiences for her as those that "draw global talent. Young people from all over the world that are happy to meet. It creates excitement, makes the atmosphere alive, awake. They're curious about life and you."

Agathe now sees how her childhood of craving to meet other people and explore new things was the early expression of her Soul Purpose. This expression of curiosity, exploration, and inclusion of outsiders seeded her purpose and her recent passion for building businesses and systems that help integrate the "outsiders," or immigrants, into societal systems. Agathe notes that she "never understood the reason to exclude people. I could understand why people resent other people . . . but not for skin color or their beliefs." Agathe cites a deep desire to include others that caused her mother to laugh for wanting to have her extended family at every meal.

Agathe was no stranger to being on the outside, having spent thirteen years as an immigrant in countries beyond the borders of Norway, starting at sixteen as an exchange student, and doing professional career stints in the United States, Netherlands, and Middle East, as well as several other countries. While in the Middle East, Agathe was in an abusive marriage in a foreign country where women were not fully integrated into the culture of power. She was isolated, alone, and felt the disparities that existed for foreigners with no safety net.

Upon returning to Norway, she quickly realized the deep disparity that immigrants faced when seeking employment or simple integration into the culture. She recounts many stories about how other Europeans or those from the Middle East were continually treated poorly in job interviews, public places, and restaurants. Agathe sums it up:

"In practical life, people from the outside are not automatically included in society. If you come from outside or have a different surname or dark skin, it's harder to get a job, be welcomed, difficult to make friends, to be a part of the greater society. I find that the society I'm in is very homogeneous and I'd like to create space for more, for the people who are here to be part of our society."

In hindsight, that Agathe's soul calling was to contribute in some way in resolving international immigration issues might seem obvious. But it wasn't even obvious a few years ago when she contacted me to coach her to uncover her purpose. Ironically, Agathe and I met at our mutual coaching training in Canada, where we gathered regularly for several years and became acquainted. As for most of us, seeing who you really are and what you're meant to contribute is much easier when you start putting the puzzle together with all the pieces on the table, which is only possible after you've found them all.

The missing pieces for Agathe, as for many, were in the resolute belief that she wasn't good enough to contribute beyond typical professional goals, much less contribute to a large societal issue. Early childhood issues that remained unresolved, which led to serious personal challenges, kept her stuck in low-risk high-performance work scenarios and in stunted relationships. As for many of us, when we can't see who we really are, we succumb to the expectations of our family or peer groups and follow the path others imagine for us.

For decades, Agathe endured the grind of the corporate technology sector without questioning the source of her misery. She knew she had an affinity for outsiders but had no true awareness of how or why she was supposed to affect their scenario. Plus, she didn't have the confidence or ambition to move in that direction.

Because of the friendship we developed during our coaching training, Agathe knew that I had come to know my own purpose in the world and became ever more curious about how to live into that. Our peer relationship in coaching training turned into a mentor-mentee relationship during my purpose work with her, which then blossomed into a deep friendship.

During our work together, Agathe's curious and inclusive nature led her to develop the startup TinkerBlue, designed as a startup hub platform that provides necessary support functions, networking, and community-building for technology entrepreneurs. The company is focused on facilitating a platform for startup phase entrepreneurs from minority groups, mainly for entrepreneurs with immigrant backgrounds. TinkerBlue's long-term purpose is integration of members of minority groups into the greater society through job creation emerging from immigrant groups—as well as making use of existing tech skills among immigrants. TinkerBlue is now a part of the Nordic Incubator for Social Innovation.

Despite the early high level of receptivity to the concept and willingness of public and private sector interest to consider funding and other support, Agathe was resistant to seeing herself as the manifester of this possibility. Then she was invited to be a founding board member (and then chair) of a second startup, DoubleYou (doubleyou.no). DoubleYou is a marketplace that gives visibility and market access to small organizations offering products and services created with a socially inclusive and environmentally sustainable focus, by connecting them with those who want to consume consciously.

After this invitation and recognition by a team of serial tech entrepreneurs, she began to recognize herself as the "insider" she truly is in her own unfolding purpose. Agathe is now contemplating her next steps, including integrating technology into business processes.

Yesterday is gone and its tale told.
Today, new seeds are growing.
—RUMI

ALL THREE HYPOTHESES AT WORK

CASE STUDY: BILL KERN

If you were watching Bill Kern—CEO, executive consultant, founder—you'd know that he's the kind of man who "knows who he is." Bill's easily one of the most handsome, confident, and successful guys in the room. He communicates with authority and greets you with that assured handshake and sense of clarity. Bill walks in a room and exudes "big man on campus" pheromones.

But you'd never know behind Bill's modus operandi for much of his life was a little boy of six left in the dirt by some bullies as he walked home from school across a football field. That day, picking himself up off the ground and spitting blood, he vowed to never let it happen again.

Bill claimed that on that day, sweaty and angry, he "must be superior in order to avoid shame and reject authority to avoid domination and alienation." Those weren't his words as a six-year-old, but more than five decades later, he's learned that the wounding generated that day kept him from living a more purposeful life that would've made him happier, more successful, and especially more impactful—which matters to him now more than ever.

When Bill started working with me in a coaching relationship, most immediately observable was the tremendous amount of success he'd had in business and in life. But he never measured up to his own high bar. He never felt as superior as he needed to be in order to recover from that incident in first grade, and a repeat incident in middle school when he was bullied again. These events reinforced his "decision in high school to play football and be big and strong and mean so [the middle school bully] would never pick on me again."

This decision, to take on a persona contrary to his true nature, effectively trampled the little boy who spent a good chunk of his childhood helping others. Bill describes this aggressive persona as his "evil twin" who's had an explosive trigger most of his life. He kept "feeding the beast," or the shadow elements of his personality, to preserve this image of dominance.

And while Bill felt the image was useful during his early years in business, it also led to his significant relational challenges at work and home, which caused career opportunities to be cut short and personal relational problems—not to mention the cloaking of a chance to be more of himself.

This "evil twin" persona was in fact the flip side of his kind and supportive nature. Bill does recall his manner in childhood as different. After finding some elementary school report cards that scored him "off the charts" in verbal proficiency, he wondered why he hadn't been on the debate team. He also recalled having been active in service clubs, once a part of a school service club that worked with inner-city kids in nature settings. In addition, he was usually the "good guy" who would stop his drunk friends from harassing others and negotiate them "out of trouble" when they were out on the town in college.

But Bill realized that his young belief systems constrained him. He felt that doing more of those activities "wouldn't have helped him be superior, didn't let me be on a high enough pedestal. Being a varsity football player was way more valued." Bill now sees that these choices created from the events of his youthful wounding were reinforcing the shadow and preventing his authentic purpose from being revealed.

But, ultimately, the "beast" also feeds the gifts. The flip side of Bill's aggressive authority persona that "would show up in a room and people would think I'm superior" helped create a skilled and tactful negotiator and facilitator. Among other things that Bill started as a result of his innate supportive nature and communication talents was a technologically based facilitation software company called GoWall. While Bill's early communication style limited his relational capacity, he began to work through those challenges. Ultimately, Bill learned to communicate with such empathy that he later became a strong mentor to peers in his Mankind Project men's group.

The paradoxical nature of how our purpose shows up in life (flip sides of the same coin) often prevents us from seeing that purpose earlier in life. While serving as Bill's coach, I helped him work on the initial threads of his childhood related to his true desire to support others, which had kept him hidden behind these fault lines of his personality. I helped Bill see the effects of his shadow on his success by creating a metaphor to guide him, suggesting that being aligned with your purpose is like floating in the slipstream of an ocean. Living from your default wounding is like having your appendages floating outside the slipstream, so that it "drags" on the flow.

Over the duration of our work together, we highlighted all the means by which Bill was deeply aligned with his purpose and in support and service to others. Through exploration of his aspirations and default belief systems, we also noted all the areas of "drag" that kept him limited, including the frustrated childhood parts that hadn't been integrated. Bill came to see that he would be best served by dropping the football hero persona to be valuable to others. He began to let go of the need to dominate in order to serve more authentically. Shortly after our work together, the synchronicity of the "purpose GPS" caught up to him, and Bill was approached to be a chair for Vistage, a peer mentoring organization for CEOs—one of his deepest dreams for serving others.

Bill now claims an expanded purpose statement of "Be of service and contribute to others," in addition to the prior knowing that he is here to "help people to see that they can and empower them so that they actually do." Bill sees these statements as serving as his "green screen" or backdrop to all other activities. In a quiet moment, he wishes someone had "helped me tune into my basic backdrop when I was a kid" so he could've expanded his innate desire to be of support to others earlier in life, as he did as a young child, rather than "swimming upstream."

Bill has learned to tease apart the gold versus the shadow to have a courageous internal authority that now lets him be the most encouraging guy in the room, while rocking his career. Bill is now a Vistage chair, bringing his capacity to serve and support dozens of leaders in the San Francisco Bay Area. Bill's facilitation software company, GoWall, is still serving dozens of tech companies.

THE UTILITY OF EXPLORING THESE QUESTIONS: THE BENEFIT OF LIVING PURPOSEFULLY

I'll explore in greater depth in chapter 3 how purpose affects us in almost every facet of our lives. One can then conjecture that aligning with our own purposeful direction yields a more coherent approach to collective society, with each of us living our greatest contribution.

CASE STUDY: SUSAN LUCCI

Susan Lucci has spent a good deal of time in her own life following in her parents' modeling of serving those in need. As a child, Susan was raised in a conventional Jesuit family in the U.S. Midwest, with values so traditional that a patina had formed. While she recalls her parents being good role models for social equity and justice, she also experienced the rigid authority insisting that she rein in her own desires to serve others. Susan learned there was "no way to argue with authorities, the priests or her parents. . . . If I stepped one toe outside of the bounds, I was punished." Susan ultimately followed in her father's footsteps and became an attorney, thinking that she could serve those who'd been unfairly penalized or mistreated. Instead, she found the profession transactional and unfulfilling.

As is often the case with rigid familial or cultural containers that confine us, she developed escape valves that represented some of her later purpose elements. Susan loved riding horses and caring for babies, both significant predictors of her current passion for creating spaces for those whose voices need to be freed.

In Susan's case, the early indicators of purpose were loud and clear. As a child, she would help her mother with her three younger siblings with tender care. Susan recalled that at age five, she would "climb into her younger brother's crib and change his diapers . . . with those huge and sharp diaper pins . . . and climb out again" by herself. She also recalls "holding a baby at a family reunion for six hours"—mystifying even to her.

Susan wanted her mother to have more babies, though rearing four kids in five years was enough for her family. She admits that she was raised to be a mother: "I know what to do to take care of people," partly because she was also raised to be a good hostess by passing out cookies and drinks to guests at the large dinner parties they threw for her father's law firm and her own huge family.

And her desire to create a supportive "net" for others didn't end when she became an attorney. In her early years as a lawyer, Susan would weekly visit a local children's hospital and rock the babies who had no one to love them. Susan suggests that these babies "had a death sentence. Some had no use of their arms or legs. They were laying in a crib all alone when I arrived, so I would pick them up and I would just sit in a rocking chair holding them." Susan wondered, "Who does this?" out loud, not yet understanding how connected this impulse was to her purpose.

Over the years, Susan also worked in food pantries, started hunger banquets, worked with interfaith programs, and created service learning programs. Susan now serves as a facilitator for some of Chicago's most dynamic interracial conversations. On top of all that, Susan raised several children of her own.

She never considered, until our conversation, that her current work of holding space for women to express their authentic lives is similar to her early childhood experiences. Susan's Circle business, 2Big4Words, literally helps birth nascent spirits who would otherwise die, much as she did for those tiny babies on Thursday nights. Most of the women who join Susan's Circles have not begun to express themselves.

As Susan tenderly guides the women in her Circles through provocative questions designed to unleash their inner selves, her clients unearth their deepest desires and core wounds. Many of her Circle members have been reined in themselves, as Susan experienced in childhood, and found the freedom to unleash their boundedness, much as Susan did in riding horses as a child. Susan suggests that her Circles are "not a comfort zone" but rather a "brave space" for people to become more of themselves.

Susan's own journey as an advocate, activist, and social artisan has been an evolutionary process. She and I trained as certified purpose guides together at the Purpose Guides Institute, and Susan is also a life design catalyst and a certified instructor of mindfulness-based stress reduction for teens, an attorney, a co-founder of the Global Purpose Leaders, and an initiator of Chicago on Purpose. Susan has described her purpose in the world as a "midwifing" process, creating safe containers from which to let new things arise, and that, recently, it's also about "hospice" work, or letting things go.

During our interview, Susan described that something was being birthed within her, but she wasn't sure what, suggesting she'd been waiting patiently for it to arise. As I queried her about what she imagined it to be, she recalled a recent book called *Figurings* by Maria Popova, in which she shines a light on the invisibility of amazing women, leading up to modern-day scientists. As Susan spoke, I noticed that she spoke of the "invisibility" of the women who begin to birth themselves in her Circles.

As Susan spoke, I connected her desire to honor the invisibility of women with her own evolving role as an activist. She spoke about her evolved approach of "bringing new ideas as an advocate and not trying to burn it down" as an activist. She noted she's learning to be "kinder, more collaborative," including, as she describes it, "going to the authorities, saying, 'Hey, what about this?' rather than previous patterns of holding my tongue or challenging them, banging down walls in systems."

As we pondered these distinctions, we realized that her childhood patterns of being repressed by authority figures kept her from speaking the truth, much like the invisible women of her Circles and the figures in Popova's book. As we circled around this notion, I suggested that Susan's evolving expression of her purpose was related to removing her own invisibility cloak, along with those she is to serve, to "uplift the invisible powers" of each of us. This potential version of a new purpose resonated very much with Susan.

In recent months since our interview, Susan is indeed removing her own cloak. She is writing her own book with the draft title, *The Upside of the Downside: How Women are Healing Their Heartache by Creating Sanctuaries of Care.* About the book, Susan shares that "amidst a culture in crisis, I am making visible the web I see women weaving, empowered by their hearts, that is creating pockets of sanctuary and together, a new culture of care. Women are not waiting; we are taking action and it is changing our experience of the world."

> *How should we like it were stars to burn*
> *With a passion for us we could not return?*
> *If equal affection cannot be,*
> *Let the more loving one be me.*
> —WH AUDEN

REFLECTIONS ON THE HYPOTHESES: WHY I BELIEVE THEM TO BE TRUE

LESSON ABOUT HYPOTHESIS ONE: PURPOSE IS OUR GPS

As the stories in this chapter show, our soul is genuinely pulling us in the direction of our purpose throughout life, even though we can't see it until later. As Bill Plotkin, PhD., depth psychologist, wilderness guide, and founder of the Animas Valley Institute (see chapter 2 for more on Bill), voiced in our interview, referencing the pull or call from our souls:

"Children shouldn't be thinking about Purpose at all . . . it could be a toxic influence to be thinking about Purpose before

*psychosocial puberty. But in early adolescence [or later for
many people who don't complete the prerequisite tasks] where
we are ready to discover our unique individual niche in the
greater earth community, the Purpose that we are born to
live, in order to discover that and explore that . . . we must go
through the adventure or soul initiation."*

And as we follow these threads as they are made explicit to
us—or to the parents, caregivers, or other adults who tend
to our developmental journeys—we are able to find more
focus and clarity about our direction. This in turn supports
decision-making about life and career choices, reduces our
nonintentional "wandering around" in careers or vocations
that seem meaningless, and eliminates unnecessary distraction from that which would create more joy, abundance, and
contribution. The world needs more people focused on creating meaningful pursuits that take advantage of their greatest
soul-level capacities. Not only will the individual benefit, but
the world will benefit from their contribution.

LESSON ABOUT HYPOTHESIS TWO: OUR
PURPOSE IS HIDDEN BY OUR WOUNDING

Just as each of us has a nuanced one-of-a-kind purpose, we
also have distinct ways of unconsciously hiding our purpose
in the "shadowed" aspects of our childhood dilemmas. As
shown in these stories, our wounded parts are represented
through unique facets of our personality. As we begin to
resolve our childhood dilemmas and accept those "parts" of
us that were fractured from our psyche, over time we can
begin to allow and integrate these very parts of us back into
our whole Being.

As we do so, we reduce the mistaken beliefs of who we are, which eliminates confusion and doubt about being able to accomplish our vision. We then move with more clarity and direction into our future, decreasing the misdirection of our own human capacity in meaningless work and reducing the waste of financial resources on poor decisions. Uncovering the blind spots, eliminating hurdles, and lining up with purpose also lessens or eliminates distractions in our lives, allowing purpose to seep into every area of our lives—work or career, relationships, creative endeavors—and manifesting a life of our dreams.

LESSON ABOUT HYPOTHESIS THREE: OUR EXPRESSION OF PURPOSE VARIES BY DEVELOPMENTAL STAGE.

As we saw from these case studies (and will see more clearly in chapters 4-6), early developmental tasks are primary so that we can prepare for our later expression of purpose in the external world. And even these childhood tasks have a nuanced expression, demonstrated through extremely unique characteristics of our identity and through actions we undertake. As we age into adulthood, our unique choices for developmentally appropriate life tasks vary by our desires to express ourselves (or not, if we're driven by conformist expectations or wounding). Regardless of the ability to express ourselves fully at any stage, we usually demonstrate some element of uniqueness that can point us to the Golden Thread of Purpose.

HOW DOES PURPOSE APPEAR IN YOUR OWN LIFE?

How do you see purpose appearing in your life's Golden Thread?

- Where has purpose shown up, pulling you uniquely along in your life?
- What elements of your childhood may still be present as "shadow" to your greatest expression?
- What patterns have you noticed related to your own unique interests over the span of your life? How may those have evolved over time in a way that could represent the unique flavor of you across your own development?

MY PERSONAL NARRATIVE: ANSWERING THE THREE QUESTIONS

You can read more about my complete story in the Appendix. As my life experiences were the spark for my personal and professional work, I also began to see the patterns and threads for these three hypotheses about purpose. Here's just a brief dissection of my own life and the three hypotheses.

Purpose as GPS, pulling me through life

As stated earlier in my introduction, my original purpose statement was "to speak powerful truths to shine love onto shadow to liberate soul's potential and reunite love and power." A more recently evolved version of my purpose statement that was offered to me intuitively is to "take people to the next stage of humanity."

Not so ironic that I'm writing about stages of consciousness and purpose.

A longing to live a meaningful life existed very early for me. You may recall my story of standing up to my mother as a young child, telling her my "truths" to protect me and my younger sister. And, simultaneously, I have always seen the good in people, able to love them because of who I saw they really were. To become "more of who I am and less of who I'm not," though, I had to learn to speak powerful truths about my own shadow in order to love myself. In doing so, I became free of the suffering and began to reunite the power within myself to experience love, which allowed me to share these gifts with others. The evolution of each of these facets of my purpose allowed me to evolve into the next stage of my own purpose and humanity.

We override our knowing of our Purpose because of our wounding.

Certainly, coming to understand the trajectory of my own childhood wounding played out like a tragicomedy. To even get to an early understanding of who I was, I had to overcome a lifetime of deep trauma and tragedy. Perhaps many of the patterns of my life—the twenty-one careers, the nomadic existence, the refusal to stop learning—were all efforts by my soul to pull me into a deeper awareness of how to resolve this complex dilemma we call humanity. The efforts have surely paid off in my own work and career to support others.

Our expression of purpose varies by developmental stage.

As the Universe supported me in my journey to resolve the crisis of my own wounding and non-individuation, I can see the distinct patterns of purpose showing up over my life trajectory. I credit the early experience of having a father who helped me live into my truth with a loving approach. While he didn't directly help me resolve my childhood dilemmas with my mother, he accepted who I was unconditionally and encouraged me to live a more courageous and "strong" life than most girls or women of my generation. True to our Texas roots, his encouragement of fishing, hunting, carpentry, sports, use of power tools (he owned a hardware store), and other generally "male-oriented" activities were well beyond the "girly" occupations that were the norm in my culture. Somehow, my soul knew that I needed to "man up" (or have more yang qualities) to be resilient enough to weather my life's storms and to be a powerful truthteller.

And, surely enough, encouraging my own now-adult daughters to be fourth-wave feminists (or, more correctly, activists advocating on behalf of social justice in many realms, including gender, racial, and climate rights) was a source of liberation for my own acceptance and individuation, as I strode into my adulthood newly ready to claim myself.

CONCLUSION: PREVIEW OF WHAT'S NEXT

The Three Hypotheses of Purpose suggest that:

- Purpose is our GPS, pulling us forward from a very early age with nuanced expression that shows up in early behaviors and preferences.
- Purpose appears to "hide" behind the wounding of our early lives and become an expression contrary to what we may believe as purposeful—that is, in fact, entirely

useful in helping us release the very constraints that keep us bound.

- Purpose looks differently across the stages of our lives, especially because we are required to complete developmental tasks in various stages that predict the type of purpose expression we're capable of.

And even if these things are true, and purpose really does live within and guide us throughout our lives, why does purpose matter? If it is as inherent and innate as eye or skin color, how does it make a difference in our lives?

In chapter 3, we'll discuss the significance of these three hypotheses of purpose and how it affects the trajectory of our lives—if we're living it. We'll also discuss various ways that purpose is seen by experts in the field, the scientific study of purpose, and the life outcomes that it affects, as well as explore more case studies and how the expression of purpose looks through these lenses.

REFERENCES

Hill, P.L., Burrow, A.L., & Sumner, R. (2016). Sense of Purpose and Parent-Child Relationships in Emerging Adulthood. Emerging Adulthood: 4(6). Accessed December 10, 2019 https://doi.org/10.1177/2167696816640134.

Jacoby, J. (1942). The psychology of C.G. Jung: An introduction with illustration. Abingdon-on-Thames, U.K.: Routledge and Kegan Paul Publishers.

Kelley, Tim. (2013). Personal communication.

Kelly, Tim. (2009). True purpose: 12 strategies for discovering the difference you are meant to make. Berkeley: Transcendent Solutions Press.

Kins, E., Byers, W., and Soenens, B. (2012). When the separation-individuation process goes awry: Distinguishing between functional dependence and dysfunctional independence. International Journal of Behavioral Development. 37(1):1-12. DOI: 10.1177/0165025412454027v.

Mahler, M.S., Pine, F., & Bergman, A. (2008). The psychological birth of the human infant: Symbiosis and individuation. New York: Basic Books.

Muehsam, D. & Ventura, C. (2014). Life rhythms as a series of oscillatory patterns: Electromagnetic energy and sound vibration modules gene expression for biological signaling and healing. Global Advances in Health Medicine, 3(2): 40-55.

Peele, Brandon. (2018). Planet on purpose: Your guide to genuine prosperity, authentic leadership and a better world. Balboa Press, 2018.

Ross, C.L. (2019). Energy medicine: Current status and future perspectives. Global Advances in Health and Medicine. 8: 2164956119831221. doi: 10.1177/2164956119831221.

Steele, C. (2017). Psychological interventions for working with trauma and distressing voices: The future is in the past. Frontiers in Psychology, 7: 2035.

CHAPTER 2

WHY PURPOSE?
PURPOSE AS YOUR GPS

———

As is true for many of us who've become purpose geeks or guides, Jonathan Gustin, founder of the Purpose Guides Institute and one of my mentors and colleagues in the field of purpose work, had an early obsession with figuring out the big evolutionary questions. In our 2019 interview, he described the second of his two early life experiences where he was "given" a mission to carry out:

"I had a soul encounter moment in junior high. I must've just gone to the bathroom during class. There was an empty hallway and no kids at the lockers. I sat down on the floor, leaning against a locker. I just had to sit there and contemplate my destiny. But I was like that, a serious little kid. This time, I had a flash."

Jonathan reflects on what he heard in this deep encounter with his soul, and what he became committed to in that moment, leaning against the junior-high lockers:

"I felt a desire to be a part of evolving the species so we could give birth to more goodness, truth, and beauty. That was what I felt. I said to myself, 'I want to heal and repair the world.' It was my second encounter, and I said, 'Holy shit, I have no idea how to do that.' So I decided then that I would like to be the wisest person I could be. Then I went back to geography class."

Like many of us in the field, Jonathan's early awakening experiences drove his fascination with searching for the maps of human development and his own soul evolution. This field is ripe with evolved experts who have brought significant heart and soul to their work to guide humanity forward.

This chapter shares the richness of these experiences from veteran voices of purpose and a few others whose lives have evolved to make their own significant contribution. Afterward, I'll also review the body of science related to aligning with purpose, to help us discern just how significantly purpose could impact our human experience.

WHAT EXACTLY IS PURPOSE? AND WHY DOES PURPOSE MATTER?

Veteran experts in the field of purpose have varying definitions, theories, and methodologies aimed at illuminating purpose. Primarily, these widely variant expressions of purpose are based in each expert's own origin of discovery and likely related to their own developmental stage of expression. These wide variations in definition of purpose, and in the methods related to finding or living purpose, may be confusing to the novice who wants to delve into an exploration of self and meaning. I hope you find it helpful to examine the various ideologies about how purpose can occur in your life, so that you can locate it from these unique frames specific to your own stage of development (see chapters 3-6).

Go confidently in the direction of your dreams. Live the life you've imagined.

—HENRY DAVID THOREAU

BILL PLOTKIN: THE SEEDS OF SOUL PURPOSE

Bill Plotkin, PhD., is a depth psychologist, wilderness guide, and founder of the Animas Valley Institute. He and his colleagues have guided thousands of women and men through nature-based initiatory passages. Bill has also authored important foundational works in the field of purpose, including the books *Soulcraft: Crossing into the Mysteries of Nature and Psyche* (2003), *Nature and the Human Soul: Cultivating Wholeness and Community in a Fragmented World* (2007), *and Wild Mind: A Field Guide to the Human Psyche* (2013). The Animas Valley Institute also offers training programs for cultural change agents seeking advanced study in Soulcraft™.

Bill speaks about the varying definitions of purpose in *Purpose Rising* (Emanuel Kuntzelman, Dustin DiPerna, Bright Alliance, 2017). He states that "what we mean by and experience as purpose depends on our stage of life and our depth of psychospiritual development." Bill acknowledges that in developing countries, purpose usually describes a mix of social, vocational, political, and/or religious goals or intentions, or a spiritual awakening.

But Bill suggests that another form of purpose "is completely absent from contemporary maps of human life." Bill describes this form as the "single most essential realm of purpose, especially in our current critical and liminal moment in the unfolding of the world's story." Bill's own conception of the soulwork required to live a purposeful life is derived from his own study and elaboration on the Four Directions Wheel, or what he calls the Eco-Soulcentric Developmental Wheel (see chapter 3).

Bill uses the east hemisphere of the Wheel to characterize the first quadrant (childhood) and last quadrant (true elderhood) of life, both of which are characterized by "being" and presence. He uses the west hemisphere of the Wheel to characterize the adolescent and adulthood quadrants, in which we are "doing"—striving to embody our essence in the world.

During our interview in 2019, Bill also distinguished his work through what he calls Eco-Awakening as one of the necessary passages for a contemporary Western person to be psycho-spiritually prepared for the journey of soul initiation. Through Eco-Awakening, we develop an awareness of and relationship with the "larger Earth community"; we come to "feel at home in the natural world in addition to the human world." His observation is that, in mainstream Western societies, most children are isolated from the natural world by parents and others who try to "protect" them from it, and that:

"This isolation from the natural world creates an existential crisis of identity because we are not rooted in the greater web of life, our primary realm of belonging."

In the absence of this rooting in the natural world, we are unable to create deeply satisfying ways of belonging to human social structures. We end up feeling alienated, isolated, and inauthentic.

Bill identifies the next major life passage after Eco-Awakening as Confirmation, which is the transition into the stage he thinks of as soul-centric late adolescence (which he calls the Cocoon). After Confirmation, we can begin to approach the deeper, more mysterious realm of purpose that is related to the soul. But the descent to soul begins only after we reach a "breaking point." He describes this phase:

"In the course of healthy human development, we are each meant to reach this breakpoint, this crisis, this divide beyond which we're no longer able to decisively define ourselves in terms of social or romantic relationships, or in terms of a job or career, a creative or artistic project, a political affiliation, a theory or philosophical perspective, a religious or ethnic membership, or a transcendental spiritual goal. We are propelled—compelled!—toward an underworld self-definition, a soul-infused experience of meaning and purpose and identity" (Plotkin, 2017).

Bill suggests that we are able to encounter our soul only after "the involuntary demise of our earlier comprehension of the nature of meaning or purpose, of the ways we developed an identity or set of beliefs about ourselves from our childhood and adolescent experiences." This is a "risky journey on which few in the West ever embark." Regarding the ways we come to know ourselves in mainstream Western adolescent and "adult" development, Bill adds:

"We have strayed a long ways from our deeper, innate, uncon-
scious knowledge of self and world, which is now obscured,
buried, unremembered. It's still there within us, but we can't
access it and we might not even know it exists" (Plotkin, 2017).

From Bill Plotkin's perspective, to encounter the soul is to
"'remember' the knowledge we were born with: our particular,
destined place in the world, our original personal instruc-
tions for this lifetime" (Plotkin, 2017). For Bill, "soul" is an
ecological concept, not a psychological one. It is our unique
ecological niche, not any kind of project or activity that
can be defined by a social role, job, or career. When people
acquire a conscious understanding of their souls, they do
so in metaphorical terms, or as what Bill calls "mythopoetic
identity"—not in social or vocational terms.

TIM KELLEY: PURPOSE ROOTED IN PARADIGM

Tim Kelley is the founder of the True Purpose® Institute
(TPI) and works with CEOs and teams from many notable
companies (e.g., Nabisco, ING, Oracle), government ministers, and international NGO leaders using his True Purpose
methods. Tim and TPI have trained over 1,000 consultants,
therapists, and coaches around the world. He is the author
of *True Purpose: 12 Strategies for Discovering the Difference*
You Are Meant to Make (2009).

Tim's approach to the purpose inquiry is to walk through
a step-by-step process that sets up communication with
one's own "trusted source," which is anything that might
already know his client's purpose (e.g., God, Source, one's
own higher self, or something in between). He guides his

clients to validate those sources and then query them for the answers to their questions about their essence, blessing, mission, and message (Kelley, 2009), the four different aspects of purpose in his system. Tim's methods continue to orient and inspire people globally to find deeper meaning and direction.

Tim describes the experience of asking the question "Why am I here?" (Kelley, 2009) as one that can:

"Shift the basic emphasis of life from one of meeting needs, dealing with fears, and seeking happiness to following a path that leads to the greatest possible fulfillment, success, and meaning in life."

I met Tim initially while serving as an executive at an online educational platform for personal and spiritual development content, where I had a chance to experience his work. He later served as a mentor to me. Perhaps because of his background in the military and as an engineer, his approach is the "meat and potatoes" of purpose work. The True Purpose approach can work for almost anyone at any developmental level as long as they're willing to listen to the guidance that comes through the process.

During our interview in 2019, Tim made a distinction between those who believe they "have" a purpose and are seeking it, and those who believe they can "choose" it. These distinctions are likely related to Tim's own early nonspiritual schema for his life and career (see Tim's life story later in this chapter) and may be related to the developmental level of his clients.

This distinction (having versus choosing purpose) is related to the location of personal power and agency of the individual. Tim added that those who don't believe in a higher power or spiritual source tend to trust their own conscious decision-making. Those who believe in a higher power have faith that a certain purpose is available to them, either stemming from their soul or in relation to a higher power or God. We can plausibly imagine these beliefs about origin of purpose are related to someone's developmental level and the perspective available to them.

As Tim's own purposeful expression has recently evolved, he is committed to working in the areas of intractable social problems (e.g., racial injustice, climate change, and white supremacy movements). His experience in working with corporations, international governmental agencies, and heads of state has allowed him to make a great dent in the intentionality among global leadership. However, he finds much work to do in these arenas that will require a more intensive and collaborative approach among other sectors that wouldn't normally be thinking about their purpose.

GREGG LEVOY: PURPOSEFUL "CALLINGS" TRANSMITTED THROUGH A LIFE

Gregg Levoy is the author of *Callings: Finding and Following an Authentic Life* (1998) and *Vital Signs: The Nature and Nurture of Passion* (2015), both texts that have been used as career publications for management and organizational leadership programs. He is a former behavioral specialist at *USA Today* and a notable blogger for national media outlets. Gregg leads workshops in higher education and industry.

Interviewing Gregg was a pleasure, as his *Callings* book was my first formal foray into purpose, after starting my doctorate and having been in the field of human potential for a decade.

Gregg paraphrased one of his favorite authors, Isabelle Allende: "She said, 'Kids should have a trunk in the basement with scary costumes' with an emphasis on the basement, to help people gain courage to look into dark places." As a former reporter, Gregg had hundreds of references at hand and shared many of them during our conversation. He spoke about Dr. Ira Progoff, whom he called "the grandfather of personal journaling"—who developed the earliest journaling methodology: Intensive Journal Method (1980). Gregg reverently shared that Progoff's method was to "go so deeply into your own well that you eventually hit the stream that is the source of all the wells. The more personal, the more universal."

Gregg described himself as "a pluralist" and believes that "people have multiple paths to purpose." His form of purpose work takes the form of helping people listen to their "callings" in different facets of their lives and exploring the idea that each of us has more than one. He believes that most people are interested in vocational callings, but that we also have relational, lifestyle, and spiritual calls. When he asks people at his workshops, "Half of the people will know they have more than one going on. And, sometimes, the vocational calling is really different, even at odds with the relationship calling."

Gregg's own life (see his story later in this chapter) and those of people he works with led him to believe that "parents are often obstacles to living purposefully." He frequently has workshop participants who tell him about the effect of parental authority on following their calling. Gregg shared that:

"Kids in college tell me that 'my father said if I didn't go to premed he would refuse to pay for my education, and I hate it.' Or I would consult with someone who said her parents sent her to her room for any display of negative emotions, such as anger or tears. And she wants to be a healer."

Gregg himself had a chip on his shoulder, originating in his own childhood repression. He's adamant that:

"It's wrong to deny people their deepest vitality."

Gregg believes that purpose is about "remembering something they already know, values they left behind." He described it as the "authentic self catching up to the social self, what a midlife crisis sounds like to me." He often hears people's stories of "way back when," that they wanted to be an artist but their parents told them such a profession was impractical so they became an accountant. It's the typical storyline. Gregg granted that purpose often relates to stuff people loved to do as children, coming back around fifty years later.

Gregg shared his belief that purpose work should address the forces that block people from expressiveness. In his own life, his parents didn't approve of significant parts of his personality, including his high energy and strong sense of self.

He suggested that we must confront the "formidable stuff that blocks expression." His advice is to "go down into the basement and process it. Reclaim your vitality. Intuitively, people know what they're up against and decide to stay where they are."

EMANUEL KUNTZELMAN:
RESISTING THE PULL OF CULTURAL CONDITIONING

Emanuel Kuntzelman is a social entrepreneur, philosopher, and environmentalist. He founded Greenheart International in 1985, through which he promoted personal and cultural understanding and social action. He's the founder of the Global Purpose Movement, a catalytic facilitator of purpose events, volunteer initiatives, and environmental advocacy projects. Emanuel contributed to *Intelligence of the Cosmos* (Laszlo, 2017) and *Purpose Rising* (Kuntzelman & DiPerna, 2017).

Most of his life, Emanuel has subscribed to the belief that we must overcome the strangling cultural conditions that prevent us from finding ourselves. During our interview (2019), as we discussed the potential Golden Thread available to all of us, Emanuel noted that:

"As an adventurer on the Golden Thread path, we must take the proverbial walk on the razor's edge, fighting every step of the way the mainstream and cultural conditioning needs of society."

He lamented that most people give up, "acquiescing to the status quo or expectations of others." He believes this outcome is partly due to the extreme amount of inner work and energy required to overcome the forces of our family, community, and culture at large. Emanuel admitted that these cultural forces have served in a protective role, creating socially normative expectations, and they also limit our advancement in the twenty-first century.

Emanuel's approach to promoting purpose has been to encourage people to explore other cultures of the world as a means to remove themselves from conformist forces. He suggested these opportunities "expand our comfort zone, open minds, and change preconceived notions of good and bad" organically, tackling the inner work on our behalf without us having to do much beyond absorbing cultural diversity. He likened it to being in a different "petri dish" of experiences, creating a milieu distinct from our natal environment.

Emanuel started traveling as a teen and has continued to resist the pull of stifling cultures by creating cultural exchange programs as an entrepreneur for thirty-five years.

JONATHAN GUSTIN:
PURPOSE EXPRESSION THROUGH MANY FACETS

Jonathan Gustin is the founder of the Purpose Guides Institute (PGI), which has assembled many purpose experts to create a comprehensive Purpose Guide training. Jonathan has served as a psychotherapist, activist, and meditation teacher and also founded the Integral Awakening Center. He has trained hundreds of students in his purpose discovery process and certified dozens of students in the last several years through the PGI curriculum.

Jonathan's approach to guiding people to their purpose includes a revelation of their "mythopoetic identity, a phrase coined by Bill Plotkin and Geneen Marie Haugen to refer to the way a human comes to consciously understand their soul, namely through metaphor" (Purpose Guides Institute). He supports people in arriving at this identity through a diverse set of tools that unveil the facets of purpose. These facets include: Vision, Values, Powers, Essence, Giveaway, Task, Message, and Delivery System, each designed to elicit an important element of how purpose is expressed in the world.

Jonathan describes purpose as:

"Something that we believe we're meant to grow into. We're called to grow into it. A human being is wired for this depth. A teenager doesn't just want to swim in the shallow end of the pool. They want to go into the deep end. It's a little dangerous, no oxygen there, but it's beautiful."

Jonathan also believes that purpose is polytheistic (as in, we have more than one) rather than the alternative monotheism (we have only one). He referred to James Hillman (1996), one of the earliest authors in the field of purpose, who described the psyche as polytheistic, and thus so must purpose be. Jonathan suggested that if we believed in the monotheistic version of purpose, then "it casts a long shadow. Find your purpose at twenty years and dive in. And that's that. That's not how it works."

He describes how he approaches his marriage as an example of how our lives shift to prompt our own evolution:

"The woman I married . . . 'til death do us part. I need to be truthful. I can't actually speak for sixty- or seventy-year-old Jonathan, so you jump in. And you don't know where your soul will lead you. You don't know where the marriage with wife or husband will lead you. So a true marriage is made up mostly of mystery. That's its main substance. It's a beautiful analogy. Marriage is so mysterious—and friendships. And some stay the same. Not everything has to be evolutionary."

And Jonathan quickly backtracked, knowing that he and I live differently than most:

"But for me, and you, that's where the juice is, on the evolutionary edge."

He agrees that purpose shows up early and evolves over time and concurred that "at a higher stage of development, it will only be better."

Jonathan himself is evolving his approach to working with purpose and teaching his students. He has recently derived a Purpose Developmental Model, interfacing with the integral stages of development (Wilber, 2000). See chapter 3 for the description of the stages model used here.

LARISSA RAINEY: PURPOSE AS SELF-DIRECTION THAT ENHANCES MEANING

Larissa Rainey's master's capstone project (2014) detailed the significant academic understandings of purpose related to positive psychology. Rainey described several key academic leanings that influenced her definition of purpose in terms of scientific inquiry. She reviewed McKnight and Kashdan (2009), who defined purpose as a "central self-organizing life aim" that serves as a stable "orienting" identity and framework to promote deliberate choices and continual targets to aspire to. These authors further suggested that for purpose to be enacted requires consistency; motivated behaviors; flexibility; an allocation of resources leading to productive cognitive, behavioral, and physiological activity; and a higher level of cognitive processing.

Rainey summarized several additional studies that give key insights into definitions and utility of purpose. These included:

- Ryff (1989) identifies that purpose is the directedness that produces a meaningful life and integration of the various facets of life into a comprehensive whole.
- Keys (2011) defines authentic purpose as having two distinct elements—the psychological purpose or sense of direction one has for their life, and the social contribution or collective benefit one's life provides.
- Rockind (2011) conceives of purpose as a unique and foundational life orientation that is active, forward-looking, and impactful in the world.

Rainey also briefly reviewed Victor Frankl's 1947 definition of purpose (2006) and its relationship to meaning, suggesting they are inextricably linked. Frankl distinguished meaning as fulfilling the life set before us, and purpose as the "why" for living, which provides us with reasons to live. Steger (2009, 2012) distinctly conceived of purpose as a motivational element of meaning, from which we can delineate the intent or reason for life and what we will do with our lives.

Rainey (2014) summarized the review of the literature with six statements about purpose:

- It is a part of our true and unique self that draws upon our unique strengths, values, passions, interests, and abilities.
- It provides direction and creates goals that serve to focus action.
- It is something we have to strive or "live" for, rather than an end goal.
- It makes life meaningful.
- It provides a benefit or connection to someone or something other than self.
- It is something that we must deliberately choose to follow or fulfill.

From a positive psychology perspective, Rainey described purpose as being an "intrinsically motivated" framework for personally and socially meaningful goals that pull one into the future (Rainey, 2014).

HOLLY'S COSMOLOGY AND DEFINITION OF PURPOSE: REMEMBERING OUR DESTINY

I've spent over thirty-five years (and many careers) in the field of human potential and transformation, including roles as a Master Coach, consultant, scientist, mediator, serial entrepreneur, and mother. Because of the huge variation in careers, roles, and expressions,

I've come to know purpose as not only the defining impetus for all our actions and focus, conscious or not, but the force behind life's most important experiences and expressions.

My own awareness of purpose integrates many of the above definitions and models, primarily because I have studied with these and other mentors. And my awareness also varies slightly, because my Soul Purpose is to liberate our souls, create an alignment of our lives, and work both to amplify our fullest expression and to take us to the next stage of our human development.

My knowing, given my soul's task to help each of us live purposeful lives (and therefore beyond my egoic conception), is that we each have an extremely nuanced, one-of-a-kind purpose that we came to express in this human lifetime, similar to Bill Plotkin's belief about our "particular destined place in the world" (Plotkin, 2017). While I do believe that we have just one purpose, I also imagine that it has many expressions, and that the articulation of our purpose can get upgraded over time (as mine recently did) as we gain capacity and live into our purpose.

This purpose transcends lifetimes, time, and space; it travels with us wherever we go beyond or in addition to the human experience. My observations suggest that we arrive here knowing who we are and what we are to do, and that our birth experience creates an "amniotic amnesia." This amnesia causes us to disremember most of our soul's knowing, though we usually recall bits and pieces through intuition and psychic doorways as we develop. Because we have mostly forgotten our purpose, our soul is forced to call or pull us through our lives in a way that serves our evolution to help us remember who we are, primarily by finding our way through the crises and the trauma of dissociating from our true selves.

It may seem like nonsense, for our journey to be this difficult and requiring more effort than most are willing to endure. However, this challenge is intentional.

We forget who we are, and are lost, so that we can find ourselves and come home.

That is the hero(ine)'s journey that our soul requires of us in order to succeed in living our fullest, most expressed lives. This "normalized oppression" of the lives and culture we live in create the "just right" circumstances that force us to do the work needed to liberate our souls.

And yet we are just a holographic particle of the vast universal quantum field. We are composed of the same particles as stars. Nassim Haramein's Unified Field Theory (Haramein, 2012) posits that the Universe is a single, entangled system, holographic in nature, which means that every single proton in the Universe contains within it the information of the entire

Universe as a whole. When this entangled nature of the Universe is illuminated, it begins to explain the extraordinary unity and coherency of the self-organizing systems all around and within us—and this phenomenon may point to the way consciousness arises. In addition, Haramein's theory provides a scientifically validated explanation for the concept that separation is an illusion, and that, in fact, we are all one (Brown, 2019).

These scientific explanations help to explain why we experience our souls the way we do, as both emergent and hidden within the dimensions of our wounding. And, we can reasonably assume that the cosmic field in which we're immersed would also be sending us signals, images, messages, insights, intuitions and beams of brilliance to find our way within the vast quantum field in an ever more aligned and expansive trajectory, which we might call purpose. But only if we listen.

Purpose, as the essential expression of our authentic nature, will unfold over a lifetime into greater possibilities because of the enhanced awareness that accompanies growing up. Developing from a child into adolescence, then into mature adulthood (something that not all people do well) creates advanced perspectives and understanding of contexts and paradox, which is essential to a full expression of one's purpose on the planet (see chapter 3). We can authentically and powerfully (and colorfully) express our purpose in all stages, though our contributions are likely to have more impact at later stages of development.

As I'll demonstrate in later chapters, my own beliefs include that purpose is hidden behind our wounds, but that this primary childhood wound serves as a catalyst to explore the authentic version of self (purpose). As a result, I often suggest that the wound is the "flip side" of purpose. As I'll also demonstrate through stories, our purpose and our wound are both expressed uniquely through time.

CASE STUDIES: HOW PURPOSE PULLS US FORWARD EVEN WITHIN VARIOUS CONTEXTS

We can see from the varying stories of people's lives that purpose lives differently within the context of the seeker yet provides direction and meaning regardless of the perceived source of inspiration.

CASE STUDY: GREGG LEVOY

As noted above, Gregg's work changed the course of my life's direction. His clear invitation to follow your path was enough to inspire and give me courage that it would turn out okay if I truly listened to my calling.

After hearing Gregg's distinct beliefs that "we must go down into the basement and process" our fears to find and live into our purpose or calling, I didn't find it surprising that Gregg's own story began with a deep curiosity about shadows and hidden rooms. He understood that the stories living behind those shadows lead us to our calling, and they led him to his. Gregg shared in our interview (2019) that one of his:

"Earliest memories was going to my grandfather's house. . . . He lived on Long Island Sound. I felt like a detective. He had a house full of secret passageways. . . . He had a bookshelf where

you pressed a button and the whole thing swiveled and opened to a series of passageways. It was fabulous for a kid's imagination and helped to turn me into an explorer. As someone who eventually wanted to dig into the shadowy realms, the hidden rooms of the psyche, and later callings and purposes, this really fit into that realm. It opened Pandora's box for me. It opened the closet for me to learn to go into the secret passageways that lead us home."

Gregg now sees that some element of his calling was designed to illuminate the "scary and dark . . . the bats . . . the stuff we find in the psyche." His purpose-seeking perspective stems from this knowing that our souls call us out. To quote Gregg, speaking on behalf of the soul, "I've got your life's work in my hands here. Please talk to me, otherwise I'm going to come to you in nightmares, body symptoms, or weird failure that's going to follow you around."

Gregg recalled that his parents proclaimed that as a very young child, he was always asking questions about everything—not just the external world but also the internal one. He chuckled as he shared how his father's favorite game to play with him and brothers was a:

"Homemade invention called 'The Alien Game,' where he was from another planet and we were his guides on earth. We had to go into the neighborhood, and he would ask questions about the planet that we saw, and we had to try to explain it to him."

Gregg described how he applied his father's fantastical game about the "alien world" to his own inner world of deep inquiry. "Instead of going 'what a jerk' when someone cuts me off in line at the grocery store, I cock my head and ask, 'Why do they do that?' It keeps me in a state of compassion."

These early memories of Gregg's indicated his fascination with what we can't see in our own lives or the world around us.

Early on, however, Gregg experienced his own life force coming up against the forces of repression and suggested that "parents are often obstacles." Gregg grew up in the 1950s, and at the time, Ritalin was commonly prescribed for children as "mother's little helper." His mother slipped Ritalin into the morning milk for him and his twin brother, starting at around age six until their early teens.

He learned later that his mother wanted a career rather than children, but that women didn't have a choice back then. She became one of the first women on Wall Street in the early 1960s. Gregg paints a vivid picture of his mother in her graduating class of account executives: "She looked like RBG [Ruth Bader Ginsburg], with fifty men in black around her." So when three boys whom she wasn't prepared to raise came along, she used Ritalin to suppress them.

Gregg thinks the repression of his native energies in fact pushed him into his deepest expression, where it was allowed. In junior high, he began writing poetry and recalls that his English teacher "Mrs. Linder ('who chopped her students to tinder') was the first person who saw the gift in me." He was into writing about dreams, poetry, and mythology, even in his preteens. He was "after a different story than most people like to tell," and consumed all the mythology stories—"Hercules, the Odyssey, the Greek gods and goddesses."

When Gregg was going through his mother's artifacts as he helped her move into a nursing home, he was surprised to find a box of letters his divorced parents had exchanged while he was in college. One specific letter stood out to him, representing the repression foisted upon him. Gregg's father wrote a scathing letter about Gregg to his mother, upon seeing Gregg's college course schedule, and claimed "from what I can see, literature, philosophy, and psychology are preparation for oblivion." Gregg acknowledges that, at the time, he wasn't sure how he would use those courses, but that they were exactly what he needed to study to be the writer of psychology he became.

Gregg's passion for writing about people took several turns, especially after he took a journalism class that he described as that moment when his "lights went on." Gregg's nuanced "callings" in his career began with what he called "service journalism," but "things called to him from the dark, in all different arenas, and I was too scared to look." He eventually left a job that told him what to write and began writing what called to him.

The clear signal to "quit the system, employment, and become a freelance writer was not designed to reassure parents, especially when they wanted me to be a lawyer. I ignored the call for half a decade. I eventually left the comfort of a regular paycheck, medical benefits, and a pension" to do what he was inspired to do instead.

While Gregg resonated with the four facets of my purpose statement, he described his purpose statement as "helping people unfold who they really are, their gifts, their passions, what they are here to contribute." As I pried deeper into how that process occurs for him in his work, Gregg acknowledged that he is "also here to be a steward for enthusiasm in any arena," which truly seemed to fit hand-in-glove with his life story and seemed a more nuanced description of his purpose. Gregg described the definition of enthusiasm as "entheos, of the god within. By following your 'enthusiasms' you are, by definition, following God, expressing God." Gregg laughs and adds, "it's just etymology, and I'm a freak for language."

Gregg also shared that he's an Enneatype 7, or the enthusiast, and that his real self has "been there all along," enthused about digging into the deeper aspects of ourselves. Similarly, he shares equal enthusiasm in helping others find their own callings in life, whether it be vocation, relationship, or other facets of life.

Gregg describes himself now as in the "neutral zone." He's been waiting two to three years for his next marching orders. He sees that in his early 60s, the:

"Eldering question is up for me. I want to work with audiences broader than students. I have a different set of questions. I know that callings grow out of people that are different than they have been in the past. I'm not just asking anymore for objects of desire, such as 'What's my next book?' or 'What's my next relationship?' or 'Where should I live?' I'm now asking, 'What would those things give me that I am searching for?'"

He described his calls as more "being" calls. He's learning "how to live in states of appreciation, in connection in everything I do. I'm trying to spread it across the whole bandwidth so I can apply it in the longest line at the grocery store or an airplane to New York."

CASE STUDY: JEFFREY SMITH

In some cases, one's purpose stands out so loud and clear in childhood that it's unmistakable what a person should set about doing and being in life. But the inherent glitch in this system is that the person usually doesn't see their own wounding on their way to purpose, which becomes a vulnerability for their fullest expression.

Jeffrey Smith, a notable activist who's spent much of his adult life crusading against the genetic modification of the world's food supply, had an early "conviction that [my] underlying purpose of life was to gain some advanced state or enlightenment," primarily because he understood, even as a child, that human potential was vast. Like most young boys, Jeffrey played superhero games. But he refused to just mimic the comic characters who usually had some shortcoming or fatal flaw. Instead, he created a personal superhero named "Molecule Man," who had unlimited control of matter, which metaphorically represented Jeffrey's knowing of human capacity.

Early on, Jeffrey understood that he was meant to help lots of people become more aware of their own power and capacity because "most people didn't know their human potential is so great." Many of Jeffrey's childhood memories were centered around his early expanded consciousness and his regular made-up practices that he used to train his mind to accomplish out-of-the-ordinary feats.

Jeffrey laughingly recounts a story from high school. He recalls how, while other kids were having a massive snowball fight, he, snowball in hand, quietly stared at a spot on a tree a considerable distance away. He was in the middle of his mental "training" when the principal appeared on the scene.

"Stop throwing snowballs!" the principal shouted at the students.

The administrator walked swiftly over to Jeffrey and said sternly, "Put the snowball down."

Jeffrey looked at him, giving no indication of having heard the demand. Instead, he replied to the principal, "Do you see that small black spot in the tree way over there?"

"Put the snowball down."

Jeffrey turned, looked directly into the eyes of the principal, and said, "Watch."

He hurled the snowball without looking. The snowball hit the tree precisely on the spot. The administrator just stared at Jeffrey and then back to the tree.

Without a word, he walked past Jeffrey to scold other kids for throwing snowballs.

This ability for extraordinary capacities, coupled with social awkwardness, left him as an "outsider" to typical peer groups, and Jeffrey faced years of shaming and bullying.

Yet his drive to live above and beyond the norm led him to circles like the Transcendental Meditation (TM) movement, where he taught people about personal development and higher states of consciousness. Jeffrey suggested that he "knew I was a communicator and that I was supposed to influence large numbers for their own good and for the good of the world," but he wasn't sure what he was being prepared for.

In 1996, Jeffrey attended a short lecture by a scientist who warned about the damaging effects of genetically modified organisms (GMOs). These new types of plants were about to be introduced into the food supply, which could have widespread health impacts. Jeffrey also learned that GMOs released in the environment would irreversibly contaminate and corrupt nature's gene pool. This lecture changed Jeffrey's life. While saving the food supply was no small task, he realized that using his talents to accomplish something so daunting was congruent with his desire to affect lots of people (and aligned with his uncommon capacities).

Jeffrey's career as an anti-GMO activist catapulted after he wrote the global bestseller *Seeds of Deception* (2003) and began to travel the world nonstop for thirteen years on behalf of the cause. He exposed how biotech companies, such as Monsanto, had an ongoing campaign to aggressively attack, threaten, and suppress scientists, reporters, and activists who investigated GMO dangers.

And Jeffrey became a target himself. Scientists and front groups were quietly paid off to try to discredit him and his work. Secret Monsanto emails made public from lawsuits confirmed the company's attack strategies. But the attempts by Monsanto to shame Jeffrey and denigrate his character bounced off the superhero armor he'd developed during years of being an "outsider" to his peers. He had learned to resist normal convention and confront a well-resourced industry and to inspire countless activists to also stand up to the shaming tactics of the industry.

Jeffrey and his nonprofit, Institute for Responsible Technology, are widely credited with pioneering the educational campaigns that have convinced 46 percent of U.S. shoppers to seek healthier non-GMO choices, which has forced the food industry to accommodate.

As we discussed the next expression of his purpose, Jeffrey paused and sighed deeply. He described his concerns that "gene editing has become so cheap and easy, it creates an unprecedented threat to the planet. Biotech companies are looking to alter practically everything with DNA. Bacteria to bees. Algae. Animals." He paused again; I could feel the weight of his thoughts. He continued, "The most common result of genetic engineering is a surprise side effect." Jeffrey is changing his focus to prevent the widespread introduction of GMOs throughout the environment, "which could irreversibly replace nature." A seemingly superhuman task.

Ironically, Jeffrey's vulnerability, or his inherent human fallibility, rather than his ability to be superhuman, gave him the resilience and much-needed armor to do the job. Jeffrey's video, "The End Game," which describes the urgent need to protect the planet's gene pool, can be found at the Institute for Responsible Technology.

CASE STUDY: EMANUEL KUNTZELMAN

While Emanuel Kuntzelman's epiphany about who he is and his purpose came early, it didn't find an expression until he was a teenager and traveled with his parents on cultural exchange programs. As his own version of the Golden Thread began to show up, it became clearer and now demonstrates itself in his role as founder of Greenheart International and of the Global Purpose Movement.

Emanuel's epiphany about his role in making a major contribution in life came when he was in the first grade. As he sat in an apple tree in his backyard in small-town Illinois, he was contemplating the gravity of being among the billions of other people on the planet that his teacher had described. He explained that "while this wouldn't be unusual for a first grader in a world that was beginning to explore space travel, it would be more remarkable in today's world of device distraction and the counting of 'likes' for a social media post."

Emanuel described his father's early open-mindedness as a catalyst for his own nature to be "different." Among his childhood expressions of this rebellion were rocking the boat of his conservative Catholic upbringing. He questioned Sister Mary Ann about "why God couldn't outfox the Devil," which got him ejected from Bible studies.

Later, as his dad tried to rein him in to fit within the culture of their small conservative town, Emanuel instead poured himself into the civil rights and anti-Vietnam war era and took a stand as a young leader in the radicalized protests. While he organized demonstrations and was a "flaming liberal," he also was a good student, athlete, and leader, learning to straddle the tension of being both radical and accepted within his own culture.

And perhaps this fact explains why much of Emanuel's youth looked more like rebellion than purpose. Among the first sentiments that Emanuel shared in our interview (2019) was his belief that "cultural conditioning is strangling us." Because of his experiences traveling abroad in other cultures, he believes that "removing yourself from the culture you live within" is among the most important means to find direction in life. Emanuel suggested that the "socializing process" of our homegrown culture gets in the way of finding our individual vision.

Emanuel's college life focused on self-exploration, as he was exposed to radical data about the dire condition of the species and the planet in his sociology class. He realized he needed to create large-scale solutions for change rather than depending on the individual approaches popular in the 1970s. This goal sent him on a long spiritual search, much like others of his era. Yet, in this process, Emanuel describes, "I lost my footing, ended my spiritual quest, and ended up as an English teacher in Madrid. I decided to face the practical circumstances of the world."

But Emanuel never really lost his thread. Even in the midst of this practical world, he wrote freelance stories about important historical moments. One of these pieces was about Picasso's 1937 depiction of the suffering caused by the bombing of Guernica, Spain, by the Nazis during the Spanish Civil War. Emanuel's writing about this anti-war piece of Picasso's, which mirrored the resistance movement in Spain, became an important centerpiece of his impulse to resist the dominant social forces.

But despite this personal success as a teacher and writer, Emanuel felt lost from his own inner compass and confused about where to go next. When Emanuel described the "hippy, wanderlust, loser" circumstances of his life to David Tiedeman, a Harvard professor who'd developed a vocational training called "lifecareer," Tiedeman responded with "Congratulations!" and suggested that he'd done everything right so far!

Following this encouragement, Emanuel became a cultural exchange entrepreneur for thirty-plus years. By doing so, he exposed people to different cultures, where they could rebel against the "strangling acculturation" of their own native culture by experiencing a new way of life.

But this work wasn't enough for Emanuel, who recalls his childhood "apple tree" moment regularly in his meditations. His need to get back to the urgency of the planetary crisis led him to found the Global Purpose Movement (GPM) to create coherence among the many voices and actors in the world working to transform society and stabilize a new paradigm in cultural consciousness.

Emanuel's last words to me during our interview included this sage advice:

"We must listen for the call of purpose, and when we lose it, we have to ask for it to come back, to keep track of it, to coddle it and make sure it keeps track of us."

Emanuel believes "it is our duty, our moral obligation and reason for being to find" our purpose. I couldn't agree more. If the appearance of Emanuel's Golden Thread throughout his life in its many expressions is any indication, he'll continue to generate even more profound expressions to keep us from being strangled by our habituated lives.

As we can gather from these distinctions yet similarities between veteran purpose teachers, guides, scientists, and mentors, and in the varied stories of these mentors and others, purpose appears nuanced, distinct, and one-of-a-kind—plus, it evolves over a lifetime into many expressions. Even more, the science behind purpose compels us, with even greater urgency, to consider the benefit of aligning with this powerful force.

THE SCIENCE BEHIND PURPOSE

The scientific field related to purpose is a relatively young area of inquiry. Relative to other domains of knowledge in the fields of psychology, positive psychology, human development, neuroscience, consciousness, or other scientific fields related to human evolution, we know less about the impact of living a purposeful life because fewer questions have been articulated and studied than these other fields. This gap is probably because purpose arose within the spiritual realm (distinct from the study of meaning), and therefore seemed "out of reach" for most scientific methods.

As humanity wakes up and grows up, moving along the developmental path toward a collective maturity, more

people will be interested in living intentional and meaningful lives that contribute to the larger schema, rather than just for their own personal wealth or well-being.

That is an artifact of advancing stages of consciousness or development, rather than a value-based definition. As we progress to more mature stages of development, we are able to see broader contexts in which we live, which we could not see before (more to be discussed in chapter 3).

And thus, as our human developmental stage advances, our inquiry expands. We personally become interested in achieving purpose and meaning, and ask questions like: How does it happen? How do I find it? Who gets to have one? From where does it originate?

McKnight et al. (2009) have proposed a scientifically derived model to understand how purpose in life creates health and well-being.

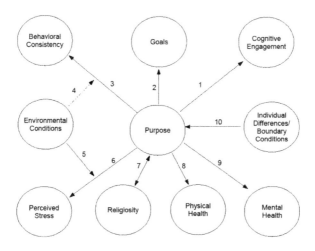

Their model suggests that purpose is the central element or unifying theme that affects and informs many facets of life, including cognitive engagement, goals, behavioral consistency, perceived stress, religiosity, physical health, and mental health (Kashdan, 2015).

While this model creates a conceptual big picture of the interrelatedness of purpose to almost every facet of life, the following overview of scientific outcomes about how purpose affects our everyday lives may entice us to consider living in alignment with purpose.

THE SCIENCE BEHIND PURPOSE-RELATED OUTCOMES

The two primary areas of study thus far that contribute to our understanding of purpose include "success" (financial and otherwise) and productivity, and health and well-being. I present here a synopsis or highlights from multiple sources to demonstrate the depth and breadth of purpose-related outcomes in every aspect of life.

SUCCESS & PRODUCTIVITY

The following are research studies that indicate the effect of having and seeking purpose on outcomes related to success and productivity.

Personal Income & Wealth

- Employees who find their jobs highly meaningful are 10 percent more likely to have received a raise in the past year and 5 percent more likely to have received a promotion in the past six months, compared to employees who consider their work relatively meaningless (BetterUp, 2018).

- Sense of purpose predicted household income and net worth (Hill et al., 2016).
- Having a purpose invokes more strategic investment and savings among individuals (Crosby, 2016).

Financial Performance

- Purpose-driven companies outperformed the market 15:1 and their peers 6:1 (Jim Collins, Jerry Porras, Built to Last: Successful Habits of Visionary Companies, Harper Business, 1994).
- Purpose-aligned cultures outperform their peers 12:1 (Kotter & Heskett, 2011).
- Purpose-driven companies outperform the S&P 500 by 400 percent over ten years (Stengel, 2011).
- Companies exhibiting higher purpose and clarity exhibit higher future revenues and stock performance (Gartenberg, Prat, & Sarafeim, 2016).
- Purpose-driven companies posted compounded annual growth rates of 9.85 percent compared to 2.4 percent for the whole S&P 500 Consumer Sector (Korn Ferry, 2016).
- Companies that have articulated and understood purpose are more likely to demonstrate 10 percent growth (58 percent) than companies who have not yet begun to articulate purpose (42 percent) in comparison (Ernst & Young Beacon Institute, 2016).
- Purpose-driven companies are more likely than "laggards" (re: purpose) to have success in 86 percent of company initiatives (Ernst & Young Beacon Institute, 2016).

Employee Performance & Engagement

- Purpose-driven salespeople outperform product-driven salespeople (McLeod, 2012).
- Purpose-driven employees have an average annual output of $9.1k higher than those without purpose (BetterUp, 2018).
- Purpose is correlated with a quadrupling of the likelihood of being engaged at work (Gallup & Healthways, 2014).
- Ninety percent of global employees in purpose-driven companies are engaged versus 13 percent of the global workforce who are engaged (Korn Ferry, 2016; Gallup & Healthways, 2014).
- People who say they're doing the most meaningful work of their lives right now were 28 percent less likely to plan on quitting their jobs within the next six months (BetterUp, 2018).
- People rank being connected to their own or the company's purpose as the highest factor in job satisfaction, and twice as important as the second factor—company leadership (Happiness Research Institute & Nordic Council of Ministers, 2018).

Leadership

- Middle managers who clarify key objectives related to purpose create more financial gain for companies (Sarafeim & Gartenberg, 2016).
- Eighty-four percent of executives believe that having shared purpose will be more successful in transformation efforts (Ernst & Young Beacon Institute, 2016).
- Employees report much higher levels of job satisfaction when their values are shared by company leadership (BetterUp, 2018).

- Purpose-oriented employees are 50 percent more likely to be in leadership positions than non-purpose-oriented employees (Imperative, 2016).

Job Satisfaction

- Employees report much higher levels of job satisfaction when their values are shared by company leadership (BetterUp, 2018).
- Employees who report company leadership as highly aligned on the value of meaningful work show a 33 percent decrease in turnover risk, compared to employees who feel leadership is misaligned on this issue (BetterUp, 2018).
- Employees will give up 23 percent of their total future lifetime earnings—nearly a quarter of their income—in exchange for work that is always meaningful (BetterUp, 2018).
- Employees who place a higher value on meaningful work occupy more senior, skilled positions and stay longer (BetterUp, 2018).
- Employees who rate their work as very meaningful report 14 percent greater job satisfaction than the average employee, and 51 percent greater job satisfaction than employees who have the least meaningful jobs (BetterUp, 2018).
- Employees who say they have the most meaningful jobs they can imagine having (about 5 percent of respondents) also take an average of two fewer days of paid leave per year than other workers (BetterUp, 2018).
- Employees who rate their current jobs as very meaningful put in an extra hour per week at work, compared to employees who feel their work is not meaningful. In a

fifty-week work year, this extra time translates to an average additional $5,437 in output per worker, per year, for an organization (BetterUp, 2018).

- Shared purpose is the most important source of meaning in supportive work cultures (BetterUp, 2018).

Strategy
- Among global executives, 91 percent link a strong corporate purpose with profitability (Deloitte, 2013).
- Eighty-seven percent of global executives believe companies perform best when their purpose is beyond profit (Ernst & Young Beacon Institute, 2016).
- Eighty-three percent of global executives believe purpose helps them stay ahead of industry disruption (Deloitte, 2014).

HEALTH & WELL-BEING
The following are research studies that indicate the effect of having and seeking purpose on outcomes related to health and well-being.

Longevity/Chronic & Acute Health Conditions
- Purpose is negatively correlated with all-cause mortality. (Sone et al., 2008).
- Purpose is correlated with reduced likelihood of developing Alzheimer's by 50 percent or mild cognitive impairment by 30 percent (Boyle et al., 2012).
- Purpose is correlated with reduced likelihood of having a stroke by 22 percent or more (Kim et al., 2013a).
- Purpose is correlated with reduced likelihood of having a heart attack by 27 percent or more (Kim et al., 2013b).

- Purpose is correlated with increased interleukin-6 (IL-6), or proinflammatory initial response of the immune system (Friedman et al., 2007).
- Purpose is correlated with lower levels of depression in the elderly (Hedburg, 2010).
- Purpose is correlated with lower levels of depression in teens (Telzer et al., 2014).

Self-Care/Screening
- Purpose is correlated with increased use of preventive screening exams and decreased use of health care services (Kim, Strecher & Ryff, 2014).
- Purpose is correlated with making healthier life choices (Kang et al., 2019).

Mental Health & Well-Being
- Purpose is correlated with more progressed identity formation (Madrozo, 2014).
- Purposeful well-being is correlated with gene expression (Fredrickson et al., 2013).
- Purpose is correlated with ability to retain commitment—grit—during challenging times (Hill, Burrow & Bronk, 2014).
- Purpose is correlated with lower levels of stress, burnout, and trauma (Singer et al., 2019).

Emotional Regulation
- Purpose is correlated with improved behavioral impulse control (Burrow & Sprent, 2016).
- Purpose is correlated with an increased ability to cope with pain (Smith et al., 2008).

- Purpose is correlated with an increased ability to cope with adversity (Malin et al., 2019).

Learning, Memory, & Cognition
- Purpose is correlated with a doubling of the likelihood of learning something new each day (Gallup & Healthways, 2014).
- Purpose is correlated with higher scores for memory, executive function, and overall cognition (Lewis et al., 2017).
- Purpose enhances "cognitive reserve," the biological strength and resilience of the brain cells to injury and degradation (Kaplan & Anzaldi, 2015).
- Purpose is correlated with faster brain processing speed, more accurate memory, and lower levels of disability and depression in aging adults (Windsor, Curtis, & Lusczc, 2015).

Sex & Love
- Purpose is correlated with higher levels of sexual enjoyment (Prairie et al., 2011).
- Purpose is correlated with increased levels of attraction (Stillman et al., 2010).

PURPOSE IS A CORNERSTONE OF A HEALTHY, SATISFYING, AND SUCCESSFUL LIFE

As you can see from the above data about the effects of purpose in nearly every aspect of life, purpose is essential to both identify with (as motivation and intention) and orient your life (or work) in order to focus, direct, and support decisions and actions. Because purpose is a cornerstone by which one's life can be lived—fruitfully—we can also imagine the profound multidimensional impact that living a purposeful life would have on your family, work life, community, and the planet in general. If we were to imagine a "tipping point," which is "that magic moment when an idea, trend, or social behavior crosses a threshold, tips, and spreads like wildfire" (Gladwell, 2002), perhaps even 10 percent of the people on the planet could save the planet if they were aligned with their purposeful lives, as Plotkin suggests above.

Plotkin also warns us that "if one has a longing to live into purpose, we must choose not to succumb to the consumer-conformist-imperial-dominator mind, to its business-as-usual" mentality (Plotkin, 2017). He suggests that seeking an encounter with soul and leaving behind the consumerist-conformist mentality is the "single most important opportunity" of our time. This requires, as a foundation, that we reshape "all human cultures so as to support every child to grow in a way that enables the uncovering and embodiment of this particular, now exceedingly rare, realm of purpose" (Plotkin 2017).

PURPOSE AS A VERB

In some cases, one person coming into alignment with their life purpose can have a significant impact. The next several case studies are examples of seemingly ordinary people who began to live extraordinary lives as they came into alignment with their purpose.

CASE STUDY: MIRA MEGS LATHROP

You wouldn't imagine that a woman as relatable as Mira Megs Lathrop, who lives in a city as alive and symbiotic as New York, would have ever felt unable to connect deeply with people.

Mira Megs (formerly known as Megan) Lathrop, whose networking energy far exceeds most power grids, has had a successful career as a certified money coach and financial planner. She co-created the Money Coaching Program at a national bank and founded her own business, Finanseer. After moving to NYC in 2018, Mira Megs quickly became a pioneer in bridging people and capital, as well as transforming people's relationship with money.

When we started working together in 2017, Mira was puzzled. Even though she'd always had a strong sense of self, she was feeling lost in her career, in a challenging relationship, in connecting with her parents, and in knowing where to go next. Even though Mira had previously launched her own business and had co-created the Money Coaching Program, she didn't have a clear vision because of the muddiness of the milieu in which she was swimming. She also envisioned that she wanted to step forward and be a thought leader around the movement to create financial freedom in the world.

While our work intended to focus on clarifying Mira's purpose, the apparent backdrop that needed resolution was the challenging partnership in which she'd been involved. With foresight, Mira suggested that she "needed a new relationship, perhaps with myself" and that she didn't care for herself in essential ways, such as choosing nourishment and acceptance. We decided that was likely a mirror for her current relationship and chose to include the relational challenges in our exploration.

As is often the case, the challenges that surface in our lives portray the very wounding that we're "blessed" with in childhood, which is also the shadow version of our greatest gifts, our purpose. In our interview (2019), Mira recalls:

"I didn't feel connected. I was always scared. I didn't like to have one-on-one time with anyone, even my father. I was anxious and didn't know what we would talk about. I didn't want to be seen because I was so self-conscious. I didn't know what I would reveal, so I didn't have close connections."

This sense of not wanting to be seen persisted into adulthood and became obvious in her closest relationships with her partner and friends.

Mira's childhood experience was marked by the birth of a baby sister when she was nine. When her mother's attention was diverted, Mira became independent and strong-willed. She remembered feeling isolated and alone, unseen by her parents, and having to let go of her own emotions to restore connection with her mom.

One of the few people Mira felt comfortable with in her formative years was a cousin, twenty years older, who had "something in her that allowed me to connect to myself. She was an artist and was kind of 'out there,' very unique. *So* herself and authentic." Mira described that as a teen she was seldom truly satisfied or happy, but in outward expression appeared to be a normal teen, if not perfectionistic. She felt connected to groups because of the shared causes and movements but was often uncomfortable alone with friends. Conversely, she could spend days alone with her cousin, with whom she had an authentic connection.

Because of the involuntary denial of her emotions in child-hood, Mira didn't trust herself. Truth was known as something outside of her own experiences. During our coaching work, Mira uncovered that she didn't have access to her own sense of "knowing," or how to hear the whispers of her body, much less her soul. She knew that the current relationship was likely a "sacred mirror" for her own way of being with herself. With great attention to her regaining access to her own emotions, body sensations, and energetic shifts, Mira began to hear her own voice and felt connected to herself again.

Mira's purpose, of course, is related to creating connections with others, or movements that transcend convention. In the emergence of a true connection to herself, a potent attribute that seemed to be missing earlier in her life, Mira proclaimed her role as a "bridge" for helping bring financial freedom to the forefront in society. As part of her current platform, Finanseer, she creates conversations with "wealth stewards" who desire to help create a new economy, aligning resources with a habitable and just planet. Mira also serves as co-founder of Women Power Our Planet, a platform empowering women to come together and deploy capital as guardians of the planet.

And, as I found in many of the interviews here, Mira's own journey shifted again before this book could be completed. The initial interview yielded a sense that she still felt more responsible for connecting to others than to herself. As is true for each of us as we come into greater expression of our purpose, our subsequent conversations further revealed the unresolved shadow, and Mira immediately set out to uncover the truth of her childhood. As she did, she experienced an expansion of her purpose to "stand in the gap" to connect traditional and new paradigm financial institutions. Mira will continue her developmental journey to bring her biggest contribution to the masses. No better place for that than NYC!

CASE STUDY: TIM KELLEY

For someone who works at a global level on intractable social problems, you'd never imagine that the impetus behind Tim Kelley's ability to help international leaders navigate conflicts was related to a childhood revelation that his parents and other adults "had no idea what they were doing and were making it up as they went along."

As noted earlier, Tim has become a leader in the field of purpose through his work across the globe. Tim currently consults with corporations, NGOs, sponsoring governmental units, and nations themselves to resolve issues such as the racial divide in the United States, the entrenched conflict between Israel and Palestine, and the rising neo-Nazi party in Slovakia.

Tim told the story during our interview (2019) of being "dragged through the streets of Manhattan by his mother, going rapidly through the crowd" as she pulled him along on her errands. When he asked his mother where they were going and why so hurriedly, he realized, at the fragile age of four, that she was making up a story to satisfy him and that she really had no idea where she was going. Tim describes that at that moment he panicked and felt empty.

Tim laughed when he suggested that "four-year-olds need a foundation of God and the Easter Bunny," rather than an awareness that their parents were clueless. The realization that his parents were "making up the answers" was cause for him to lose faith and hope that the adults knew what they were doing. This shift ultimately did cause Tim to "reject God, religion, and anything else that smelled of it."

Despite the fact that Tim didn't believe his family was normal or that his parents were adequate to raise him, he pretended that everything was fine and continued to ask questions even when they provoked conflict. Because life at his home often did not go well, he "suppressed unpleasant emotions and became very logical, like (the fictional characters) Sheldon Cooper in *The Big Bang* or Data in *Star Trek*."

Earlier in his career, Tim found himself in the safe world of numbers, obtaining a mathematics degree from the Massachusetts Institute of Technology. He later became a director at Oracle, where he established international software centers and then served as a commanding officer in the U.S. Navy, where he commanded reserve units of an amphibious assault craft unit, a submarine repair unit, and an ammunition-handling team.

As the "meaningless world" that Tim experienced in childhood led him to be detached and created a fracturing of psychic parts (similar to many of us in this book, as we experience childhood wounding), this detachment also propelled him forward in the career experiences that were relatively devoid of personal flavor or passion.

This experience of "not giving a crap about the paradigms people live in," similar to his childhood, ultimately catalyzed Tim's ability to make a difference in systems where "stakeholders can't talk to each other and [their issues] get wound up around the axle," referring to stubborn corporate and global dilemmas.

While Tim's detachment from disillusionment served him well into his adult career, it became a handicap in his adult relationships, and he went through a "catharsis and emotional intelligence training to get my wiring hooked back up again." The gift of his childhood experience was that, through his own healing, Tim learned to use the innovative techniques (which he loosely refers to as "voice dialogue") to be used as the healing of these fractured parts.

For decades, Tim's purpose statement had been to "Create and Reveal Heaven on Earth," which is somewhat of an enigma for a man who doesn't believe that purpose has an implied spirituality. Tim's evolved expression, likely related to his advancing awareness, is related to solving racial and cultural tensions around the world. Tim's desire to create coherence in conflict zones originated in a childhood lacking direction or meaning and has fueled his global work to bring purpose and direction to nations and organizations in crisis.

CASE STUDY: KATHLEEN

[Client's last name withheld to protect anonymity.]

Kathleen's childhood was anything but comical, but she used the experience of distracting her alcoholic father with humorous antics to save herself and her family from harm.

And while Kathleen developed a gift to see what was needed to resolve situational challenges, she was less adept at seeing what she needed in her own life. The irony is that if our purposeful traits aren't used for the benefit of all, including ourselves, they can become filled with shadow elements in addition to the gifts they offer. Kathleen's story shows how purposeful traits can amplify our own lives if we're willing to live into our ultimate expression.

As a means of dealing with the violent nature of her alcoholic father, who often turned his rage against his children and wife, Kathleen developed a perceptive and adaptive capacity that was unusual for a child. She learned to watch for the signs when situations would start spiraling downward, and then to turn on the comedy to evoke laughter.

She became extremely adept at "listening to all the voices in the room" to figure out what was needed. As part of this adaptive ability, Kathleen learned to be the "good girl" who was flexible and accommodating. She was an A+ student, even when the subjects didn't matter. She helped her dyslexic sister with schoolwork and elevated her sister's stature as an athlete at her own expense.

Her perceptive and adaptive ability led her to see what was needed and to provide that to others. In childhood, this tendency looked like "goofing off," which made her family laugh and lightened tense situations. She's used this tactic since childhood to sense what was needed and "pull the strings" behind the scenes to create good endings to challenging situations. In her profession as a project manager, she became essential to her bosses, adapting to their needs and making them look good for the sake of the project.

As part of our coaching work together, we determined that part of Kathleen's purpose was to "turn lemons into lemonade," making the best out of every situation. She has been a peacekeeper, a collaborator, a strategist, and a supportive ally to her colleagues and superiors.

However, the consequences of only serving others with her purpose were that Kathleen became allergic to the limelight, preferring to remain unacknowledged and unseen. When Kathleen was elevated to executive positions in her career in the technology industry, she suffered from the stress of being thrown into the front seat of decision-making and from a lack of confidence. She eventually developed a brain aneurysm and stepped down from the elevated ranks to regain her health and reduce her stress level.

After her self-demotion, she described that it "became painful when I wasn't valued. They put me in a corner where

I would have minimal impact" as a means of limiting the scope of her impact. She was truly feeling unseen and worthless. Having spent a lifetime serving and adapting to others' visions, she felt lost and unfulfilled. She experienced a "knot in my stomach when I go to work every day."

Kathleen had spent so much of her life turning lemons into lemonade for others, as a means of gaining external approval and feeling valued, that she'd forgotten to include herself in the gift of her purpose. As we worked toward an understanding of her purpose, Kathleen began to see that the extraordinary capacities she'd used in childhood and in serving others' visions would be useful in doing work that provided her meaning and purpose. She began to see that the perceptual and adaptive capacities she'd used as a child were the same strengths that would enable her to listen to all points of view, assimilate information, help a team develop a thorough strategy, and accomplish goals and tasks effectively and efficiently.

Shortly after Kathleen joined me in my Purpose Masterclass, she began searching for other work opportunities to put her "yes-can-do" spirit to work for good. She was searching for work high and low. During this interview (2019), she truly saw that she hadn't blessed herself with another level of own purpose and began to believe that she too could turn her current work scenario, where she was being belittled, into opportunity. Within a month of our conversation, Kathleen had a new job working for a globally innovative company aimed at altering the climate crisis through disruptive agricultural practices. She has become a remarkable team player by turning lemons into lemonade, and now her approach will benefit her own life and the planet.

NOTES FROM THE FIELD

After more than thirty-five years in the field of transformation—as a scientist, practitioner, and consultant—I've observed that no other transformational shift or personal attribute has more potency than when people live into the potential of their authentic selves. The nascent field of purpose science already demonstrates that finding and aligning with purpose yields greater clarity, focus, direction, and impact, likely resulting from the effects of synchronicity from living one's essential life. The case studies presented here just add flesh to the bone, depicting the nuances and possibilities when we live according to the impulse emerging from within.

Living into my own purpose, with direction and nuance, supports others to make their greatest contribution and expression. Many of my clients have powerful lives that unfold after they name and claim their purpose, and then get out of their own way by resolving their "shadowed" wounding. As they take small pivots into their future, learning to overcome their limiting beliefs and self-doubt, as well as the expectations of their social and cultural milieu, they become more of who they are, and less of who they are not. They are propelled into their purposeful futures by the rocket fuel that is purpose.

The best way to find yourself is to lose yourself in the service of others.

—MAHATMA GANDHI

SELF-REFLECTION: WHAT WOULD CHANGE IN YOUR LIFE IF YOU WERE FULLY ALIGNED WITH PURPOSE?

Our inner compass can affect not only our own life but a broad swath of humanity—if we live into our greatest contributions.

QUESTIONS TO CONSIDER:

If you knew your purpose and could live with greater distinction and life direction, which areas of your life would likely be affected? How would you, and your life or work, be different?

How do you imagine those changes—in you, your life, or work—would also affect others? The planet?

CONCLUSION: PREVIEW OF WHAT'S NEXT

This chapter has reviewed many fascinating lives of veteran purpose mentors who have had more than their share of soul encounters to guide them to own nuanced systems for guiding people to live more authentic and purposeful lives. In some cases, we demonstrated their Golden Thread through their stories, revealing their unique way of helping humanity evolve. We also shared stories of several extraordinary people whose life experiences included early challenges that may have precluded their contribution, had they remained stuck in their stories of victimhood and adversity.

And, although the field of purpose science is young and emergent, already we have overwhelming evidence that a purpose-driven life yields significant rewards for those who choose to follow their paths. I chose to review here the two major areas of study in which the evidence is clearly pointing to positive outcome. Other areas of inquiry are unfolding rapidly.

REFERENCES

Animas Valley Institute. https://animas.org.

BetterUp. (2018). Meaning and purpose at work. San Francisco, CA: BetterUp.

Boye, P. Buchman, R., Wilson, R., Yu, L., Schneider, J. and Benett D. (2012). Effect of purpose in life on the relation between Alzheimer Disease pathologic changes on cognitive function in advanced age. Archives of General Psychiatry, 69(5): 499-506.

Brown, W. (2019). Unified physics and the entanglement nexus of awareness. NeuroQuantology, 17(7): 40-52.

Burrow, A., & Spreng, R. (2016). Waiting with purpose: A reliable but small association between purpose in life and impulsivity. Personality and Individual Differences, 90, 187-189. doi: 10.1016/j.

Collins, J., Porras, J. (1994). Built to last: Successful habits of visionary companies. Harper Business.

Crosby, D. (2016). The laws of wealth: Psychology and the secret to investing. Harriman House.

Deloitte. (2013). Culture of purpose: A business imperative. 2013 core beliefs & culture survey. https://www2.deloitte.com/content/dam/Deloitte/us/Documents/about-deloitte/us-leadership-2013-core-beliefs-culture-survey-051613.pdf.

Deloitte. (2014). Culture of purpose: Building business confidence; driving growth. 2014 core beliefs & culture survey. https://www2.deloitte.com/content/dam/Deloitte/us/Documents/about-deloitte/us-leadership-2014-core-beliefs-culture-survey-040414.pdf.

Ernst & Young, (2016). The business case for purpose. Harvard Business Review. https://www.ey.com/Publication/vwLUAssets/ey-the-business-case-for-purpose/$FILE/ey-the-business-case-for-purpose.pdf.

Fredrickson, B.L., Grewen, K.M., Coffee, K.A., Algoe, S.B., Firestine, A.M., Arevalo, J.M., Ma, J. & Cole, S.W. (2013). Proc Natl Acad Sci USA 110(33): 13684-9. doi: 10.1073/pnas.1305419110.

Frankl, V.E. (2006). Man's Search for Meaning. Boston: Beacon Press.

Friedman, E., Hayney, M., Love, G., Singer, B., & Ryff, C. (2007). Plasma interleukin-6 and soluble IL-6 receptors are associated with psychological well-being in aging women. Health Psychology, 26(3), 305-313.

Gallup & Healthways. (2014). State of global well-being: Results of the Gallup-Healthways Global Well-Being Index. Gallup, Inc. & Healthways.

Gartenberg, C., Prat, A & Serafeim, G. (2016). Corporate purpose and financial performance. Harvard Business School Working Paper No. 17-023, September 2016.

Gladwell, M. (2002). The tipping point: How little things can make a big difference. New York: Back Bay Books.

Global Purpose Movement. https://www.globalpurposemovement.org.

Levoy, G. https://www.gregglevoy.com.

Gustin, J. (2019). Personal interview.

Happiness Research Institute & Nordic Council of Ministers. (2018). In the shadow of happiness. Analysis 01/2018. Denmark: Nordic Council of Ministers. http://norden.diva-portal.org/smash/get/diva2:1236906/FULLTEXT02.pdf.

Haramein, N. (2013). Quantum gravity and the holographic mass. Physical Review & Research International 2013: 270-292.

Hedburg, P., Gustafson, Y., Alex, L., & Brulin, C. (2010). Depression in relation to purpose in life among a very old population:

A five-year follow-up study. Aging and Mental Health, 14(6), 757-763.

Hill, P.L., Burrow, A.L., & Bronk, K.C. (2014). Persevering with positivity and purpose: An examination of purpose commitment and positive affect as predictors of grit. Journal of Happiness Studies, 17(1): 267-269. DOI 10.1007/s10902-014-9593-5.

Hill, P. L., Turiano, N. A., Mroczek, D. K., & Burrow, A. L. (2016). The value of a purposeful life: Sense of purpose predicts greater income and net worth. Journal of Research in Personality, 65, 38-42. doi: 10.1016/j.jrp.2016.07.003.

Hillman, J. (1996). The soul's code: In search of character and calling. New York: Warner Books.

Imperative, LinkedIn. (2016). Purpose at work: The largest global study on the role of purpose in the workforce. 2016 Purpose Workforce Index. https://cdn.imperative.com/media/public/Global_Purpose_Index_2016.pdf.

Kang, Y., Strecher, V.J., Kim, E., & Falk, E.B. (2019). Purpose in life and conflict-related neural responses during health decision-making. Health Psychology.

Kaplan, A and Anzaldi, L. (2015). New movement in neuroscience: A purpose-driven life. Cerebrum: The Dana Forum on Brain Science, 2015: 7.

Kashdan, T.B. (2015). What do scientists know about finding a purpose in life? The psychology of ultimate concerns. Psychology Today 2/24/2015.

Kelly, T. (2009).pTrue Purpose: 12 strategies for discovering the difference you are meant to make. Berkeley: Transcendent Solutions Press.

Kelly, T. (2019). Personal interview.

Keyes, C.L.M. (2011). Authentic purpose: The spiritual infrastructure of life. Journal of Management, Spirituality & Religion, 8(4), 281–297.

Kim, E.S., Strecher, V. & Ryff, C.D. (2014). Purpose in life and use in preventive health care services. www.pnas.org/cgi/doi/10.1073/pnas.1414826111.

Kim E., Sun, J., Park, N., & Peterson C. (2013a). Purpose in life and reduced incidence of stroke in older adults: The Health and Retirement Study." Journal of Psychosomatic Research. 74: 427-432.

Kim, E., Sun, J., Park, N., Kubzansky, L., Peterson, C. (2013b). Purpose in life and reduced risk of Myocardial Infarction among older US adults with Coronary Heart Disease: A two- year followup." Journal of Behavioral Medicine 36, 124-133.

Korn Ferry. (2016). Purpose powered success. Korn Ferry Institute. https://www.kornferry.com/institute/purpose-powered-success

Kotter, J.P., & Heskett, J.L. (2011). Corporate culture and performance. New York: Free Press.

Kuntzelman, E, & DiPerna, D. (editors). (2017). Purpose rising: A global movement of transformation and meaning. Occidental, CA: Bright Alliance.

Kuntzelman, E.(2019). Personal interview.

Laszlo, E. (2017). Intelligence of the cosmos: Why are we here? New answers from the frontiers of science. Rochester, VT: Inner Traditions.

Lewis, N., Turiano, N., Payne, B., & Hill, P. (2017). Purpose in life and cognitive functioning in adulthood. Aging, Neuropsychology, and Cognition. 24(6).

Levoy, G. (1998). Callings: Finding and following an authentic life. New York: Harmony Publishers.

Levoy, G. (2015). Vital signs: The nature and nurture of passion. New York: TarcherPerigee Publishers.

Levoy, G, 2019. Personal interview.

Madrozo, V.L. (2014). Identity, purpose and well-being among emerging adult hispanic women. Florida International University Digital commons. DOI: 10.25148/etd.FI14071157

Malin, H., Morton, E., Nadal, M., & Smith, K.A. (2019). Purpose and coping with adversity: A repeated measures, mixed-methods study with young adolescents. Journal of Adolescence 76, 1-11.

McLeod, L.E. (2012). Selling with noble purpose: How to drive revenue and do work that makes you proud. San Francisco: Wiley Publishers.

McKnight, P.E. & Kashdan, T.B. (2009). Purpose in life as a system that creates and sustains health and well-being: An integrative, testable theory. Review of General Psychology, 13, 242-251.

Peele, Brandon. (2018). Planet on purpose: Your guide to genuine prosperity, authentic leadership and a better world. Balboa Press, 2018.

Plotkin, B. (2003). Soulcraft: Crossing into the mysteries of nature and psyche. Novato, CA:New World Library.

Plotkin, B (2007). Nature and the human soul: Cultivating wholeness and community in a fragmented world. Novato, CA:New World Library.

Plotkin, B. (2013). Wild mind: A Field guide to the human psyche. Novato, CA:New World Library.

Plotkin, B. (2017). The realm of purpose least realized: But most essential in our time of radical, global change. In E. Kuntzelman and D. DiPerna (eds), Purpose rising: A global movement of transformation and meaning. Occidental, CA: Bright Alliance.

Plotkin B. (2019). Personal interview.

Prairie, B.C., Scheier, M.F., Matthews, K.A., Chang, C.C. & Hess, F. (2011). A higher sense of purpose in life is associated with sexual enjoyment in midlife women. Menopause, 18(8), 839-44. doi:10.1097/gme.ob013e31820befca.

Progoff, I. (1980). At a journal workshop: Writing to access the power of the unconscious and evoke creative ability. New York: TarcherPerigee.

Purpose Guides Institute. https://www.purposeguides.org.

Rainey, L. (2014) The search for purpose in life: An exploration of purpose, the search process, and purpose anxiety." Master's thesis. Philadelphia: University of Pennsylvania.

Rockind, C.L. (2011). Living on purpose: Why purpose matters and how to find it. Unpublished Master's thesis. Masters of Applied Positive Psychology Program. Philadelphia: The University of Pennsylvania.

Ryff, C.D. (1989). Beyond Ponce de Leon and life satisfaction: New directions in quest of successful ageing. International Journal of Behavioral Development, 12 (1), 35-55.

Sarafeim, G. & Gartenberg, C. (2016). The type of purpose that makes companies more profitable. Brighton, MA: Harvard Business Review. Retrieved on October 21, 2018. https://hbr.org/2016/10/the-type-of-purpose-that-makes-companies-more-profitable.

Singer, J., Cummings, C., Moody, S.A., & Benuto, L. (2019). Reducing burnout, vicarious trauma, and secondary traumatic stress through investigating purpose in life in social workers. Journal of Social Work.

Sone, T., Nakaya, N., Ohmori, K., Shimazu, T., Higashiguchi, M., Kakizaki, M., Kikuchi, N., Kuriyama, S., & Tsuji, I. (2008). Psychosomatic Medicine. 70(6): 709-715. doi: 10.1097/PSY.ob013e31817e7e64.

Steger, M.F. (2009). Meaning in life. In C. R. Snyder & S. J. Lopez (Eds.), Oxford handbook of positive psychology (2nd Ed.)(pp. 679-687). New York: Oxford University Press.

Steger, M.F. (2012). Experiencing meaning in life: Optimal functioning at the nexus of well

being, psychopathology, and spirituality. In P.T. Wong (Ed.), The human quest foR meaning: Theories, research, and applications (2nd ed.)(pp. 165-184). New York: Routledge.

Stengel, J. (2011). Grow: How ideals power growth and profit at the world's greatest companies. New York: Crown Business.

Smith J. (2006). Seeds of deception. Portland, ME:Yes! Books.

Smith J. (2019). Personal Interview.

Smith, B.W., Tooley, E.M., Montague, E.Q., Robinson, A.E., Cosper, C.J., & Mullins P.G. (2008). The role of resilience and purpose in life in habituation to heat and cold pain. Journal of Pain 10(5): 493-500. doi: 10.1016.

Stillman, T.F., Lambert, N.M., Fincham, F.D., & Baumeister, R. (2010). Meaning as magnetic force: Evidence that meaning in life promotes interpersonal appeal, Social Psychological & Personality Science.

Telzer, E., Fuligni, A., Liberman, M., & Galvan, A. (2014). Neural sensitivity to eudaimonic and hedonic rewards differentially predict adolescent depressive symptoms over time." Proceedings of the National Academy of Sciences. 111(8): 6600-6605).

True Purpose Institute. http://www.truepurposeinstitute.com.

Wilber, K. (2000). Integral psychology: Consciousness, spirit, psychology, therapy. Boulder, CO: Shambhala Publications.

Windsor, T.D., Curtis R.G., & Luszcz, M.A. (2015). Sense of purpose as a psychological resource for aging well. Dev Psychol. 51(7): 975-86. doi: 10.1037/dev0000023.

CHAPTER 3

PURPOSE AS IT SHOWS UP OVER THE LIFE SPAN

One can choose to go back toward safety or forward toward growth. Growth must be chosen again and again. Fear must be overcome again and again.

—ABRAHAM MASLOW

As you've probably witnessed, as humans we evolve gradually, and in many cases not so gracefully.

We use the terms infancy, childhood, adolescence, adulthood, and elder adulthood to suggest that we "grow up."

But in fact, these general categories are only useful as rough depictions of what happens in different stages of life, primarily representing chronological age and the accompanying bodily changes.

These broad categories are less useful for discerning whether an individual develops "as expected," or just moves along the continuum as they get taller, morph body parts, grow, and lose hair and other common (and sometimes unpleasant) changes in physique. In many cases, it seems a violation of the label "adult," when someone hasn't accomplished developmental tasks much beyond adolescence.

Living into our purpose can be a difficult task—if we don't make our way along the developmental trajectory. As you'll see below and in more detail in later chapters, purposeful expression emerges through the developmental objectives of each stage or remains hidden if the staged tasks are not mastered.

But what if we could see purpose from a utilitarian standpoint, as a means to accomplish developmental tasks?

What if instead of denying our purpose, we embraced it from the get-go and used our unique expressions as a means of growing through the developmental tasks?

In this chapter, you'll learn about Jacqui, who loved the "sensual nature" of water and other natural elements. When small, she put pebbles in her mouth because they were so beautiful; she loved to feel them rolling around in her mouth, a tactile and sensory experience. How many of us would ever consider that these childhood curiosities would turn into a purposeful career? I'll show you how that happened for Jacqui.

And, most notably, this chapter will review several "staged" developmental models to examine the unique conceptions of how we grow up to express ourselves over the span of our lives. Through several case studies of Jacqui, Jane, Carol, and Brandon, you'll read about how purpose exposed itself early and evolved into later tier expressions.

PURPOSE SHOWS UP DISTINCTLY IN THE STAGES OF OUR LIVES

To help characterize how we grow up, the concept of "stages" was derived by early developmental psychologists Erikson (1968) and Loevinger (1976). These stages were defined by stage-specific developmental tasks required to successfully "complete" each stage. The completion of these "tasks" actually predicts whether we'll move along the developmental spectrum at age-appropriate timeframes.

Unfortunately, many of us are stopped in our tracks or "stunted" developmentally when we experience trauma, disease, injury, tragedy, or seemingly unnatural incidents (e.g., dislocation, injustice, bias, financial crises) in life.

Attachment disorders are one of the most common byproducts of these early life "interrupters," as evidenced in my own journey in childhood. The lack of healthy bonding, secure attachment, and sufficient nurturing greatly affected my own relational trajectory from childhood into adulthood and has taken significant focus and commitment to repair and recover so I can now have healthy and nourishing relationships.

In chapter 4, we'll discuss early childhood wounds and social acculturation patterns that can affect task completion. And, as the world slips into greater levels of chaos, these "unnatural" incidents are becoming more natural, as climate change, migration patterns, and extreme weather events cause dislocation of families, communities, and large populations of people—which wreaks havoc upon normal child development.

Even in normal circumstances and in families where life just "happens" with some regularity, normal childhood developmental tasks "supersede" (and/or are critical to) any pull or call from our soul. In fact, Erikson and Loevinger suggested that adolescence is the first period in life when we begin to dedicate ourselves to finding meaning. As more recent developmental experts suggest, adolescence is when we begin to create "systems of belief that reflect compelling purposes" (Damen, Menon, Bronk, 2003).

These belief systems, often formulated in adolescence (and more rarely in childhood), are what affect identity formation and later life choices. A commonly held belief, in the human development arena, is that we don't begin to experience anything "purposeful" in early parts of our lives because we are focusing on the age-appropriate developmental tasks required to successfully "complete" each stage of our lives.

However, my own work with clients (and in my lifetime) suggests that we are "called" by our soul distinctly to accomplish our developmental tasks so we can develop in the unique and nuanced ways only we are capable of, reflecting our soul's purpose.

Damon et al. (2003) suggested that an earlier purpose in life "plays a positive role in self development as well as a generative one for the person's contributions to society." Given that, what would happen if we could recognize the Golden Thread, or our "through-line," earlier in life? Would we accept the challenge to live as ourselves and make our greatest contribution earlier, instead of waiting until it's too late (or not at all)?

My conception of purpose is that our unique expression of purpose evolves, but that purpose itself remains the same most or all of our lives.

We can also imagine that the evolved "versions" (or expressions) of purpose might coincide with the advancing stages of human development. Thus, we could reasonably assume that purpose looks different in different stages of our lives, as we complete developmental tasks, gain new capacities, and advance in perspective-taking. And for each of these new expressions to emerge, we must also liberate the shadow that originates in our childhood wounding so we can catalyze a more expanded version of our unique purposeful expression.

Learning to allow whatever version of you most wants to express itself next is the surest way to let purpose unfold in your life.

This premise would lead us to believe that part of why many people remain confused about purpose is because it looks so different at different stages of life. You may see someone focused and impactful in their middle or later stages of life and wonder, *How in the world did they figure that out?* Generally, we think that "purpose" only occurs as a significant and world-changing impactful career. You may also believe the myth that some people are lucky enough, or smart enough, or talented enough, to live at that level of purposeful impact.

Let's just assume that we all have a purpose. And if our soul is really pulling us forward in all stages of our lives, then everyone is always already on purpose, more or less (mostly less). Hints of purpose alignment have been suggested to be "authentic happiness" (Seligman, 2002), "flow" (Csikszentmihalyi, 1990), or positive emotion, engagement, meaning, positive relationships, and accomplishment (Seligman, 2011). These "states" themselves suggest that we are "Living On Purpose," so our contribution and its impact may be more apparent. But these are just indicators of purpose, not evidence of what purpose itself is.

Purpose can look and feel hopeless, demoralizing and destructive, or less-than-inspired if we're:

- in the muck and mire of ego deconstruction (a necessary element of purpose work that leads to liberation and further alignment), or
- struggling with a developmental task requiring critical capacities that don't come easy.

Living a Life On Purpose sometimes means we're walking the "razor's edge" (Kuntzelman, 2019).

But if indeed we all have a purpose, and we have found and felt it, then more likely we experience that purpose is what we do without trying, or:

Purpose is that which we *must* do.

This creates the tension of having to walk that razor's edge to live into the essence of who we are. And we often don't see it or know it because it just looks differently at different phases of life, and/or because it may be hidden by the wounds of our upbringing.

And, sometimes, it's scary to imagine that something is pulling us forward that we "can't not do" (Linda Ronstadt, *The Sound of My Voice*, 2019), which may require us to give up what we are currently doing.

In my own life, the day (or moment, really) I got really clear about my purpose, I had this sense of something I would die for. I was contemplating the value of my own gifts and talents and wondering what the effect would be if I weren't here to share them (like Jimmy Stewart in *It's a Wonderful Life*, when he contemplates suicide and Clarence, the angel, makes him reflect upon a life in his absence). I had this gut-wrenching awareness that if I couldn't "do the thing" that I came to do, my life wouldn't be worth living. I spontaneously emitted this primal cry. It's almost the same experience I have when thinking about my children, but from a grander/broader perspective: the gift I give humanity.

And we each have one of those—something you "can't not do" that could change the course of history if you're living it fully.

So I got to work and began cleaning up my life in a way that gave me clarity and confidence that I could make my greatest contribution from a place aligned with love and freedom. The developmental tasks that somehow I'd skipped over became apparent, and parts of me that weren't integrated called out for support. I began integrating all that I had not dealt with, so I could live fully from my stage of awareness and make my greatest contributions.

This chapter will provide some detail about three different models of "development" that will attempt to explain why and how purpose varies by developmental stage.

CASE STUDY: JACQUI WEBB

When I met Jacqui Webb, she was unequivocally disengaged from any professional life. She was a relentlessly busy mom with a need to find something more meaningful. But with three of her own kids at home (and others that she routinely fostered), she had no idea where to start. Working with Jacqui would ultimately change the way I understood how the deeply nuanced facets of life that intrigue and entertain us are keys to the locked door of our Soul Purpose, as they vary over our stages of life.

In our early exploration of various facets of Jacqui's life while we were engaged in purpose coaching, she couldn't see any clear connection between the different parts of her life. It all seemed random and haphazard. She was certain she would be an abysmal failure at finding something purposeful to do.

Jacqui routinely suggested that "the only skills or talents I have are being a mediocre mom." Much of Jacqui's life was disappointing to her, including strained relations with some of her children and a marriage that was shaky at best. And yet, she was willing to explore her purpose, if only to see if our work together could yield a path that would be more fulfilling.

Jacqui's early interests included a love of swimming and being in nature. And as noted above, she found delight in the sensuality of nature. Little did she know that the practice of rolling pebbles around in her mouth would help her develop a keen tactile and sensory experience. In late childhood and early adolescence, she also had a deep curiosity about mysticism and mystics, and her affinity for prayer and solitude would lead her to sit silently in nature for long periods. Even though unusual for her age, her natural tendency in childhood was to "counsel" others. She would sit patiently with other children who were in tears or troubled as a means to console them.

But none of these experiences helped Jacqui to focus her efforts on a particular career path, which caused her to feel isolated and be labeled as disengaged or lazy. When motherhood came early for Jacqui, her innate desires for solitude and contemplation took a backseat to the intense demands of caring for several children. Jacqui eventually came to see herself as "not worth it" because of her seeming lack of value.

As she abandoned her innate sense of self, she eventually learned to dissociate from her life (and body) and ultimately rejected religion and a belief in God.

Despite the fact that she felt she had few tangible skills, Jacqui decided to pursue being a coach, and she and I met during our mutual coaching training. Jacqui was quite certain that she would never make a good coach, though her early days of counseling others and her experience as a mother were intriguing to her as a career option. When I started working with Jacqui a few years later after we'd both been certified as coaches, she was trying to sort out who she was amidst the overwhelming nature of her life, the "ups and downs and boredom of endless rush mealtimes" along with childcare and myriad other domestic chores. Despite all that, she had a deep desire to find herself without rejecting all the goodness that had emerged in the life path she'd inadvertently chosen.

During the time we worked together, Jacqui continued to seek activities and practices that would engage her passion, like she'd experienced in childhood. One aspect of life that had emerged for Jacqui in the midst of the mother-housewife groove was her desire for physical intimacy, which had been unavailable in her busy routines. She felt this type of intimacy would bring her back into her own life.

Jacqui began to explore intimacy with others and herself through tantric practice. Tantra is an ancient Indian practice that honors and celebrates the body and enriches the sensual pleasure of being in your body. Breath, meditation, mindfulness, and movement can enhance intimacy with yourself and others. Jacqui found that the physical intimacy of tantric practices, even without sex, provoked a presence between herself and others that caused other limited aspects of her being to just drop away. She described being able to:

"Find the intensity of the experience, which was just presence to me. . . . [This] very quickly became a supernatural journey, where the walls of the room would fall out and there would just be presence, just two people and vastness."

Ultimately, that sensual presence she'd found through tantric practices allowed Jacqui to be with herself, to hold herself in her own deep intimacy without the story of her feelings of inadequacy. As she did so, she allowed the developing voices to "settle and drop away." She described that "without presence to allow, the voices sit under the floorboards and keep hammering so you'll hear them." Through our work together, Jacqui began to regain her instinctive desire to be silent and to reattune to the organic wisdom within her silence. She learned to let the internal voices of shame and unworthiness to "drop of their own accord."

And she found a desire to get back into nature. Jacqui's first experience of "baring her soul" in nature happened during a desert Soul Quest near her home in Johannesburg, which I had prescribed during our coaching work together. She was called by the natural world to be witnessed and held intimately. A circling eagle spoke to her of her fears of the darkness. A caterpillar slithered into her red-cloth-draped "bush altar" to help her settle into her desert cocoon. Frogs startled her out of her skin as they leapt in front of her. Baboons called out to her as they witnessed her journey. A moon changed phases right before her eyes. And a discontented elephant cloud helped her realize the inherent opportunity of her life, rather than her belief of her unworthiness. In nature, as in her tantric experiences, she started to find her way back to herself.

As happens for so many, when the repression of her essential nature dropped away, synchronicities showed up to engage Jacqui in a fuller engagement in her own life. Almost like magic, during the summer of 2018, she was invited to a camp of fifty people at the AfrikaBurn (satellite of the original Burning Man). Ironically, no one had been assigned as camp cook, so Jacqui volunteered and took it on with enthusiasm and trepidation. As she described the experience during our interview in 2019, I could hear the lingering magic in her voice as she revealed how:

"I loved it! I was so energized. I was seen. I was central to community. People told me it was the best Burn they'd ever been on because of the food."

Jacqui speaks reverently as she unearths an important truth of her purpose: "I realized I wanted to anchor the spiritual community. I never had a specific teaching that I birthed" before, but it seemed right because "people need a loo and a kitchen."

Over time, Jacqui has become adept at invoking her deep presence in the hearth of many retreats, taking on the mantle of a tenzo (the title given to a chef in a Buddhist community) to nurture and hold a container for sacred and impactful work in the world. She's now held the kitchen space for a number of retreats, including an African Bush Retreat at a Private Game Reserve and a Women's Empowerment Retreat aimed at aligning around issues of racial division.

Jacqui's early curiosity of sensual pleasures, her forays into contemplative mysticism and in nature, in seeking serenity and intimate connection, along with her multitude of years as a kitchen goddess, so thoroughly prepared her for her role as an anchor for spiritual community through her artful cuisine. Jacqui writes in her bio:

"As my children leave home I'm finding such delicious, sensuous joy in slowing down and really enjoying flavours and textures. I can find myself lost in the glorious sunshine falling through the window onto a lemon exploding with colour. The smell and the curling juiciness in my mouth are the meeting of joyous sensuality and spirituality for me."

While her current purposeful expression might not have seemed predictable from her childhood fascinations, we can see her purpose unfolded organically over the stages of her life. Her purpose expression seems congruent for a child who enjoyed stimulating her tactile senses, held a safe container for those in need, loved the serenity of nature and simple sensual pleasures of life, and who learned to unearth those same pleasures as an adult.

You've got to think about big things while you're doing small things, so that all the small things go in the right direction.
—ALVIN TOFFLER

HOW PURPOSE LOOKS DIFFERENT IN VARIOUS STAGES OF HUMAN DEVELOPMENT

I will outline three different models to examine why and how purpose shows up differently in life. In later chapters I will use the first model, the Stages of Consciousness, to explore specific nuanced examples of purpose by stage. I am most familiar with this model and have done several years of study at the time of this writing.

This model was conceptualized and meticulously examined and validated by Terri O'Fallon PhD., and is a rigorous and practical extension of the good works of many others, including most notably scientists (Loevinger, 1976, 1998; Cook-Greuter, 1999, 2013; Graves 2002), philosophers (Ken Wilber, 2001, 2006; Kegan, 1994; Gebser, 1985). See www.stagesinternational.com for in-depth detail about the model, the validation studies, and its application.

STAGES OF CONSCIOUSNESS: TERRI O'FALLON, PHD., STAGES INTERNATIONAL

The Stages of Consciousness Matrix

PERSON PERSPEC-TIVE	The Object of Aware-ness Is Concrete, Subtle, or MetAware	The Social Preference Is Indi-vidual or Collective	The Learn-ing Style Is Receptive, Active, Re-ciprocal, or Interpene-trative	STAGE NAME
1.0	Concrete	Individual	Receptive	Impulsive
1.5	Concrete	Individual	Active	Egocentric
2.0	Concrete	Collective	Reciprocal	Rule-Ori-ented
2.5	Concrete	Collective	Interpene-trative	Conformist
3.0	Subtle	Individual	Receptive	Expert
3.5	Subtle	Individual	Active	Achiever
4.0	Subtle	Collective	Reciprocal	Pluralist
4.5	Subtle	Collective	Interpene-trative	Strategist
5.0	MetAware	Individual	Receptive	Construct Aware
5.5	MetAware	Individual	Active	Transper-sonal
6.0	MetAware	Collective	Reciprocal	Universal
6.5	MetAware	Collective	Interpene-trative	Illumined

The Stages of Consciousness model, developed by Terri O'Fallon of Stages International (www.stagesInternational.com), is described as:

- Comprehensive: Includes many dimensions of human experience.
- Predictive: The precision of the model allows clarity in navigating life stage transitions.
- Dynamic: Recognizes the fluid nature of human development and works well with other models, such as business, therapeutic, and spiritual.
- Actionable: Allows precise actions to be taken to gain concrete results.

I found the Stages of Consciousness model when I served as an executive at a startup company offering online personal and spiritual development courses. I wanted a framework that could assess 1) the developmental stage of the content being offered, and 2) for whom the course content would be most useful. While we did not move forward in that application of stages, I pursued exploration of the model for my own work with purpose coaching and consulting clients. It has been among the most practical, predictable, and flexible tools that I use in my work and career. I find that when I apply it as a framework for seeing the world, almost everything makes sense!

Additional elements of this model are appropriate to discuss in the exploration of how and why stages of consciousness matter for uncovering purpose. Each of these elements are described in the basic teachings of Terri O'Fallon and summarized or paraphrased here: (www.stagesInternational.com).

**BASIC ELEMENTS OF THE STAGES OF
CONSCIOUSNESS FRAMEWORK**

Consciousness as Perspective-Taking

The Stages of Consciousness model primarily reflects the expansion of "perspective-taking" across the span of development in a human life. As infants, we only have available a first-person perspective, then grow into a second-person perspective in childhood and adolescence to encompass our new awareness of parents, siblings, and others, and eventually we include family, peers, tribe, and community in our awareness. A third-person perspective develops when we can witness ourselves or our group. Third-person perspective is also when we begin to experience subtle energies both within ourselves and in our external world. This pattern of expanded perspective-taking evolves into a worldview that captures a fourth-, fifth-, and sixth-person viewpoint, though among a smaller proportion of adults. Purpose will vary widely among these different stages, dependent upon the vantage point of each stage.

Cyclical Being and Doing

Each stage tier reflects four iterative stages, cycling between Passive and Active stages, or Being and Doing. This back-and-forth flow between receiving and learning (being) and practicing and acting (doing) reflects our organic ways of evolving in the world. In each stage of our lives, we must observe and explicitly make meaning of what is modeled for us. We practice it as individuals, then integrate those meanings in extended contexts, such as in families, communities, or networks. Then we make discernments and practice again in those expanded "collective" or community contexts. As you can imagine, purpose will occur uniquely in the context of whether we are in a receptive or active stage.

Objects of Awareness Distinguish the Tiers

The repetition of these four iterative stages (receptive, active, reciprocal, interpenetrative) occurs throughout our lifetimes and looks different depending on the "objects" upon which we're focused. In early stages, we're focused on Concrete objects (what we can see and touch in the material world— e.g., our bodies, other people, food, elements of the natural world, or objects that make up our everyday lives).

In middle stages, we're focused on Subtle objects (that which we cannot see but shapes our world nonetheless—e.g., emotions, intellectual and creative domains, strategic plans, social or legal agreements, conceptual models, expectations, beliefs, projections).

In the third MetAware tier (which is comprised of fewer than roughly 5% of the humans on the planet), we are focused on an awareness itself that all human experience is based on a social or individual construction of meaning, or in essence, doesn't exist as we formerly knew it to exist. The object of focus is "as awareness," and the initial awareness in this tier causes the reconstruction of self, identity, meanings and relationships between all things formerly known as concrete or subtle.

Because this developmental framework uses the "object of awareness" as the distinction for the tiers and is based on scientific understanding of human development, the stages are not a representation of any "spiritual" progression. The experience of "non-duality" or "causality"—both terms used in spiritual lineages to denote "oneness" with the Universe—do not equate to a later stage of consciousness in this framework.

Those of us who may be considered "awake" (or enlightened, in spiritual jargon) may in fact have a perspective-taking capacity of an earlier tier (Concrete or Subtle). In Integral Theory jargon, "waking up" (becoming spiritually adept) is independent of "growing up" (evolving to later stages of human development) or "cleaning up" (resolving earlier wounding). To accomplish a later stage of development in this framework, you'd need to do all three.

All Stages Are Perfect, Wherever You Are

This framework allows that each stage of development occurs organically and "right on time" for the person experiencing it. In other words, it is perfect, wherever we are. You can attempt to accelerate your movement through the stages, but generally it requires integrating the "fractured parts" of our wounded childhood and lots of practice in the current stage.

I hold that wherever we are is perfect for our time of life. No stage is "better than" or "worse than" any other; they just constitute differences in how we perceive the world from whatever frame is represented in that stage. Our most important task is to fully complete the developmental tasks of each stage (see chapters 3-7), so that we can evolve to the next stage with a full complement of capacities (and resolution of earlier wounding, which is what generally causes our suffering) for our next iterative expression.

Perspective-Taking and Purpose in Each Tier

In the Concrete Tier, we experience a first- or second-person perspective, which means that we can see ourselves and the "other" but don't easily see others looking in on us from the outside. This tier focuses on early individuation, early egoic needs attainment, sensory development, relationship tasks, and social construction of identity, among other facets. In this tier, we have little ability to witness ourselves beyond our physical experience and basic emotions, much less witness others.

Purpose, in the Concrete Tier, would appear primarily as self-oriented and related to the material world (more on this in chapter 4).

Those of us who advance to the Subtle Tier (which is not all adults) develop a witness or "standing outside of self" capacity and can see others and sense their experiences. As we evolve to the perspectival capacity of this tier, we also begin to explore the stories that our minds create, and participate in planning and deep subtle intimacy with others and their interior ego states. We also have an awareness of the contexts of life that we live and work in, and ultimately see and live in complex-adaptive systems (e.g., systems that are related and interactive, such as climate, ecosystems, social networks, markets, political parties).

Purpose in the Subtle Tier varies from the exploration of the unique self, to initiatives aimed at global transformation and everything in between (more on this matter in chapter 5).

While we have no known data to cite to suggest how many people live in the third or MetAware Tier, we do know that a very small number of people on the planet exist in this tier, in which the object is Awareness itself. People in this advanced stage of consciousness, who are capable of fifth- and sixth-person perspective, hold life as an illusion in their daily lives and an expansion of themselves beyond their physical boundaries. They are required to regularly deconstruct and reconstruct their identity and capacities. People at this stage are capable of connecting paradigms and integrating boundless and timeless (and infinite and eternal) fields of awareness.

Purpose at this stage will often appear as initiatives, businesses, or global networks that span boundaries or paradigms and defy social definitions through massively creative expression (more on this subject in chapter 6).

ECO-SOULCENTRIC HUMAN DEVELOPMENT:
BILL PLOTKIN, PHD., ANIMAS VALLEY INSTITUTE

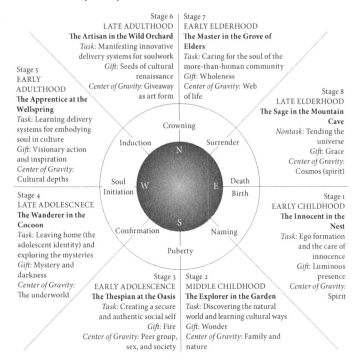

Stage 6
LATE ADULTHOOD
The Artisan in the Wild Orchard
Task: Manifesting innovative
delivery systems for soulwork
Gift: Seeds of cultural
renaissance
Center of Gravity: Giveaway
as art form

Stage 7
EARLY ELDERHOOD
The Master in the Grove of
Elders
Task: Caring for the soul of the
more-than-human community
Gift: Wholeness
Center of Gravity: Web
of life

Stage 5
EARLY
ADULTHOOD
The Apprentice at the
Wellspring
Task: Learning delivery
systems for embodying
soul in culture
Gift: Visionary action
and inspiration
Center of Gravity:
Cultural depths

Stage 8
LATE ELDERHOOD
The Sage in the Mountain
Cave
Nontask: Tending the
universe
Gift: Grace
Center of Gravity:
Cosmos (spirit)

Crowning
Induction — Surrender
Soul Initiation — N — W — E — Death / Birth
Confirmation — Naming
Puberty

Stage 4
LATE ADOLESCNECE
The Wanderer in the
Cocoon
Task: Leaving home (the
adolescent identity) and
exploring the mysteries
Gift: Mystery and
darkness
Center of Gravity:
The underworld

Stage 1
EARLY CHILDHOOD
The Innocent in the
Nest
Task: Ego formation
and the care of
innocence
Gift: Luminous
presence
Center of Gravity:
Spirit

Stage 3
EARLY ADOLESCENCE
The Thespian at the Oasis
Task: Creating a secure
and authentic social self
Gift: Fire
Center of Gravity: Peer group,
sex, and society

Stage 2
MIDDLE CHILDHOOD
The Explorer in the Garden
Task: Discovering the natural
world and learning cultural ways
Gift: Wonder
Center of Gravity: Family and
nature

From the book *Nature and the Human Soul*. Copyright © 2008 by Bill Plotkin. Reprinted with permission of New World Library, Novato, CA. www.newworldlibrary.com.

Bill Plotkin's "Eco-Soulcentric Developmental Wheel" understands purpose as derived from the ego's interactive journey in the natural and human world. Bill describes his wheel as a:

"Model of soulcentric ego development, not soul development. We descend into this world from spirit and develop a functional, or primary, ego in stages 1 through 3, an ego that is grounded primarily in human society. Then our ego further

matures as we align it with soul in stage 4, in time giving birth to a second-stage (soul-rooted) ego at Soul Initiation. Our second-stage ego carries us through stage 7. At Surrender, we release our soul-rooted ego and achieve a third-stage (spirit-rooted) ego in Stage 8" (Plotkin, 2008).

Bill's work, primarily conducted through the auspices of the Animas Valley Institute, "honors the deeply imaginative potentials of the human psyche" and suggests that human development is best guided by nature and the soul (Plotkin, 2017.) The Eco-Soulcentric Stages of Human Development Wheel are arrayed around a nature-based circle, and each stage and its attributes are based primarily on the qualities of nature found in the seasons, the cardinal directions, and the times of day. Each stage includes developmental tasks that are both nature-oriented and culture-oriented, indicating the balancing of influences required of humans to develop attuned to the prescriptive aspects of being human on a living planet.

Plotkin's model also reflects the inherent challenges in becoming soulcentric (or ecocentric) in a world that primarily suppresses the natural dimension of human development. He suggests that "most humans are alienated from their vital individuality—their soul—and humanity as a whole is largely alienated from the natural world that evolved us and sustains us."

Having "mapped" the Stages of Consciousness and Eco-Soulcentric Human Development models onto each other, I have noted some overlap between the models in the defined stages themselves and their developmental tasks, despite the distinct foci of each model. O'Fallon's model is primarily based on empirical and observational research, and Plotkin's model could be considered primarily pre-empirical, employing the template of the natural world. Both of these methods are valid means of understanding the deeper patterns in humanity. One major distinction in the models is related to the attribution of beingness and doingness, and the individual and collective tasks.

As noted earlier, the Stages of Consciousness model ascribes a cyclical and repetitive pattern of being and doing, being and doing—throughout our lives. This model also suggests (and data supports) that the individual precedes a collective stage within each tier (suggesting we receive-learn-practice-act).

In Plotkin's model, he suggests that the stages in the first half of life (stages one to four, childhood and adolescence) are individually oriented—the emphasis is on individual needs and potentials, on personal growth with a focus on the *ripening* individual. After that ripening, Plotkin's model depicts that we travel into the world as an agent for soul and enter the collective-oriented stages (five to eight, true adulthood and genuine elderhood) with the emphasis on collective needs and potentials, on personal growth with a focus on serving the whole.

Like O'Fallon's model, Plotkin observes that not all adults arrive at the latter stages unless they succeed with the earlier ones. For Plotkin, similar to O'Fallon's model, a person must have adequate success with the developmental tasks of the previous stages, have progressed through the life passages between stages, and have developed the capacities required to make the contributions that are possible in the later stages. Plotkin also describes "beingness" as characterizing the first two and last two stages of life, and "doingness" as characterizing the middle stages three through six.

Plotkin also specifically identifies and describes the developmental tasks of each stage, indicating that the first four stages focus on ego formation, exploration, development of an authentic social self, and identity exploration, respectively. These stages roughly "map" onto the first Concrete Tier of the Stages of Consciousness model. Plotkin depicts what I call purpose, in stages five to seven, as an embodiment of soul (cultivating a delivery system for soul in stage five; innovating never-before-seen delivery systems in stage six; and caring for the soul of the more-than-human community in stage seven, early elderhood)—similar to O'Fallon's second Subtle Tier. Plotkin denotes that stage-eight elders don't have developmental tasks (any more than we do in early childhood) but that the stage-eight elder, the "Sage in the Mountain Cave," "tends the universe" (similar to the later stages of O'Fallon's third MetAware Tier).

Plotkin's wheel emphasizes the importance of maturation within the context of not only the cultural world but also the natural environment, where a human ego can be nurtured and nourished in its developmental trajectory. He describes this process as foundational for human development—and "missing" from most human development models (2019)— foundational in part because the human soul, as he understands it (as a person's unique ecological niche), is a feature or dimension of the natural world. Bill believes that only when we fully experience our innate membership in the earthly world can we begin the initiatory journey through which we might discover or remember our ultimate contribution to the world.

FOUR WAYS OF LEADING: CONSCIOUS LEADERSHIP GROUP

The Conscious Leadership Group, founded by Jim Dethmer and Diana Chapman (https://conscious.is), offers leadership services and resources to companies based in the Four Ways of Leading model.

Four Ways of Leading: Conscious Leadership Model

TO ME: Life Happens to Me
• **Posture**: Victim • **Experience**: Blaming, complaining • **Beliefs**: There is a problem. Someone is at fault. Someone should fix this. • **Key Question**: Why me? Whose fault is this? • **Benefits**: Experience separateness, drama as entertainment, adrenaline high. Supports empathy toward others.
BY ME: I Make Life Happen
• **Posture**: Creator • **Experience**: Curiosity, appreciation • **Beliefs**: Problems are here for me to learn from. I created the problem, so I can solve it. • **Key Question**: What can I learn? What do I want to create? • **Benefits**: Personal empowerment. Define your wants & desires.
THROUGH ME: I Cooperate With Life Happening
• **Posture**: Co-creator • **Experience**: Allowing flow, wonder, and awe • **Beliefs**: I am the source of all meaning I experience. Things are perfect, whole, and complete. Life handles all apparent "problems." • **Key Question**: What wants to happen through me? • **Benefits**: Non-attachment. Unlimited possibility, plenty of everything.
AS ME: Life Is Me
• **Posture**: At one with all. • **Experience**: Peace, spaciousness • **Beliefs**: There is just "oneness." There are no problems, and no one to solve them. • **Key Question**: No more questions—just knowingness. • **Benefits**: Experience oneness and non-dualism. Unlimited freedom and peace.

While the Four Ways of Leading model defined by the Conscious Leadership Group is not a human development model per se, it has a staged approach to leadership that is being used primarily among leadership teams in corporations. The model is simple and can be used to describe the phases of development that may occur within a company or other group. Because many corporations are now attempting to integrate purpose into their culture, I chose to include a leadership model that assesses "perspective taking" of leaders, similar to the Stages of Consciousness framework. This model gives us a window into what frameworks are being used in corporate cultures, and how leaders may be guided toward purposeful endeavor.

The Conscious Leadership Group (CLG) defines four types (or stages) of leadership:

To Me or Life Happens to Me, whose posture is a Victim that blames and complains, similar to the early egocentric stages of infants through early adolescence, and among adults who don't advance past their wounding or limited environments. Generally, this type of leadership resembles the first Concrete Tier of O'Fallon's model, in which individuation and identity are formed. As a person assumes responsibility for their life (and work), they progress to the next stage.

By Me or I Make Life Happen, whose posture is a Creator, corresponds to O'Fallon's early second Subtle Tier stage. Upon recognition that much of life is outside of the control of the individual, surrender occurs, and a developmental progression ensues.

Through Me or I Cooperate with Life Happening, in which the posture is a Co-creator, corresponds to O'Fallon's late second Subtle Tier. As a person experiences a more collective "oneness" experience, they make a shift to the next stage.

As Me or Life is Me, with a posture of At One With All, is the last stage in the CLG model. We can make an assumption that this model intends to suggest a similar stage as O'Fallon's early stage MetAware Tier, though the actual depiction here is "oneness," which is a state rather than a stage. The object of focus in this CLG stage is not clear.

IN SUM

All three of these models present a unique and overlapping frame for viewing the stages of human development. The Stages of Consciousness framework lends itself to examine the perspective-taking ability that occurs and expands over time as developmental tasks are "completed," which is useful for discerning how our unique and nuanced purpose is recognized and claimed—or not—across the stages of life.

I present another case study here to analyze the unique characteristics that "showed up" early to suggest the Golden Thread and progress through the developmental stages.

CASE STUDY: JANE SHEPPARD

We can easily imagine that childhood adventures could parlay directly into a meaningful career. What's challenging is that child's play could come full circle after a destructive downward spiral related to cubicles, corporate burnout, and a wild young adult phase.

But that's exactly what happened with Jane Sheppard, now a functional medicine-certified health coach and an epidemic answers health coach. Jane helps parents understand and resolve their children's underlying issues related to serious behavioral, chronic health, and other social issues (e.g., ADHD, anxiety, depression, allergies, autism).

Jane's current work is not so distinct from the healing she provided to her dolls and injured animals as a child, but a far cry from the near decade of fast-paced high-pressure work in the emerging telecom and other industries, where she set out to prove herself because she didn't see herself as lovable, acceptable, or worthy.

Jane's childhood wasn't exactly easy, as for many of us. In fact, her early childhood left her without an early childhood individuation, or sense of self. Despite her early traumas, Jane attempted to "find herself" through her childhood play. In the early Concrete Tier, she nurtured sick animals: feeding birds who had fallen from their nests, or sick puppies who had been abandoned. She cared for her dolls with special leaves and bright glittery objects. Later, she was a highly sought-after babysitter. She envisioned having four children of her own to care for, but her own lack of self-worth kept her from imagining she was good enough to do so.

As she entered the middle or Subtle Tier, Jane locked away her gifts of caring for the sick and attended college, first majoring in interior design and later business. She left college with two unfinished degrees, never imagining success in either.

Jane was sidetracked by the pull of social pressures into the lucrative corporate world, where she remembers that she "went along with it. I didn't have any sort of ideas about who I was or any sense of myself. I was shut down, really shut down. I was following what everybody else was doing, the drugs and alcohol and stuff." Without a strong GPS, Jane describes that she was liable to follow whomever wanted to influence her: "Just pull me wherever direction you want to take me because I don't know who I am."

That is, until she realized that she was "letting people take advantage of her" by making extreme requests to both party and work too much, which depleted her and led to a serious illness. She realized she needed to "stop killing" herself with work that wasn't fulfilling. She quit the corporate world and committed to "never going back to that, but to find work that fed me. Meaningful work."

At this point, Jane began to heal some of the unresolved childhood tasks to become a more authentic version of herself and move more wholly into a later stage of development. She moved to Arizona, where she began work as a healer. She found that she still had "a deep core belief that I was unlovable, not valuable, and not worthy." She couldn't even imagine being good enough for a nurturing relationship that would've yielded the promise of a fulfilling relationship and family.

Because she'd had this childhood desire to care for animals and children, she decided to have a child on her own, to help satisfy those early childhood longings. As Jane began to explore how to be a good parent, her research on child development and items she would need to care for her own child triggered her desire to share some of this information with other parents.

In this more evolved stage of consciousness, in which Jane was developing expertise to satisfy her intellectual curiosity, she began to write the Healthy Child Newsletter and ultimately wrote hundreds of articles and a book about her findings. She developed a business as an adviser and purveyor of products that promote healthy and safe childhood development, establishing herself in a worthwhile career role.

Jane became a consummate parent to a remarkable child and ultimately found the rewarding relationship in which to nurture herself and her daughter. Through this time, she continued to heal herself into greater wholeness with deep inquiry into her past childhood traumas. In her own personal work, some of which came about through her participation in my Masterclass, she then came to see how she could support and provide feedback to other mothers to explore their own relationships with their children. At this stage, she began to see how her own traumas had given her the capacity to support her clients.

Jane's most recent expression of her Soul Purpose came about through a series of organic events. While this situation is not unusual for someone with a strong and loud childhood desire, navigating the many stages of development and awareness required to yield a purposeful career and meaningful work as Jane has still requires deep commitment and intention.

I have two significant points to articulate here. First, by Jane's own admission, she "had a lot of communication with the spirit world [as a child], but I didn't allow myself to . . . talk about it." Jane describes that she "was overly sensitive and . . . [my family] broke me down with that. So I shut it off." She also had "access to the natural world, because we lived in a place where there was a lot of nature around. And that fed me."

Her early connection to her truth through nature and a connection to something greater led her to have a "knowing" about what mattered to her, even as a child. Despite her inadequate individuation as a child, because she had early access to her inner world and the broader "subtle" world around her, she was able to discern that her soul was pulling her along in her own life.

Jane later acknowledged that she is now "being in the energy and allowing that, which is really what I'm trying to tap into now . . . because I had lost that for so long." Through her deep connection to her Soul Purpose, Jane is able to listen to what feels right for her own alignment.

Second, Jane sees that much of her adult life was about:

"Trying to make myself worthy . . . such a deep pain that I had, that nobody could love me . . . I don't have it anymore. . . . The more I can really honor and love myself . . . that's the only way

I can truly help someone else. The sense of self and value of who I am that's taken me so long to get to that place."

Despite the fact that Jane has moved into coaching with parents, which finally feels to her like she's living into her greater potential, Jane stated that "none of it has really been successful; I haven't really been able to do anything." Even at this stage of her advanced development, Jane imagines she's less accomplished than she'd like to be.

At the end of the interview, I helped her reframe this misconception, that any stage is better than the one before or that her current work has more meaning. In fact, each stage has its own sense of meaning, depending on the lens through which we view it.

Jane's earlier-than-normal access to her inner world and the subtle energy world around her, including the awareness of those around her who didn't approve of her own callings, created the paradoxical challenge of staying true to herself amid her social contexts that wanted her to be something else.

CASE STUDIES RELATIVE TO STAGES OF PURPOSE

CASE STUDY: CAROL
A Long Journey to Achieve Natural Connections

You may recall Carol's [anonymous] story in chapter 1. Carol went from loving nature and being outdoors as a child to working at a startup company focusing on sustainable agriculture. The following are specific elements of Carol's journey that indicate the Golden Thread in her life, evident at different stages of her journey.

When Carol was a child, she demonstrated elements of the Concrete Tier through a deep love of nature—creeks, streams, meadows. She would spend hours and hours there as a little girl, to escape the bullying nature of her brother.

As she aged, Carol didn't want to migrate into the "real" world of business, day jobs, and constraints. So she opened up a vegetable business and simultaneously raised her children, learning the ins and outs of running a business and tending to the budding nature of her business and her children. She describes that she had an affinity for soil science and studied farming techniques dutifully. As money was tight during the child-raising years, she was forced to reconsider her role and realized that going back to school for a degree might be a good idea.

In this process, Carol migrated into the Subtle Tier. She earned her undergraduate and graduate degree in business and found herself capable of taking a management job at a university. Even though Carol felt repressed in her corporate managerial job, she knew she was doing good work and contributing. During this time, Carol also began her personal and spiritual development journey and gained insights into her inner journey and the outer contexts of her world. She began cataloguing and connecting people's important work around the world. She also became entrenched in learning about indigenous people and their connection to the land. Carol also had health issues that stymied her and caused her to study different therapeutic approaches.

Carol did migrate into the MetAware Tier, as she went on a soul-searching journey to rediscover herself after retirement in a much larger context of loss of meaning. As she made this transition, she pulled together disparate pieces of life as a coherent tapestry, including her connection to nature, use of her capacities in business and management skills, and her desire to promote a healthier connection between people and the land.

CASE STUDY: BRANDON PEELE
Reclaiming Gender Balance for True Self

You may recall Brandon Peele's story in chapter 1. Brandon went from a young boy exploring both his masculine and feminine characteristics, experiencing the repression of the feminine aspect of himself, to ultimately reclaiming his sovereign nature and eventually helping men and women find their true selves within a purposefully balanced gender equanimity. The following are specific elements of Brandon's journey that indicate the Golden Thread in his life, evident at different stages of his journey.

During Brandon's childhood and Concrete Tier, he enjoyed creating friendship bracelets, forming healthy relationships with girls, expressing himself through art and drawing, but also building things, participating in all types of games and sports, and even playing war. Brandon had a healthy overt expression of both elements of his masculine and feminine side. When his dad encouraged him to move away from showing his feminine nature, this facet of himself became repressed and he began to demonstrate more aggressive and masochistic patterns.

In the Subtle Tier, as Brandon made his way into his academic and career world, the repressed parts became hypermasculine behaviors that challenged his own inner compass. As Brandon began to do personal development work, he gained an awareness of the contextual representation of the male ego that dominated so much of his world and life. Ultimately, he began to integrate parts of himself to achieve his own internal balance and bring that into the world via his purpose work to assist men and women in achieving their own form of gender balance.

Brandon, currently in the late stage of the Subtle Tier (and beginning to express MetAware capacities as his leading edge) is navigating the paradox of balancing the desire to become his true self in a world that diminishes the wholeness we desire within and among us.

NOTES FROM THE FIELD

Tim Kelley and I dialogued about my hypothesis that the type of purpose one experiences is likely related to their developmental stage. In our conversation, Tim described his experience that the early childhood stages are a "victim stage" (things happening to you, or Concrete Tier in the Stages of Consciousness framework) where, from his perspective, purpose may not have much utility at all. He suggests that in this phase, people can "think about something happening to them, and a sense of purpose provides justification, or an external locus of control, like religion. Or a child wants something larger than their real parents, who may not be doing such a great job." Tim believes that among children, there is "rarely a clearly articulated purpose . . . but one of adopting a purpose of a system or another person. They take on whatever purpose the person or social structure explicitly articulates for them."

While Tim's assessment of children expressing the "purpose of a system or another person" seems valid, I also see this as the childhood/adolescent adoption of social norms, expectations, and boundaries. Children experience this normative adaptation to their families and peers as they migrate into the Rule-Oriented and Conformist stages of the Concrete Tier (see chapter 4).

In my own observations, I see the nuanced expression of purpose distinctly in the patterns of childhood or adolescent play, interests, curiosities, and patterns of behavior that lay outside the normative expectations of their context. The Golden Threads show up early, and sometimes these distinct nuanced expressions of purpose in the "conformist" stages are what gets kids into the most trouble with parents who can't yet see their child's purpose!

When speaking about the middle Subtle Tier (in the Stages of Consciousness framework), Tim described the role of "self-authoring" as a phase in which someone "chooses a purpose as a strategy for my ego's need for fulfillment, to make full use of your gifts, manifesting in the world. It's a great way to go into the world, feeling satisfied. At that stage, a purpose statement becomes useful."

Tim described that business leaders like the approach he uses to engage the ego, which creates a tool to help them manifest their vision. He also notes that learning purpose from a Trusted Source makes the ego more permeable and less dominant. Tim noted that this outcome creates a win-win because it accelerates the loosening of rigid worldviews and frames, as the ego starts to be less solid if a person is talking to a trusted source all the time. This would accelerate a person's move through stages of development because it is ego-friendly rather than ego-hostile.

As we discussed purpose in later stages, Tim described that people can begin to see that it's "not just me, that other stuff is happening and that we're participating in larger forces at work. Now purpose from Trusted Source is better than the one I chose." Tim's experience with his clients affirms that in the Subtle Tier, we begin to be more aware of the contexts of our lives and that circumstances beyond our control are at play, including the "others" who hold critical roles in our lives.

The case studies represent some early indicators that purpose does show up uniquely and distinctly early in life. As demonstrated in these stories, the nuances are not readily seen in the present moment if one doesn't know what to look for and are often hidden behind the early wounding of childhood.

SELF-REFLECTION: WHAT EVIDENCE CAN YOU BEGIN TO GATHER TO CREATE CLARITY ABOUT WHERE THE GOLDEN THREAD SHOWS UP IN YOUR LIFE?

The evolving nature of our purpose, as it shows up across the span of our lives, lives within the memories and stories of our childhood, adolescence, and adulthood.

QUESTIONS TO CONSIDER:
How has your awareness of purpose changed over your lifetime?

What evidence do you have that your purpose may have existed in different stages of your life?

CONCLUSION: PREVIEW OF WHAT'S NEXT

This chapter revealed several unique models of purpose-related development or perspective taking, each with unique features and some overlapping commonalities. Most notably, these models cohere around the "staged" concept of human development, with the evolving ability to perceive, learn, and take action with greater capacities over time. While the application of these principles to purpose is somewhat novel, examining purpose through the lens of a staged approach is sensible. If purpose can be deemed simply the ability to contribute our most authentic talents and gifts throughout our lives (with some indication of those gifts being inspired, spiritually or otherwise, rather than chosen), then we can examine how purpose comes to be experienced, expressed, and contributed through expanded contexts and more complex applications in each subsequent stage of life.

I've demonstrated these early portrayals of purpose through-out the stages through the case studies of Jacqui, Jane, Carol, and Brandon in this chapter. As we delve into each staged tier of the Stages of Consciousness model in chapters 4-6, I'll share additional case studies and note the progression of nuanced purposeful expression.

REFERENCES

Cook-Greuter, S.R. (1999). Postautonomous ego development: A study of its nature and measurement. (habits of mind, transpersonal psychology, Worldview). Dissertation Abstracts International: Section B: The Sciences and Engineering, 60(6-B), 3000.

Cook-Greuter, S.R. (2013). Ego development: Nine levels of increasing embrace in ego development. A full spectrum theory of vertical growth and meaning making. www.cook-greuter.com.

Csikszentmihalyi, M. (1990). Flow: The psychology of optimal experience. New York: Harper & Row.

Damon W., Menon J., Bronk, K.C. (2003). The development of purpose during adolescence. Applied Developmental Science, 7(3): 119-128.

Dethmer, J. & Chapman, D. 4 ways of leading. San Francisco: Conscious Leadership Group. (https://conscious.is)

Erickson, E.H. (1968). Identity; youth and crisis. New York: Norton Books.

Gebser, J. (1985). The ever-present origin. Athens, OH: Ohio University Press.

Graves, C. (2002). Claire W Graves: Levels of human existence. Santa Barbara: ECLET Publishing.

Kegan, R.L. (1994). In over our heads: The mental demands of modern life. Cambridge, MA: Harvard University Press.

Kelley, T. (2019). Personal Interview

Kuntzelman E. (2019). Personal communication, interview.

Loevinger, J. (1976). Ego development: Conceptions and theories. San Francisco: Jossey-Bass.

Loevinger, J. (1998). Technical foundations for measuring ego development: The Washington University Sentence Completion test. Mahwah, NJ: Laurence Erlbaum Associates.

Murray, T. (2017). Sentence completion assessments for ego development, meaning-making, and wisdom maturity, including STAGES. Integral Leadership Review. August-November. www.integralleadershippreview.com.

O'Fallon T. Stages International. www.stagesinternational.com.

O'Fallon, T. (2013). The senses: Demystifying awakening. Sonoma, CA: Integral Theory Conference. www.terriofallon.com.

O'Fallon, T. (2015). Stages: Growing up is waking up—interpenetrating quadrants, states and structures. Retrieved on August 20, 2017 www.terriofallon.com.

Plotkin, B. (2008). Nature and the human soul: Cultivating wholeness and community in a fragmented world. Novato CA: New World Library.

Plotkin, B. (2017). The realm of purpose least realized: But most essential in our time of radical, global change. In Kuntzelman & DiPerna, D. (eds), Purpose rising: A global movement of transformation and meaning. Occidental, CA: Bright Alliance.

Plotkin B. (2019). Personal interview.

Ronstadt, L. (2019). Quote from The Sound of My Voice. Greenwich Entertainment. Filmmakers: Rob Epstein and Jeffrey Friedman.

Seligman, M.E.P. (2002). Authentic happiness: Using the new positive psychology to realize your potential for lasting fulfillment. New York: Free Press.

Seligman, M.E.P. (2011). Flourish: A visionary new understanding of happiness and well-being. New York: Atria.

Wilber, K. (2001). A theory of everything: An integral vision for business, politics, science and spirituality. Boston: Shambhala.

Wilber, K. (2006). Integral spirituality: A startling new role for religion in the modern and postmodern world. Boston: Shambhala.

CHAPTER 4

EARLY STAGES AND HOW PURPOSE SHOWS UP

I have this vivid memory of being quiet, almost motionless, standing in the middle of a kindergarten Sunday school classroom, listening to my mother and the teacher talk about me. My mother had just deposited me in the classroom, late again after all the other kids had started playing. She was explaining something about me to the teacher in her syrupy-cover-something-up voice. My ears tuned in to the teacher's words as I heard her say,

"Oh, but she seems like such a quiet child. So shy. Is she always like this?"

My mother laughed loudly. "Oh no. I would never call her shy." She summarily dismissed the teacher's assessment of my emotionless presence.

I don't recall what else my mother went on to share as she excused my dissociated experience that looked like "shy." The teacher was kind enough to usher me to play with some other children.

On most Sunday mornings before Sunday school, my mother would spend an hour or more dressing me and my two sisters in perfectly matching dresses, tights, and patent leather shoes. She would comb out our long hair from the pink rollers and dippity-do placed them in the night before while watching *The Carol Burnett Show*. The Saturday night hair treatment itself would take thirty to forty-five minutes, designed to produce three little girls with long curly hair ultimately to be topped off with ribbons to match our dresses.

We were required to approach a level of beautification that resembled a Madame Alexander doll from my mother's own doll collection. The back of the hairbrush served as disincentive when we complained the brushing was too brutal or the ribbons too tight. The process was a ritual, certainly, but didn't seem to have much to do with my friend Jesus. The ceremonial end of the ritual was always a Polaroid taken of my mother with her three beautiful dolls, staggered by height, before we were ushered into the station wagon and off to church. Theoretically, our tears would dry before we got to the church.

The fact that I became purposeful at all is a testament to my soul's insistence that it be allowed to breathe. In so many ways, my uniqueness and individuation were shut down in childhood. And yet my soul insisted—no, demanded—that it be allowed to experience the light of day rather than the safety of the quiet dark spaces that protected me from the insidious contours of my childhood.

In this world you're either growing or dying. So get in motion and grow.

—ROBIN SHARMA

THE UNIQUE EARLY EXPRESSION OF YOUR GOLDEN THREAD

Can you imagine being allowed to express yourself so adequately early in life that everyone you know—parents, siblings, playmates, friends—recognize those things that you enjoy, get enthused by, are curious about, or pick uniquely out of the sandbox? And even more so, being encouraged and supported to continue following those curiosities, even when they lead down dark alleys or dead-end streets, in search of yourself?

The primary reason most of us don't live our greatest expression of our purpose is because we aren't able to accomplish the primary developmental tasks of childhood. Parents don't get a handbook that describes how to change the oil or check the filters for their children. We (as parents) primarily depict the parental modeling we experienced during childhood. Thus, the patterns of inadequate nurturing and imposed systemic expectations and suppression become the dominant parenting behavior for many children. And that's if we're lucky and have parents who demonstrate positive intent at all.

I'm hoping to demonstrate that even in cases of this suppression or neglect, most of us actually do demonstrate the

Golden Thread in every stage of life, distinctly by developmental stage, and often express it even more overtly because of our early wounding patterns.

THE REPEATING PATTERNS OF THE TIERS IN THE STAGES OF CONSCIOUSNESS FRAMEWORK

The Stages of Consciousness Framework details repeating patterns, associated with the developmental trajectory in each tier, to show how our human development proceeds in cyclical phases distinguished by the "objects of focus": Concrete, Subtle, MetAware (O'Fallon, Stages International). The repetitive stages are depicted below:

Structure Pattern	Receptive/ passive	Active/ agentic	Reciprocal/ exchange	Interpenetrative/ integrated
	New identity	Either/or choice	Both/and	All ways of seeing are merged
	Imitation	One-way seeing	I see you see me	I see you are me
	Horizontal	Hierarchical	Horizontal	Hierarchical
	New class of objects	Parallel play	Relativism	Interpenetrative (merged)
	One side of the coin	Agree to disagree	Agreements	Principles
	Early individual: cause/ effect	Individual case/effect, universalizes	Construction of reality	Developmental
	Individual	Individual	Collective	Collective

O'Fallon, T and Barta, K. (2019). Stages Certification for Coaching, Counseling & Psychotherapy Diagnostics Manual. Stages International.

THE GOLDEN THREAD IN THE CONCRETE TIER

In this chapter, we are describing the stages of the Concrete Tier to identify how the Golden Thread may show up in each stage. These same repeating patterns also occur in the Subtle and MetAware Tiers, but with different objects of focus (i.e., Subtle objects, MetAware objects).

Basically, all members of the human population experience the first stages in the Concrete Tier as they emerge from the birth canal. Most people progress through the end of the Concrete Tier to the 2.5 stage, though some do not (those who become developmentally disabled for numerous cognitive or physiological reasons, or in cases of severe abuse, neglect, or injury, or when a cultural context prevents growing up into adulthood). Even more rarely, some children progress through the Concrete Tier at a very rapid clip and reside in the next tier at very young ages (in metaphysical circles, some of these children might be referred to as "indigo children" for their uncommon abilities).

The Concrete Tier demonstrates the repetitive patterns as such:

Person Perspective	TIER: Object of Awareness	SOCIAL STYLE	LEARNING STYLE	STAGE NAME
1.0	Concrete	Individual	Receptive	Impulsive
1.5	Concrete	Individual	Active	Egocentric
2.0	Concrete	Collective	Reciprocal	Rule-Oriented
2.5	Concrete	Collective	Interpenetrative	Conformist

O'Fallon, T, Barta, K. (2017) Essentials Course Manual, Stages International.

In the Concrete Tier, children, adolescents, and early adult stages focus primarily on concrete objects: things they do, see, hear, and touch, and concrete objects they have or want, such as their homes, clothing, food, nature, family, peers, relationships. A Concrete individual is an actual human in a body; the Concrete collective is a group that would fit in a physical structure (e.g., neighborhood, business, religious group, sports team). The Concrete interior refers to emotions you can see on the outside, such as sad, glad, mad, or related to the rules imposed by the group (e.g., guilt or shame). The Concrete exterior relates to concrete actions and physical development, such as brain development or the growth of the body.

The following are the specific stages in the Concrete Tier, from birth often until early adulthood (or later adulthood, in many cases).

Concrete Tier, Stage 1.0: Impulsive Stage
A baby's general experience of life is an immense awakening of concrete self-identity and interior emotions. Babies learn in this stage by copying speech and action. They can only see concretely from their own perspective. They learn about their own bodies and think that others only see what they see. In this stage, bonding or healthy attachment is the primary task, and caretakers need to provide a safe, loving, and engaged environment for the baby to wholly complete this stage. Babies become engaged through their senses of sight, sound, touch, taste, smell, and movement. Any of these experiences when not offered with enough consistency or safety create an attachment disorder, often leading to deep childhood wounding that sets up lifelong

challenges (American Academy of Child & Adolescent Psychiatry, 2014).

While purpose per se does not become discriminate in this stage, babies and young children will demonstrate affinity or curiosity toward certain objects of play, which gives an indication of their innate objects of interest. Babies and children gravitate toward certain toys, animals, books, nature, plants, types of people, specific kinds of touch, or other sensory experiences as a means to satisfy their curiosities. Babies will put these curiosities in their mouths, roll around on them, explore the touch and smell, and attach themselves to the items of interest. The more a parent or caregiver can encourage the specific "wonderment" at this age, the more likely the baby will grow into a more curious child seeking their own fulfillment.

Concrete Tier, Stage 1.5: Egocentric Stage

Children at this stage begin to understand that they have a body unique from yours (and they become "me"). In the early part of this stage, they do not have the capacity to see that others could have similar experiences, because it's still "all about me." They have concrete thoughts, feelings, and needs, see things as either/or (right or wrong, good or bad, not yet both/and). We hear toddlers adamantly and frequently use labels of "my" and "mine." Children at this age generally only see through their own eyes and don't yet know that others can see them, which limits their ability to receive feedback about themselves. Have you ever heard a toddler ask a parent whether they liked their tantrums, or have empathy for the parent after the tantrum ended?

Children in this stage cannot visualize and therefore cannot imagine the future or perceive the past. Expecting a young child to wait patiently for a parent to come home or for a special treat is generally imposing healthy rules rather than teaching perceived logic. Just don't expect the child to be able to apply it globally in different scenarios.

EGOCENTRIC: EARLIEST INDIVIDUATION OCCURS

Children at 1.5 are exploring the boundaries of their power: physical, intellectual, emotional, and social; they need safe containers to explore all aspects of themselves.

This stage involves the earliest type of individuation (beyond the birth and individuation from the mother's womb), a critical task for childhood. Caregiver support to allow the child to fully express themselves, their interests, curiosities, and uniqueness will have a lifelong impact.

In addition to the requirements of a safe container for children to explore their ever-expanding awareness and boundaries of this Concrete stage, developmental tasks that need to be completed in this stage include the accomplishment of:

- Autonomy: Knowing I have a choice
- Initiative: Taking a step to act on that choice
- Follow-through: Continuing the effort, no matter how hard
- Completion: Completing the task
- Celebration: Celebrating the completion

EGOCENTRIC: PURPOSE AS TENSION BETWEEN BOUNDARIES AND CURIOSITY

Purpose in the 1.5 Stage might look like the ability to adequately (and safely) explore the boundaries for the Concrete object of curiosity. If a child is deeply curious about nature and allowed to explore in wonderment—what do they find most fascinating? Trees, dirt, rocks, animals? What do they touch, pick up, stick in their pockets, talk about to their playmates, draw once they get home? What are their multiple curiosities: Is there a unique combination or relationship among their objects of interest? Do they have a special interest that captivates them enough to take initiative and follow through in ways they can't with other objects?

Purpose at this stage only reflects what the child is capable of achieving given their limited perspective and task orientation, and yet the thread of purpose will be more apparent as a child is given the right environmental support to express their curiosities.

Concrete Tier, Stage 2.0: Rule Oriented

This is the first collective stage that we experience as humans and thus, the most difficult. In a collective stage, we are practicing those things we have barely just mastered in the prior stage, and applying them in social contexts with the intent to reciprocate with others in a way that preserves both my individual nature and our collective interests.

RULE-ORIENTED: I BECOMES WE

Children cross over into the collective realm in the Concrete Tier generally at four to six years old in healthy development, taking on the capacities of second-person perspective. The focus is no longer "all about me" but now also "I see you see me," though still only on the exterior. Thus, children can start to distinguish which of their friends may have black or blonde hair, brown or blue eyes, dark or bright clothes, and a multitude of skin tones.

RULE-ORIENTED: LEARNING INTIMACY AND BOUNDARIES
Children move from playing separately with others (parallel play) to playing or talking easily with others (reciprocity). Children generally mature in this stage until early adolescence (twelve to fourteen years), and here they learn basic social skills and ways of interacting with others in the social world. Developmental tasks in this stage include learning about intimacy and boundaries and maintaining relationships (including repair, feedback, acknowledgement, apology, making changes).

Trust, care, friendship, motivation, communication, fairness, feedback, and love all develop here, as this stage is where children and adolescents learn the rules of social conduct and expectations to be well-received in the world. Often, when a child struggles with making friends, sharing, "playing nice" with others, or communicating their needs or interests, this difficulty indicates that some kind of trauma has occurred in either the 1.0 or 1.5 stages and developmental tasks were not fully met there.

Children learn and adolescents practice a "both/and" thinking in this stage, seeing beyond their own early ego needs to consider that someone else's needs are also important, creating room for negotiation and agreements. In the later part of this stage, peer pressure becomes a primary influence. It is, in fact, a developmental task for children and adolescents to learn to navigate the "rules" of these peer relationships, with their caregivers' support, through a balance of freedom and adult management.

RULE-ORIENTED: PEER RELATIONSHIPS AS A JOB

Caregivers should expect that children require significant time with their friends to accomplish these tasks (and care should be taken to encourage healthy friendships). I often tell parents who lament that their tweenagers spend too much time with friends that, in fact, it's their "job" to be spending this much time at work developing their social skills.

RULE-ORIENTED: DEMONSTRATING PURPOSE WITHIN THE TENSION OF ME AND US

Purpose at this stage often includes navigating personal interests and curiosities as held within or juxtaposed to peer relationships. How does a blooming adolescent express their sacred (and possibly secret) desires and curiosities in the context of new friendships and maintain their own autonomy while being seen as cool? Remember how hard your late primary/elementary school and early middle-school years were?

The Rule-Oriented Stage is one of the most intense periods of human development.

And if you've ever raised a middle-schooler (or been one), you'll remember how so. The identity formation stretch from early individual (practicing to be "me," and learning about "you") to the early collective (who are "we" and how do "we" become "us" without losing "me"?) is a huge jump requiring significant faith that "I am someone who matters."

We can see that if early individuation didn't go well at 1.5, then navigating the territory of the organic tension of "self within group" may be an impossible task. An aspiring artist or scientist or horticulturist (fill in the blank) may be pressured to follow the dreams of a best friend (or parent) to be a doctor or banker or filmmaker.

However, this is the stage at which purpose gets more demonstrably revealed, as children and adolescents are routinely asked to express themselves—most often at school and sometimes at home. Children and adolescents will use art projects, writing assignments, journaling, song, science projects, sports teams or casual play, dress-up, field trips, outdoor adventures, or spontaneous eruptions of delight to convey their deep interests and the thread of purpose.

A caregiver and other adults should shepherd the nascent interests of children and adolescents to encourage the curiosity, special talents, and wonderment that erupts when they're allowed to just "be themselves." It is indeed unfortunate when children or adolescents are required to give up their native interests for the prodding of parents who aspire to help their children become "more or different" than they are.

Adolescent rebellion (which shows up in behavior, dress, peer groups, anger or depression) is generally a means for the young person to express how repressed they feel at not getting to live their authentic lives. As is often the case, the greater the repression, the more extreme the statement.

Concrete Tier, Stage 2.5: Conformist

In this stage, we learn to prioritize the rules. We learn that some rules are more important than others, depending on the context of our lives and environment. We preserve our status in life, and status in social groups, by following rules and avoiding straying too far from the norms. We experience being "in" or "out" of groups, initially in adolescence and then into adulthood.

CONFORMIST: FOLLOW OR LEAVE

This stage generally starts in mid-teens and includes many adults who don't develop beyond this point. It is generally where we find our "tribe" that often becomes our mates for life (if we're not evolving rapidly). In isolated or traditional demagogic communities, often the entire social network follows the rules of the clan in order to keep the peace. Those who hear the beat of a different drum generally leave the community, causing it to stagnate due to the lack of differentiation in ideation.

Contrasted with teens who are susceptible to peer pressure because they are learning to follow the normative rules, in this stage, we begin to accept and integrate the rules of our group, but only if they are aligned with our true selves, beliefs, and values. If we are "in-group," we tend to look, dress, act, speak, and feel like others in our group. If we reject a group, or have chosen for some reason to be "out" of the group, we no longer conform and thus reject the principles of that group (and find another group more aligned with our true selves to be "in.")

If developmental tasks have been accomplished sufficiently (key distinction here, because this happens so seldom), peer pressure begins to diminish in this stage as adolescents define "who they are" and stabilize into a lifestyle, philosophy, or set of principles that align with that.

CONFORMIST: LOYALTY, BELONGING, AND COLLECTIVE VALUES PERSIST

In whatever group we find ourselves, conformists tend to be very loyal and appreciate status symbols of many kinds (badges, certificates, money, property, clothing, cars, or other material items) as expressions of fitting into the group. Little room exists for individual behavior in this stage, as people tend to see each other as "common" rather than unique (even among radical groups or one's "fringe" to mainstream society, this loyalty is paramount to group norms.)

People "belong" in this stage—to families, tribes, communities, social groups, and belief systems. When developmental tasks haven't been accomplished sufficiently, we often find ourselves trying to fit "in" with a group that is sufficiently distinct enough from our innate desires that we must hide some part of ourselves to belong. A healthier adaptation would be to accept ourselves and go find the "in" group that really fits us.

In this stage, the rules are hierarchical and based in past traditions, as people cannot see subtle objects and therefore can't project well into the future. Routines, order, and stability are means of safety, rules are followed strictly, and everyone on the outside is typically a threat.

CONFORMIST: PURPOSE "FITS" WITHIN
BOUNDS OR BECOMES RADICALIZED

For an adolescent or adult to express purpose in this stage, they would have needed to complete significant developmental tasks in earlier stages. We can see how the extreme pressure to fit in and live according to the rules requires one to either a) give up their unique self and potentially their purpose, or b) find a group that allows them to respect their authenticity, which may require rejection of childhood social groups. They can't "move past" this stage, and it is often a very messy time for anyone who wants to live an intentional life.

"Finding yourself" in the context of group normative expectations can be as simple as standing up for what we believe in or yield radical acts like isolating ourselves from family, moving across the country (or world), taking on a new name, rejecting the family fortune or legacy, or taking on a career that our parents would despise. These radical behaviors are not always aimed at living purposefully and are more likely to be stimulus for creating authentic expression.

However, generally purposeful expression follows such acts and can look like vocation or avocation, and the beginning pursuit of an authentic life may follow. This stage is an informal rite of passage in which many of us "conform" to the status quo of social expectations (when we may have difficulty truly expressing our unique purpose) and are unlikely to move past this stage. Or, if we don't conform to the social expectations of our childhood groups, we find a way to individuate again into something more purposeful and meaningful to savor the one life we came to live.

PURPOSE REQUIRES ALLEGIANCE TO SELF

One of the challenges of living a purposeful life is that we are required to be "allegiant" to our souls, as opposed to the many voices and contexts of our lives. If we want to remain true to ourselves, in many stages of childhood or adolescence we are required to remain unyielding to the forces that would subsume our unique essence. To make our unique and most significant contribution, we cannot abandon our purpose as it is exhibited throughout our young lives.

This reality is especially challenging in the context of the developmental tasks we need to complete to become whole, healthy adults. Finding our way through the maelstrom of individual to collective requires navigating complex human interactions and dynamics, suggesting that either caregivers are extremely attentive to the needs of their children, or adolescents gain negotiation skills rarely present even among adults.

I remember, as far back as in my late childhood, being told by my parents that I was among the most stubborn and hard-headed people they had ever known. I wanted to do things my way—perhaps because of the extreme repression in which I found myself. In hindsight, my instincts and desires were often in alignment with my essential traits, but different than my parents' expectations of me. I wore the label of "stubborn" as a suit of armor, which created its own shadow characteristics ill-suited for relationships of all kinds.

No wonder so many adolescents and adults abandon their dreams and live disappointing lives. To live purposefully, we must accomplish the developmental tasks to allow the fulfillment of our childlike, wide-eyed enthusiasm for unfettered curiosities.

And living purposefully is not at the expense of the collective. Living purposefully is always about finding our unique Golden Thread that offers our greatest contribution to the larger tapestry of humanity and the planet.

EXAMPLES OF PURPOSE IN THE CONCRETE STAGE

The following are brief examples of how the Golden Thread weaves itself in the story of people's lives through the stages of the Concrete Tier.

JACQUI WEBB: CREATING CONTAINERS FOR SENSUAL CONNECTIONS

1.5 Egocentric stage: Jacqui Webb, whose story is told in chapter 3, is just one example of a child whose fondest early memories are being entirely connected to herself, putting pebbles in her mouth because they were so beautiful, resting in long hours of swimming, and otherwise connecting to nature. Nature and concrete objects were both sensual experiences and created a container for Jacqui to come to know herself intimately.

2.0 Rule-oriented: Jacqui found her way to be accepted in the world, learning how to be of use to others by offering support and counseling her peers—even when "kids didn't do that."

As a result, she created supportive containers for her friends' emotional expressions.

2.5 Conformist: As a young mother, Jacqui acquiesced to social expectations that she drop everything and fit within the parameters of motherhood. Even then, she tried to find goodness in her life, "but the ups and downs of endless meals, boredom, and rushed mealtimes" along with childcare and other chores kept her disillusioned about whether she'd ever find herself again. While Jacqui described the relinquishing of her own deep desires in this stage, she also managed to derive pleasure from the sensual experiences of preparing food for her children and the touch and intimacy that motherhood offered her.

GREGG LEVOY: DIVING INTO THE SHADOWS

1.5 Egocentric stage: Gregg Levoy, whose story appears in chapter 2, was always asking questions and wondering why things were the way they were. Despite his inquisitive nature, his mother attempted to suppress his boyish energy with Ritalin. Very early on, Gregg was seeking how and why things are the way they are, to uncover the truth behind the story.

2.0 Rule-oriented stage: Gregg spent many long summer afternoons exploring the secret passageways of his grandfather's house with his brother. He also played a fantastical Alien Game that his father invented, negotiating rules of relationship in his neighborhood. Gregg was also into writing about dreams, poetry, and mythology, even in his preteens. He was "after a different story than most people like to tell," and consumed all the mythologic stories as he was beginning to navigate the rules that bind humanity through archetypal stories. Gregg's exploration of the secret passageways and stories that define us constituted his initial foray into the dark shadows of humanity.

2.5 Conformist stage: Because of the early repression from the Ritalin, Gregg describes how he didn't have a clue what he wanted to major in in college, but ultimately his "lights went on" in a journalism class, and he rejected the career path his parents wished upon him. He eventually left a job that told him what to write and began writing what called to him. Gregg eschewed conformity to his parents' expectations and created his own "in" group among writers, choosing to write about liberating the self.

NOTES FROM THE FIELD

My own observation of these and many other client stories is that the developmental trajectory is the same for all of us, but the details vary widely. If we experience a childhood that allows us to accomplish our developmental tasks, with adequate nurturing, bonding, attachment, allowance for free expression, and exploration of self within and through boundaries, then we are then more likely to come to know ourselves more authentically and assert our purpose earlier in life.

That's perhaps the biggest "if" on the face of the planet.

Or, as in many case studies in this book, when the wounding is deep and complex, it does not allow the full (or even partial) conveyance of purpose. Early developmental tasks are most significant because this timeframe is for the original and subsequent (more informal) individuation phases. If this individuation does not occur at birth, in early childhood, in adolescence, and then into early adulthood, the next tier will require significant healing and integration of fractured sub-psychic parts.

SELF-REFLECTION: HOW DID YOUR ABILITY TO INDIVIDUATE AFFECT YOUR EXPRESSION OF PURPOSE IN THE CONCRETE TIER?

Individuation is a psychological term for becoming an individual, or healthy separating from other important figures in your life (parents, peers, or social groups). Imagine the phases of individuation you may have experienced thus far. These would have occurred in early childhood (roughly one and a half to two years old), in early adolescence (twelve to fourteen), late adolescence (nineteen to twenty-one), and roughly coincide with the transitions between stages—which most of us cannot demarcate well enough for that to be useful. As we consider the Concrete Tier, imagine the demarcations from the Individual 1.0 Egocentric to 1.5 Impulsive, then again to the Collective 2.0 Rule-Oriented and finally to the 2.5 Conformist stages.

QUESTIONS TO CONSIDER:
Remember and explore the childhood experiences you had when beginning to express your innate curiosities, passions, talents, gifts, and ways of being.

As you conjure up those memories, what do you recall of those innate expressions of you? What do you recall through your senses about the experiences that evoked delight or aliveness?

What in your life may have kept you from fully experiencing this aliveness? How did that affect who you became, the trajectory of your own development, and how you were able to learn about and begin living your purpose?

CONCLUSION: PREVIEW OF WHAT'S NEXT

This chapter begins to explore the early demonstration of the Golden Thread in the Concrete Tier as a depiction of the nuanced expressions of ourselves, both within healthy and functional childhood settings, and despite—and sometimes because of—the constrained environments in which we grow up. This succinct review of the patterns of child, adolescent, and early adult development provides an overview of the major milestones accomplished when things go well. We can see that purposeful expression shifts significantly over the timeframe within the Concrete Tier, which encompasses birth to an entire life for some.

While no data exist to depict global estimates of numbers of people within the Concrete Tier, I've used global population patterns and age ranges (Worldometers, 2020 projections) and suggest that approximately one-third or more of the human population falls within the Concrete Tier. And while purpose does begin to be expressed in very early stages of life in important and fundamental ways in the Concrete Tier, the depictions generally are reflected within self-oriented and rule-bound and conforming parameters. As we examine the significant enhancement of strategic capacities within evolved states in the next chapter, we'll be able to project why some of the intractable social challenges exist on the planet and within our species. Purpose begins to take on more strategic, contextual, and ultimately systemic attributes in the Subtle Tier, which is more likely to contribute in a way that can resolve deeply challenging global issues.

I've demonstrated the early portrayals of purpose in the Concrete Tier through the case studies of Jacqui and Gregg, and a few stories from my own life. In the next chapter, we'll delve into the Subtle Tier of the Stages of Consciousness model, where I'll share additional case studies and note the progression of nuanced purposeful expression.

REFERENCES

American Academy of Child & Adolescent Psychiatry (2014). Attachment Disorders, No. 85. https://www.aacap.org/AACAP/ Families_and_Youth/Facts_for_Families/FFF-Guide/Attach-ment-Disorders-085.aspx.

O'Fallon, T. Stages International.

O'Fallon, T, & Barta, K. (2017) Essentials Course Manual, Stages International.

O'Fallon, T, & Barta, K. (2019). Stages Certification for Coaching, Counseling & Psychotherapy Diagnostics Manual. Stages International.

Worldometers (2020).

CHAPTER 5

MIDDLE STAGES AND THE THREADS OF PURPOSE

My earliest memory of "talking to myself" was during my teens when I started comparing myself to other women and consciously deciding who I wanted to be and what I wanted to look like. While this compare-and-contrast behavior was not itself a Subtle Tier experience (given that comparison begins in the Concrete Tier, as we mimic peers and familial contexts), but the notion that I could cognize the distinct voices and choose to be someone independent of my family or friends was a deviation from the Concrete's 2.5 Conformist stage.

At around age fifteen, I recall pulling out magazine pages of women I wanted to portray. Most of them were advertisements of slim models with expensive clothes who appeared to have successful and powerful careers (obviously long before media literacy was a thing). And I also read stories of courageous, heroic, noble, brilliant women who made great contributions to the world, and I wanted simultaneously to be like them. I had a complex array of externalized ideals (physical beauty, influence, and power, along with courage, generosity, intellect, and magnanimous contribution) that composed my sense of the "ideal woman" I wanted to become.

This complex interplay of competing aspirations came to a head one day when I found myself in the bathroom, age fifteen, staring in the mirror behind a locked door. I was staring at the petechiae (pronounced puh·tee·kee·uh), the tiny red dots that appeared on the skin around my eyes. My capillaries had erupted and bled into the skin during an intense bout of purging. No hiding my eating disorder now.

I realized no amount of makeup would hide the glaring red spots dotting my eyelids and the soft skin below my eyes—especially from my already suspecting few best friends who'd noticed my unusually rigid eating patterns. As I focused on the dots, I simultaneously peered into my own eyes, trying to find an answer to the several competing voices in my head demanding to be heard.

The confused adolescent wanting to be sexy/attractive:

You can't quit purging. Unless you can go back to not eating, and you know how hard that is. You get too hungry. You won't fit into your clothes if you gain any more weight. You have to be pretty to be loved. You'll just have to find a way to hide the spots.

The smart, practical, responsible voice:

You know there has to be a better way to stay at a healthy weight. You have to stop compromising your health. You know this practice is so bad for your body. Why are you so ashamed of who you are?

The feminist activist who wanted to create powerful change in the world:

You know you shouldn't care about your body weight anyway. You have way more important things to do with your life than worry about your weight or how you look. Stop this ridiculous habit now!

I stood at the mirror for about an hour, listening to my internal voices debate how to resolve this complex dilemma. They were arguing the pros and cons, trying to make sense of the challenges of being a woman in a world with expectations that the more evolved parts of me didn't want to meet. I had a compulsive sense of perfectionism in all areas of my life, living in a home with an inordinate amount of chaos and neglect. I was treating my body as just one more subject to master.

Obviously, these voices were perspectives from a range of stages, Concrete to Subtle, and most certainly represented some unresolved shadowed wounding from childhood.

I decided to jump in the shower to see if I could spark a different conversation. I wanted to focus on who I would become and how I would steer my life toward ideals that mattered to me, rather than someone else. Somehow, as I changed the context for the internal conversation, the voices began to negotiate and support each other, wanting to work together to confront and resolve this formidable problem.

Later, as a senior in high school, I began to confront my eating disorders and the shadowed wounding that led to the crisis of self-image. A fairly rebellious late individuation occurred, which had other "unpleasant" repercussions at home but resolved the struggles related to controlling my body as a means of managing my out-of-control family context.

I had no idea how hard the task to live into more realistic and appropriate ideals would become over the years for someone like me, as I very slowly began to deal with my childhood wounding. I needed several decades and a commitment to allow the voices to speak their own truth. These voices that had been repressed during childhood would need to reemerge and be heard, to allow the benefit of integration. Ultimately, these and other gifts of my life's trauma-blessing paradox would eventually allow me to work my way through the Subtle Tier and become more of myself.

We often think we're "crazy" when we first encounter the multitude of internal Subtle voices that speak loudly—sometimes vehemently and often competitively—about what and who we should be and do. The ability to hear and process our thoughts and feelings is an indicator of a rich Subtle awareness, even while it can be initially distracting and later rewarding as we come to know ourselves due to this interactive internal dynamic.

OPPORTUNITY FOR UNDENIABLE PURPOSE IN THE SUBTLE TIER

We enter the Subtle Tier at a wide range of ages. We migrate there primarily in our twenties to forties, and in rare cases in the teen years; some of us show up there in our elder years, as entering this tier is dependent on awakening of the Subtle senses, not age. Given the huge variation in age, we obviously see a wide variation in how purpose is demonstrated in this tier. The Golden Thread can show up as a nuanced expression in any stage of the Subtle Tier, though the style, tone, voice, and execution will vary based on the perspectival awareness at each stage and the egoic personality still intact in this tier.

Expression in this tier is steeped in purpose, especially if we complete most of the developmental tasks of the earlier tier and become committed to our own sovereign expression.

The Subtle Tier demonstrates these repetitive patterns:

Person Per-spective	TIER: Object of Awareness	SOCIAL STYLE	LEARNING STYLE	STAGE NAME
3.0	Subtle	Individual	Receptive	Expert
3.5	Subtle	Individual	Active	Achiever
4.0	Subtle	Collective	Reciprocal	Pluralist
4.5	Subtle	Collective	Interpene-trative	Strategist

O'Fallon, T., Stages International. www.stagesinternational.com.

We should remind ourselves that not all adults reach the Subtle Tier. Before we make it into the Subtle Tier, we "cross over" from primarily Concrete objects of focus to Subtle objects of focus. These experiences of the world in the Subtle Tier include:

- interior Subtle objects (e.g., complex feelings, thinking, planning for the future, assumptions, interpretations, judgements) and
- exterior Subtle objects (e.g., bodily feelings, subtle energies and systems, contexts, complex systems).

THE GOLDEN THREAD IN THE SUBTLE TIER: OBJECTS OF FOCUS WE CANNOT SEE OR TOUCH

In this chapter, we are describing the stages of the Subtle Tier to identify how the Golden Thread may show up in each stage. These same repeating patterns also occur in the Concrete and MetAware Tiers, but with different objects of focus (i.e., Concrete objects, MetAware objects).

Some of us in the Concrete Tier (or even early Subtle Tier) have disdain for or completely discount perspectives of those of us in the later Subtle Tier, because the objects of focus are imperceptible to those who only see with their eyes. When we cannot yet see the invisible, we either:

- disbelieve those who can,
- feel intimidated by their experiences, or
- consider them nuts.

While early Subtle Tier inhabitants (e.g., doctors, lawyers, accountants, engineers) are often revered by much of society because they are following a "rule-bound" paradigm of the Concrete 2.5 Conformist collective, late Subtle Tier inhabits are often referenced as "the intellectual elite" or "spiritual woo woo" because their rules or parameters are context-based and not perceptible to all.

Early in my doctoral studies, in what some academics discounted as the "soft" sciences (e.g., methodologies related to human behavior and human and organizational development), I recall sitting at dinner with my husband, the soon-to-be father of my first child. I was sharing some of what we'd discussed in class that night. His engineering mind couldn't wrap itself around the concepts I was describing.

He looked at me cynically and said, "I don't believe in what you're doing."

I was puzzled. What did he mean? I sat still, listening to the competing voices in my own head. Did he mean he didn't understand the concepts or methodologies of humanistic studies? Did he want to know why I was in school in my mid-thirties with a baby on the way? Was he intimidated by my learning?

I finally asked, "What do you mean?"

He stated very matter-of-factly, "There's no way you can measure that stuff. It's not measurable. You can't study what you can't measure."

My own mind couldn't embrace the idea that my husband of six years had such divergent perspectives from mine. His incredible linear problem-solving capacity that served him as an engineer and chemist in a manufacturing operation constituted a very different skill set (mostly early Subtle Tier) than what I'd begun to use in the complex systemic and context-laden human dilemmas that I studied as a social scientist (mostly late Subtle Tier).

The Subtle Tier includes third- and fourth-person perspectives, and we begin again, focusing on Subtle objects, in the cyclical pattern of:

- creating a new identity in 3.0,
- taking on either/or choices at 3.5,
- integrating both/and perspectives at 4.0, and
- merging all ways of seeing at 4.5.

No firm epidemiologic data exist about how many or who evolves to this tier, though generally we can make assumptions that people who migrate to this tier have "moved beyond" at least some of the limited notions of themselves in their childhood context and begun to explore "what's true" for them in the broader world.

And, certainly, not all adults who enter the Subtle Tier evolve into the later stages of the tier. As in the Concrete Tier, a person is "had by" their experiences of the newly discovered Subtle world in the early stages and later has a greater command and utility of those experiences.

SUBTLE TIER: MASTERING OUR INNER SELVES TO EMBODY IT IN THE WORLD

Mastering the stages of the Subtle Tier requires not only practice and commitment to exploring the unknown territory of one's inner milieu, but also a commitment to integrating it into broader contexts of our lives. We "merge" aspects of our lives, inner and outer, in ways that someone in the Concrete Tier cannot fathom.

Some part of the mastery of our inner milieu includes integrating childhood wounding and shadow. We often migrate to the Subtle Tier with unfinished tasks from the Concrete Tier related to the wounding of childhood, which explains why some of us may have an uncanny ability to appear competent and polished in a work setting yet have disastrous relations at home, or vice versa. Our wounding shows up in the relational dynamics or settings in which we are most triggered by the circumstances where the wound was formed.

The origin of these non-integrated parts starts in less-than-ideal circumstances in childhood. When we do not have access to all the attachment and nurturing we need, some part of our egoic personality unconsciously decides that it cannot "go along for the ride" and survive the experience. This "part" of ourselves basically "splits" from the whole personality and begins to reside in a submerged or shadowed expression. The "part" doesn't leave us, but instead serves as background noise to the rest of our personality attempting to move forward without it.

We are never wholly ourselves until we have integrated these split, projected, or introjected sub-psychic parts. As

I resolved the childhood attachment wounds related to my mother, I began to integrate these many sub-psychic parts of myself. This process ultimately also reduced and eliminated the passive-aggressive traits I brought to relationships with both intimate and authority figures, and thankfully severed a long-standing resonance with narcissistic personalities.

As we age and/or develop without these fully integrated parts, we demonstrate personality quirks or traits that demonstrate our nuanced woundedness and create challenges for a full, authentic expression of purpose. Many methodologies are now available to reclaim and integrate these sub-psychic parts and become a more whole being.

As I worked with the clients included here and many others, my most common observations of these fractured parts related to purpose were that:

- The suppressed or rebellious voices tend to take charge when faced with stressful situations, as a means of controlling risk and creating safety, which in turn causes our authentic self to remain hidden.
- Usually the parts suppressed are some of the most unique and special parts, as they were the most distinct from the childhood container (that rejected authenticity), and so the suppression often targets significant purposeful gifts.
- Our particular personality quirks are directly related to the distinct parts, as we are attempting to hide ourselves and our neuroses but end up showing our true colors (e.g., an anxious person may laugh obnoxiously).
- As we move toward wholeness, we may unconsciously "project" onto others the very trait we are needing to

integrate to make it consciously known to ourselves; thus, the others in our lives who trigger us are mirror (mere) reflections of ourselves.

The significance of integrating unresolved childhood parts is none other than having available to us all of our time, energy, passion, and intention, which allow us to be fully present and purposeful. Abraham Maslow, father of humanistic psychology and the Hierarchy of Needs, once noted:

"The civil war within the average person between forces of the inner depths and the forces of defense and control seems to have been resolved in my subjects and they are less split. As a consequence, more of themselves is available for use, for enjoyment and for creative purpose. They waste less of their time and energy protecting themselves against themselves" *(Maslow, 1943).*

The following are the specific stages in the Subtle Tier, and all cases assume that someone has grasped many of the developmental tasks in the Concrete Tier.

Subtle Tier, Stage 3.0: Expert Stage

As the Expert stage is an upshift of the 1.0 "birthing" stage of infancy, we enter this stage wanting to imitate Subtle Experts who command our attention and respect (much as we imitated our parents or caregivers in childhood).

In this stage, the maturing of the brain and subtle senses permit us to visualize and imagine things we haven't seen.

EXPERT: RELIANCE ON CODES & PRINCIPLES TO ORGANIZE NEWLY DEVELOPING SUBTLE ABSTRACTIONS

We enter into this stage and believe ourselves to be Experts because we can move beyond concrete operations and linear thinking and create new rules and parameters that are abstractions. We view ourselves as superior because of this ability to see things newly and distinctly from those in our "tribe" or concrete collective.

As Experts, we tend toward perfectionism because we don't yet have the capacity to prioritize what we're "seeing" (which would create a hierarchy of knowledge and allow us to loosen our need to "get it all right"). You might picture a recent college graduate whose specialized skills are far superior to their peers or family because of their recent studies and imagine the cockiness that accompanies this recent acquisition of knowledge.

As we enter the Subtle Tier, we also can't envision the distant future because of the limitations of our newly developing Subtle skills. So we rely on professional and expert explanations, codes and principles to guide us, resisting feedback and strongly defending our professional knowledge. We don't value others' ideas easily, because we can only experience what we know ourselves, not yet able to experience others' interior Subtle experience.

Experts also still utilize the Collective of the Concrete Tier, as our Subtle Collective has not yet formed. This fact means that we remain primarily Conformists in our group experiences (and vehemently argue for the rules and procedures associated with our expert professions), until the late Subtle Tier when we enter the Subtle Collective (in the 4.0 Pluralist stage).

As Experts, we generally have highly innovative and entrepreneurial skills because of our new visualization capacity. Experts also tend to have a strong desire for continuous improvement and are often involved in building new products or the execution of projects or businesses. Many people in this stage are in occupations or industries based in technical or professional knowledge that requires licensure or certification (e.g., medical, legal, financial, technological, academic/education).

EXPERT: EARLY WITNESSING CAPACITY ARISES

In the Expert stage, we begin to experience our subtle self, and so can witness ourselves and also "see ourselves in someone else's shoes." Because we only have early capacity to visualize, we can see the past and future for a few years but are not yet strategic thinkers (and thus cannot see far enough out or see multiple perspectives). We are also not usually good team players because we don't have access to "either/or" viewing and can't hear others' viewpoints. People in this stage often reject their conventional peers in the Conformist 2.5 stage because of their limited thinking and inability to visualize beyond their traditional principles.

EXPERT: PURPOSE SHOWS UP AS TRAITS AND SKILLS

Purpose in this stage is often defined by exploring the traits and skills we want to express as our Unique Self, which has begun to come online. Despite the fact that we are still enmeshed in the 2.5 Conformist Collective, we see that it may repress our unique identity and thus attempt to resolve the rifts between our 2.5 Principles and the expanded 3.0 Subtle perspectives. We may discard prior associations (e.g., religious, social, familial, trade) and follow a path that allows us to project ourselves in the world through a vocation or avocation. We do so by perfecting our new Subtle skills, supported by the experts who lead us. Purpose often looks like professional mastery in this stage yet hosts the unique and nuanced flavor of the threads of our essential purpose.

Subtle Tier, Stage 3.5: Achiever Stage

ACHIEVER: PRIORITIZATION ALLOWS
STRATEGY AND SCIENTIFIC METHOD

As we make our way into the "practicing" stage of the Subtle Tier, Achievers gain mastery over our Subtle visualizations and can prioritize them. This practice is distinct from the lack of ability to prioritize in the Expert stage, which required us to rely on codified rules and procedures. This prioritization of subtle experience allows us to create goals and strategic plans with outcomes of up to five years. At this stage, we can also visualize linear cause and effect, and therefore Achievers believe strongly in empirical sciences and natural laws, including as applied to people. We believe here that everything can be improved through the scientific method.

ACHIEVER: ENHANCED SUBTLE EXPERIENCES
PROMOTES EMOTIONAL/SOCIAL EXPLORATION

At this stage, we are able to see others but may not "feel seen" by them, living parallel lives without necessarily feeling the reciprocal relationships. We move into subtle either/or choices, allowing our individual priorities to become focused and strategic. We begin to experience that the interior subtle states are paramount, thus material objects fall out of focus and priority. Houses, cars, clothing, and credentials become less significant, though still important given we're still in the 2.5 Conformist Collective. We become interested in "owning" things beyond the Concrete, and intellectual property, brands, copyrights, and trademarks become significant assets here.

We become more malleable team players, as we can see others' perspectives, and take feedback well, especially if it relates to our goals and accomplishments. Because we have begun to claim the power of our Subtle self, we explore the physical, intellectual, emotional, and social power (similar to the 1.5 Egocentric stage) available in the Subtle Tier. This process looks like the power of communication, body language, emotional expression, feedback loops, and use of our subtle energy, though we are not masterful at using any of these yet, often intruding into others' own subtle systems.

Because we have mastered our one-way and either/or subtle seeing, we can envision, follow through, and complete complex strategic plans, even if they're not entirely useful for the broader human condition.

Achievers generally learn to manage many aspects of life because they can view a broad perspective, begin to see what they do not know, and not get bogged down in details.

The 3.5 stage is a mature upshift of the 1.5 egocentric toddler who insists that their way is the right way. Depending on the extent of completion of prior developmental tasks of the Achiever (e.g., including childhood wounding), their Subtle interior may decide that anyone who gets in the way of the Achiever's accomplishments may be considered a problem.

At this stage, we tend to resent people in the advanced 4.0 stage who have ability to prioritize and use reciprocal Subtle energies. As Achievers, we see the 4.0 Pluralists attempting to "rein in" our powerful expressions beyond the "this is how we do it" social conventions (of the 2.5 Conformist Collective) because we're not yet in the "both/and" or "we're all correct" seeing (of the 4.0 Pluralist Collective).

ACHIEVERS: PURPOSE AS PROJECTS AND POWER

Purpose in this stage begins to take on dominant structures in society, as Achievers who have accomplished many of their developmental tasks are masterful at building and scaling projects, businesses, and social and professional networks. Many unique expressions of purpose are initiated by those who have mastered the skills necessary to implement their visions into the world.

This stage is where "manifesting" from the juicy fruits of early expression of purpose would begin to occur. Just as successful enterprises are built that maximize profits and power in this stage, so too can purposeful entrepreneurs, activists, changemakers, thought leaders, parents, innovators, students, and agents of change capitalize on their meaningful intent as Achievers who desire to impact the world with their nuanced contributions of purpose.

Subtle Tier, Stage 4.0: Pluralist Stage

PLURALIST: SOCIAL JUSTICE ARISES DUE TO
SHARED SUBTLE EXPERIENCES

People in the Pluralist stage begin to interact reciprocally with others in subtle ways because they are able to see others' own interiors (e.g., thoughts, feelings, assumptions, interpretations, judgments) and also experience empathy for others' lives. The recognition of suffering and the broader human condition begins to take on new meaning here, as we become connected to the Subtle Tier collective and realize that we all have unique and valid ways of seeing the world. This new awareness, that reality is based in experience, creates an understanding that we are all embedded in and shaped uniquely by the context of our lives and all worthy of respect and dignity.

For the first time, the Pluralist can see that life is ambiguous and that everything is relative.

"Respect and protect all beings" become the new "Subtle rules" through which the world is viewed, as opposed to the 2.5 rules of social expectations of family, clan, and cultural community (and often nation). This second shift away from a "me-first" identity occurs only if most developmental tasks have been completed.

Indeed, context itself becomes the new Collective, so that as Pluralists (we seldom occur individually!), we define ourselves and our beliefs by the context through which they occur. We begin to see how our experiences have been shaped by hidden cultural and social expectations and we desperately need to make this matter overt.

We begin to see that others can reciprocally see us and our subtle ideas, visions, and behaviors. Because we now experience subtle energies as more important than even our physical ones, we begin to experience the collective perspective and co-create containers where everyone shares power, responsibility, creative potential, and decision-making. A shadowed aspect of this new recognition is that in the Pluralist stage (ironically), we begin to believe our values are the only correct ones because of the inability to prioritize our internal subtle voices.

PLURALIST: TENDENCY TO DISREGARD GOALS, RULES, AND HIERARCHY

While this democratization of the social order optimizes equanimity and distributes power, it also challenges goal orientation and progress and can limit the ability to get things done. Pluralists often have an "allergy" to earlier (e.g., conformist, hierarchical) stages because we harshly judge the lack of two-way both/and seeing in the earlier stages. The whole world would benefit from having Pluralists learn to better co-create with Achievers and Experts for their goal orientation and technical capacity, respectively. Because of the resentment and disdain these stages have for each other, people in them seldom work or interact together easily.

Because of Pluralists' broader context awareness, we tend to focus on all kinds of social justice issues (e.g., gender, racial, income disparities), environmental and climate issues, and animal rights. Because of our now well-practiced capacity for visualization, we are futuristic.

We are also process-oriented because of our need for reciprocal dynamics; we see and constantly question our own and others' assumptions, ambiguities, and interpretations. However, because we do not yet have hierarchical prioritization of subtle awareness, nor the capacity to merge perspectives in this stage (which happens at 4.5 Strategist), we easily make projections onto others of our own limited perspectives.

PLURALIST: PURPOSE AS ACTIVIST FOR UNIQUE AUTHENTIC SELF

This stage is where the authentic self emerges strongly out of the orientation of the Subtle rules to "respect and protect" all humans uniquely. Our internal Collective (voices from childhood or adolescence that were suppressed since the 2.5 Collective) emerges newly and begins to voice its truths, just as we allow all repressed or marginalized people to express themselves.

We become more tolerant, understanding, and respectful of divergent ways of seeing the world and celebrate the uniqueness that is each one of us. Purpose in this stage often appears as an activist orientation, as the arising of two-way both/and seeing creates a radicalization of former values into a collective stream of consciousness. This emerging orientation for every soul to find its unique expression and place appears as a more open and inclusive society, and can produce a collective identity through which co-emerging groups, clubs, projects, and businesses are formed.

Subtle Tier, Stage 4.5: Strategist Stage

STRATEGISTS: PRIORITIZE CONTEXTS TO
CREATE SYSTEMIC INTERDEPENDENCE

The Strategist stage of the Subtle Tier has the distinction of being able to prioritize the contexts that were the backbone of the somewhat rigid and democratized "rules" of the Pluralist stage (e.g., political correctness, inclusion and diversity, reparations for societal injustices). Strategists are able to prioritize commitments, opinions, and beliefs, and thus "value those perspectives that are developmental, people-oriented, inclusive of other levels of development, dynamic, and which foster continuous learning" (O'Fallon & Barta, 2017).

Because Strategists can see and value the reciprocal relational qualities of the systems and contexts in which they work, they create a safe container for the voices of each stage to be heard, thus including the gifts of each stage in any co-creation. Because it is an interpenetrative stage in which all perspectives merge, Strategists tend to see how different systems interact with each other—as opposed to seeing independent systems.

Strategists, like Conformists at 2.5, create operating agreements to reflect the Collective and develop Principles that can serve to accomplish outcomes. But a Strategist's principles are based on ethics, rather than tradition or social norms.

A Strategist sees that reality is constructed socially and can help prioritize goals and create contexts to support a movement from this awareness rather than "how it's always been done."

STRATEGISTS: SYSTEMIC AWARENESS CAUSES VALUING
OF HUMAN CAPACITY AND AUTHENTICITY

In this stage, because of the broader and deeper awareness that we are each unique (based on our contexts and awareness of the human frailties), we begin to imagine that each person has a right to develop to their highest capacity, and that becoming our authentic selves is the foundation for our greatest contributions.

STRATEGISTS: SYSTEM DYNAMICS ENHANCED
BY SEEING NUANCE AND CONTEXT

As a Strategist, we also have unique capacities to zoom in (focus) and zoom out (expand awareness) to see both the nuance and the broader context. We embrace paradox and projections, and look for patterns of underlying principles to guide us. As Strategists, we want to better understand how systems work, both in specific contexts and in a broad array of life circumstances (including internally). This leads us to accept and integrate feedback, and is how systems are sustained. In this stage, we experience a rapid integration of the previously fractured ego states and also the creation of interconnected systems in the material world.

The 4.5 Strategist stage is a very advanced stage of consciousness or human development. According to theorists, if more people on the planet could advance to this stage, we could resolve most of the volatile, uncertain, complex, and ambiguous (Bennett & Lemoine, 2014) dilemmas on the planet because of the capacity to see and develop systems.

STRATEGIST: SUPER-WITNESS STANCE ALLOWS
COMPLEX PROBLEM-SOLVING AND INNER PEACE

Evolving to this tier means integrating and relinquishing much of the human dilemma. As Strategists, we will have expanded our consciousness enough to see beyond even the Subtle reciprocal dynamic of the 4.0 Pluralist and thus can witness the patterns that stymie us within the Pluralist stage. From that witness stance, we can derive Subtle Principles (to replace 2.5 Concrete Principles) that explain the patterns of the subtle human mind and in systems. These complex skills would contribute greatly to resolving complex human systems.

The benefit of this perspective is to both offer support to individual human expression (and purpose) and create internal (e.g., individual transformational programs) or external (e.g., businesses, networks, social movements) systems that result in efficient and powerful change dynamics.

The personal benefit of the Strategist stage is that internally we grow incredibly quiet.

We begin to integrate the fractured sub-psychic parts. We begin to see how our internal and external systems have affected our lives, and we have great compassion for how we have navigated the complexity. As this self-compassion arises, wisdom emerges, distilled from the lessons of life, allowing us to have acceptance and compassion for people at all levels, in all contexts, in all reaches of humanity. We can then construct new systems internally that let us find greater peace for ourselves and build external systems to support others.

STRATEGIST: PURPOSE DEMONSTRATES
UNIQUE MULTIDIMENSIONAL CONTEXTS

The expression of the Unique Self at this stage includes what emerged in the 4.0 Pluralist stage and refinements based upon the ability to see and prioritize all perspectives. So rather than a long list of attributes that define our purpose, we begin to ferret out that which speaks most loudly about who we are and how it "fits" in the internal and external systems of our lives.

Purpose may have been articulated in an earlier stage, but we come to see it within the multidimensional contexts of our internal and external systems. By now (if we have accomplished most of our developmental tasks), we will be able to utilize our increasingly agile skills to build systems to accommodate our wildest dreams, and to take into account how those systems fit within the systems of others' dreams. We encounter few limits here in expressing our purpose—if we've done our developmental work.

PURPOSE REQUIRES BREAKING OUT
OF CONTEXTS AND IDENTITIES

One of the challenges to living a purposeful life at this tier is that the developmental tasks in these stages are usually accomplished in cultures, workplaces, or communities where very few people have reached these stages (given the low prevalence of people who make it into the Subtle Tier, especially the latter half). This fact means few role models exist, and even fewer mentors, especially at the later stages.

Being confined to systems or structures that present a developmental "glass ceiling" can keep us from evolving, much like too-tight shoes or a box that's too small. Thus, completing the required developmental tasks is especially challenging in contexts where people have disdain for anything different (or beyond) their own level of maturity.

Because of this reality, we either find new contexts to support us outside of our traditional structures or are often forced to abandon our traditional contexts (e.g., workplaces, social groups, families). Either solution can help us become "more of who we are and less of who we are not."

However, leaving existing structures can be disruptive, and isolating, as we become more and more removed from all that we previously knew as safe and certain. I've become acutely aware that most of us who dream of living a purposeful life also are unconsciously aware that living into purpose can require "leaving behind" parts of our identity that have felt safe or stable. That fear keeps us stuck in old patterns and contexts, living out the status quo rather than an authentic version of ourselves.

In the context of finding our unique self and purpose, we must attempt to find containers that can hold a broader and deeper version of us, so that we can complete the developmental tasks in each stage and be less fearful of creating a new identity.

To live into healthy developmental tasks and choose a purpose-driven life, we need to find support systems that can serve in several ways.

- First, we need support systems—friends, colleagues, community—that will provide a mirror for our evolving selves, as purpose continues to "show up" in more and more complex, nuanced, and powerful expressions.
- Second, we need contextual support to help us remain curious and to allow deep inquiry into the wounded parts of us, so we can do the vulnerable shadow work required to liberate the next stage of our purpose.
- Third, we need to find encouragement and enthusiasm for the new expressions of ourselves, as each stage brings trepidation when we attempt to step into much larger versions of ourselves.
- And, lastly, we need partners with whom we can bring our complex and nuanced work into the world—full of integrity, love, and compassion for all that we are attempting to be.

There is nothing noble about being superior to your fellow man; true nobility is being superior to your former self.

—ERNEST HEMINGWAY

EXAMPLES OF PURPOSE IN THE SUBTLE TIER

The following are brief examples of how the Golden Thread weaves itself in the stories of people's lives through the stages, starting in the Concrete Tier and evolving into the Subtle Tier. Notice that our thread is always representative of the exact type of healing/longing we are required to overcome ourselves.

SUSAN LUCCI: CREATING SAFE CONTAINERS
FOR HUMAN LONGING

CONCRETE TIER: My purpose colleague, Susan Lucci, whose story is in chapter 1, spent much of her childhood and early adolescence tending to others: first her siblings (recall her changing her youngest brother's diapers in his crib), then extended family's babies, and later orphaned children. Susan was socialized around strict Jesuit values and "toed the line" all during her adolescent years, learning volunteering and "hostessing" capacities.

3.0 Expert stage: When Susan went off to college, she began to rebel against the strict norms of her upbringing but continued in the service vein by finding her roots in social activism. Susan eventually followed in her father's footsteps and became an attorney, thinking she could serve those who'd been unfairly penalized or mistreated, but instead found the profession transactional and unfulfilling.

3.5 Achiever stage: Susan served as an attorney until she began to raise her own children, then excelled at parenting and becoming a community leader in social networks and volunteer activities. She also started a business helping students with college essays.

4.0 Pluralist stage: Susan worked in food pantries, started hunger banquets, worked with interfaith programs, and started service learning programs; she now serves as a facilitator for some of Chicago's most dynamic interracial conversations. One of Susan's business endeavors is her Circling business, with her having run more than 700 Circles with women searching for meaning in their lives.

4.5 Strategist stage: Susan has played an important role in moving forward the nascent group of Global Purpose Leaders, serving as the facilitator of the group's Well of Wisdom (a community council for the GPL) and also on the leadership council. Susan continues to be engaged in creating transformative regional networks related to political and social issues. Susan's evolving nature has her easily pushing into the next stage.

JANE SHEPPARD: NURTURING YOUNG MINDS (AND SOULS)
CONCRETE TIER: As a child, Jane Sheppard, a former client whose story appears in chapter 3, provided healing to her dolls and injured animals. She fed birds who had fallen from their nests or sick, abandoned puppies. She cared for her dolls with special leaves and other found objects. As a result, she became a highly sought-after babysitter. She envisioned having four children of her own to care for, but her lack of self-worth kept her from thinking she was good enough to do so.

3.0 Expert stage: Jane's college experience was an unfulfilling experience, and she left college with two unfinished degrees. She worked in the tech industry but left when she outgrew the rules of the corporate world. As she began to heal her own early wounding (and decided to have a child), she was intrigued to learn more about healthy products for children.

3.5 Achiever stage: Jane started a *Healthy Child Newsletter* and ultimately wrote hundreds of articles and a book about her findings. She developed a worthwhile career advising about and selling products that promoted healthy and safe childhood development, establishing herself in a worthwhile career role supporting parents. She also became a skillful parent to a remarkable child and found the rewarding relationship nurtured her and her daughter.

4.0 Pluralist stage: She gained a deep subtle intimacy of the many facets of herself and also came to see how she could support and provide feedback to other mothers to explore their own relationships with their children. She became an activist, taking a stand for healthy products for parents, and also participated in many nurturing community groups.

4.5 Strategist stage: Jane evolved into a full awareness of her own internal stories and systems and how that impacts her effectiveness. She has also created complex external systems and partnerships to mobilize her business.

BILL KERN: EMPOWERING OTHERS TO LEAD

CONCRETE: Former client Bill Kern, whose story is told in chapter 1, was "off the charts" in verbal proficiency as a child. He was also active in service clubs and found himself eager to support others' exploration of themselves—once taking inner-city kids into nature and doing experiments with them. But mean childish pranks in his early school years created a wounding that shut down his facilitative instinct, and he instead became a "big man on campus" to protect himself from bullies.

3.0 Expert stage: In college, Bill gained exposure to international business principles while playing big-league football and emerged as a major player in business settings, supporting large corporate teams with technical and management skills. Bill admits that he struggled to find his way in navigating conflict.

3.5 Achiever stage: Bill's corporate and entrepreneurial savvy created many opportunities to grow and scale companies, including founding several startups, serving on C-suite teams, and owning a change management consulting firm.

4.0 Pluralist stage: Eventually Bill realized how his childhood wounding was affecting his corporate career and began to take a stand for the personal development of his peers and himself. He became very active in leading men's groups and other social networks.

4.5 Strategist stage: Bill recently moved into leadership of CEO peer groups by coaching and empowering leaders to run businesses from a place of integrity, purpose, and personal transformation.

NOTES FROM THE FIELD

SUBTLE TIER AS A KEY STAGE FOR RESOLVING DILEMMAS OF CHILDHOOD

As we come into contact with our internal milieu in the Subtle Tier, we become acutely aware of how our internal voices are limiting our potential. Over time, as we progress into the later stages, a longing emerges to begin resolving these hurdles and barriers to success so that we may express ourselves more authentically.

For those of us who enter the Subtle Tier during adulthood, we have plenty of grist for the mill to explore here. Most of us humans don't make it to the latter part of the Subtle Tier, because we find it tempting to stay in the safer and more secure (and seemingly predictable) confines of the Expert or Achiever stages.

As we come into contact with our early Subtle experiences and the discomfort of these voices, we can tend to "shut down" or shut off the voices, which may also cause a physical disembodiment, or dissociation, because of the desire to repress the memories or experiences that feel too painful. The early Subtle experience (Expert stage) is often accompanied by repression or denial of the voices that emerge with our new subtle awareness. Many of us choose to use mood-altering substances or adrenaline-heightening experiences ("adrenaline junkies") as a means to get past the discomfort.

In the middle stages of the Subtle Tier, as we develop capacity for metacognition in the Achiever stage (and the ability to contemplate our thinking and feeling and to recognize the feeling states), we start to cognize how these experiences may occur, and we may enter psychotherapy or coaching, or access other "healing" modalities to support our early inquiry.

As we enter the Pluralist stage, we start to see that everyone else also has these experiences, and they become normalized and therefore safe to discuss and "process" our internal state. A greater curiosity is at work here for "cleaning up" the childhood wounding and shadow, and even karmic experiences (e.g., with energy work, plant medicine, psychedelics, and other modalities that create opportunity for regression to past-life experiences).

In the latter Subtle stage, the Strategist, we see a desire to rid oneself of the wounding that keeps us from being liberated or moving into our full potential. As the interpenetration of either/or and both/and seeing emerges, and we begin to see all the perspectives with equanimity, we can find more clarity about how our life trajectory is affected by our early experiences and the many ways we've replayed these scenarios repeatedly throughout life.

The increased awareness of psychosocial, energetic, neuropsychological, spiritual, and other resources to help us move past the discomforts and come to know ourselves better has dramatically shifted our ability to be present to and resolve the complex early wounding. As human and spiritual development have become prevalent in many contexts (including even corporate), more people are moving into the Pluralist and later stages.

From my own work as a human development scientist, coach, and mentor, I've noted that the basic steps for this process of liberating our childhood wounding, or shadow, usually includes the following steps, which are also usually iterative:

- awareness of the belief systems that hold us back,
- witness of these belief systems and the associated patterns of behavior,

- deconstruction of the underlying beliefs and emotions, psychologically and energetically,
- integration of fractured parts,
- imagining a new possibility and identity, and
- developing new habit patterns.

GETTING STUCK IN SUBTLE STAGES

It's useful to note a caveat for sojourners in the Subtle Tier. As we enter this tier, we find almost an addictive quality that happens as we gain access to our interior Subtle experiences. In the early part of the tier, we begin first thinking and feeling about our thinking and feelings (leading to metacognition and a "busy" mind). These habits of "processing" are perfectly normal for this stage of development. The childhood wounding that accompanies it can preclude a healthy metacognition and focuses instead on the personality quirks of "limiting beliefs." We can almost never fully reconcile the limiting beliefs or create a "mindset" (popular in today's personal development offers) unless we also focus on integrating sub-psychic parts or shadow elements.

The later Subtle experience can be slightly addictive or "yummy"—an expression often heard especially among Pluralists who have left the material comforts of the Concrete Tier and enjoy the deep escape of meditation or the community experience of sharing subtle energies (e.g., dance, meditation, song, sound healings, festivals, rallies). Because the Subtle experience can become preferred over the Concrete experience, some people choose to "escape" the foundational elements of leading lives of productive endeavor (of the Concrete or early Subtle Tiers) and begin to flounder in their roles and responsibilities in the "real" world. This "bypass" can be tempting, and also indicates the presence of earlier wounding that needs to be addressed, as generally the material world has as many delights as the Subtle world—if the developmental work has been tackled adequately.

And, lastly, we sometimes get stuck in the Subtle stages because the work to release our wounding is too challenging for us to do, as noted throughout this chapter. We're reluctant to face our demons (Allione, 2008), even though deep down we know that we can't escape the Demons 'R' Us. Generally, we do not shift to the MetAware Tier until we have made enough progress in resolving our shadow that we can squeeze through the gate to the universal portal.

INCLUSION OF A RANGE OF STAGES

I should clarify that the Subtle Tier represents a vast array of human experiences—although, from the outside, we may not appear so distinct to the observer. We each have what's called a Center of Gravity (Beck & Cowan, 1995) for our primary stage of consciousness that represents our general perspective-taking capacity. This Center of Gravity stage serves as a fulcrum for our actions and decisions, no matter what tier we inhabit. However, we also have a range of stages from which we act. This range can be across all three tiers or concentrated in one tier.

If we've accomplished our developmental tasks at earlier stages, we generally "include" those stages in our every action.

This tendency may show up as:

- being grounded in our physical presence (1.5),
- relating well to others (2.0),
- abiding with appropriate social expectations (2.5),
- offering up our expertise (3.0),
- building strategic endeavors (3.5),
- providing inclusive opportunities and networks (4.0), and
- delivering innovative solutions to complex problems (4.5).

When we "transcend and include" all the stages of our experience, we are more able to occupy the full range of our genius in a purposeful way.

As human culture has begun to make this shift to the latter Subtle Tier, we have started to see extremely innovative, complex adaptive systems present themselves to move us all forward into a new paradigm with wide-reaching solutions. These solutions are emerging in every significant sector in society and hold promise of large-scale repercussions. And yet these innovative solutions are not enough to tackle the volatile, uncertain, complex, and ambiguous problems of our world. The challenge will be to harness the collective spirit of the Pluralist and Strategist stages (and beyond) to both include and transcend the more stable and hierarchical structures and solutions of the Expert and Achiever stages. It's a both/and, not an either/or.

The world is shifting, and many more opportunities exist for people to break out of the confines of their contexts now more than ever. Startup incubators are more common, teaching people how to launch their own meaningful endeavors.

Culture shifts are beginning to occur in the boardroom, when women are now required to occupy board seats and more women and people of color occupy executive roles. Diversity and inclusion among employees are paramount in most companies, especially as we recognize that the global workforce is affected by migration patterns, recognition of gender fluidity, racial bias, and economic disparity.

SELF-REFLECTION: HOW DID YOUR ABILITY TO WITNESS YOUR INNER WORLD ALLOW YOU TO MIGRATE INTO AND WITHIN THE SUBTLE TIER?

Entry into and progression in the Subtle Tier require an awakening to the interior Subtle experiences of thoughts, feelings, emotions, and ultimately the complex inner world we all (consciously or unconsciously) inhabit. These metacognitive capacities then unfold into more ordered, prioritized, and systemic processes that help us make sense of and serve in the complex adaptive systems in which we live.

As you contemplate where you may live most of the time in one or more of these stages, think about the ages or phases of your life when you may have begun to explore and witness your own complex thoughts, feelings, and emotions. Also, reflect upon how you used those capacities in your personal and work life over time.

QUESTIONS TO CONSIDER:

Remember and explore your experiences when you began to stand "outside" yourself enough to witness your internal subtle experiences. When do you remember first thinking about your thinking or feeling, or feeling something in response to what you were thinking?

What are some other experiences you recalled as you read through the stages that may have reflected a time in your life?

What do you think may have made it challenging to be in or move beyond one of these stages? What were the containers of support (e.g., friends, family, colleagues) that enhanced or detracted from a healthy experience of that stage?

CONCLUSION: PREVIEW OF WHAT'S NEXT

This chapter begins to explore how the Golden Thread may arise in the Subtle Tier as we begin to have an expanded human experience with the addition of our "inner world" of thoughts, feelings, emotions, and subtle energies. In the latter part of this tier, we also become aware of the distinct contexts that greatly influence our life trajectory.

As we begin to experience our nuanced lives in a contextualized world, we develop a deeply enhanced understanding of how we can live with greater purpose and intention to reflect our distinct and true nature over time. It is psychically imperative at this point—as we make our way into the Subtle Tier—to fully express ourselves to complete the mandate for meaning.

Choosing to live into purpose may appear optional for some, but not for others. However, the tension that arises when we deny why we're here is that our innate capacities go unexpressed and create additional recessed sub-psychic parts, which become additional personality shadows. The more extreme our denial of self, the greater the wounding that goes unresolved and the more our life path becomes ego-driven as we repress or manipulate our longing to be ourselves.

As we examine the significant enhancement of strategic capacities within evolved states in the next chapter, we'll be able to project why some of the intractable social challenges exist on the planet and within our species. Purpose begins to take on more strategic, contextual, and ultimately systemic attributes in the Subtle Tier, which is more likely to contribute in a way that can resolve deeply challenging global issues.

I've demonstrated the early portrayals of purpose in the Subtle Tier through the case studies of Susan, Jane, and Bill, and a few stories from my own life. In the next chapter, we'll delve into the MetAware Tier of the Stages of Consciousness model, where I'll share additional case studies and note the progression of nuanced purposeful expression.

REFERENCES

Beck, DE & Cowan, CC. (1995). Spiral dynamics: Mastering values, leadership and change: Exploring the new science of memetics. Maiden, MA: Blackwell Publications.

Bennett, N. & Lemoine, GJ. (2014). What VUCA really means for you. Harvard Business Review. Jan-Feb 2014. Retrieved on January 1, 2020

O'Fallon, T. & Barta, K. (2017). Essentials Course Manual, Stages International.

Maslow, A. H. (1943). A theory of human motivation. Psychological Review, 50(4): 370-96.

CHAPTER 6

LATER STAGES AND THE ROLE OF PURPOSE IN OUR LIVES

My migration into the MetAware Tier was not a fairytale experience. You don't gain access to this vast awareness by knocking on the door to heaven and having it opened. Far from it.

In fact, the navigation of this immense deconstruction is challenging for most. Many of my clients find me as they're making their way into the MetAware Tier, perhaps because I fell into and climbed out of the chasm myself. They are usually slightly or significantly lost, confused, alone, and clueless as to what is occurring—or "indecisive and flip-flopping," as one recent client shared, just as I was in this stage, and as most of us are as we make our way into a slightly barely human realm. Waking up to life as an illusion is similar to being in a lucid dream, with a few nightmarish elements for some of us.

As our transition through these stages is not documented, nor transparent, it's hard to say exactly when I began making the shift into MetAware. As I was experiencing the dissonance with the culture and ways of being of my life in Colorado prior to my move to California, I began having experiences of being "guided" during my waking moments, distinct from the states of non-dual connection during meditation and other contemplative practices. I had focus and direction, a new joy and internal peace, and experienced gratitude and love for all things.

During this time, I'd had a middle-of-the-night "calling" to Petaluma ("What is a Petaluma?" I asked, as I heard the word at 3 a.m. and got up to Google its definition). Petaluma turned out to be a town in Northern California. Home of the Butter & Eggs Festival, according to the Chamber's website. Having developed clairvoyant, clairsentient, and clairaudient capacity by this time, I heard and sensed that I was supposed to move to California, but being married and having children in high school did not seem an opportune time to pick up and leave. So I tabled the idea and went about my life.

But within a couple years, after many attempts to reconcile a marriage and invite in new opportunities within my current domain, I realized that the life I'd been living no longer served my evolving self, my children, or the planet, and I decided to follow the call and launch a new life. My eldest daughter was going off to college, and my youngest begged me to reconsider the "dream" to move to California. As I contemplated this possibility, I realized I was supposed to be there.

Not decided. Not pondered. Just realized—as in, I was drawn there.

"I couldn't not go," as goes the story of one pulled along by their purposeful endeavors. I even wrote a blog about (figuratively) "leaping naked" into my new life . . . which is exactly what we shouldn't do as we begin to enter the MetAware Tier (more on this later).

When I arrived in California (near Petaluma), I started to record the miraculous synchronicities that happened every day. I posted on social media about #everydaymiracles. One of the hallmarks of being connected and aligned with purpose is the magical way goodness just flows to you. I found new clients, was invited into an amazing job, developed new relationships. All things seemed heavenly.

And then, the other shoe dropped. In hindsight, I still had much shadow resolve, which drove me to the flip side of purpose so quickly after arriving in California. I had arrived in the exact right spot to complete the next stage of my evolutionary work. I "called in," through resonant energies, the people and experiences who could mirror for me the patterns and fractured parts that still needed focus, so I could move closer to liberation. This transitional time wasn't pretty, but it was useful.

Despite having some "leading-edge" MetAware experiences, at this point I was "stuck" in the Subtle Tier, as described in the last chapter. I couldn't move the engine any faster down the roadway until I removed the roadblocks. It was a painful, messy, chaotic time—though also filled with huge quantum leaps forward and some side streets of delight.

This phase lasted possibly two years, as I cleared most of the shadow and roadblocks and finally found my way fully into the MetAware Tier.

I live on Earth at present, and I don't know what I am.
I know that I am not a category.
I am not a thing—a noun.
I seem to be a verb—an evolutionary process—in integral function of the universe.

—R. BUCKMINSTER FULLER

FROM EMPTINESS TO FULLNESS IN THE METAWARE TIER

Adults in the MetAware Tier are usually middle-aged or older, having experienced life in its fullest. A small number of thirty- to forty-year-olds progress to this tier because of their early access to subtle experiences and contexts that promote their evolution. In some ways, we see an enormous variation in how purpose is demonstrated in this tier.

The Golden Thread will show up as a nuanced expression throughout this tier because of each of our uniqueness, though the style, tone, voice, and execution will look more similar than in other stages because the egoic personality is much less intact in this tier. Expression will be imbued with elements that might be called love, oneness, awareness, unity, timeless, flow, joy, essence, full, empty, cosmic, or other words that indicate an alteration in orientation of self on the planet.

Purposeful expression shows up as incredibly simple or ridiculously complex, as people in the MetAware Tier have access to both a reconstruction of self and awareness of awareness. As one moves into 5.0, and especially into later stages, the facets of personality that formerly inhibited or stymied us disappear as the shadowed aspects of personality usually resolve. It is the emptiness and fullness of no self within the Universe. As we arrive in this tier, we will have accomplished almost all of the prior developmental tasks, integrated our wounding, and begun to align with our essential self. As we do so, purpose is easily expressed in this tier. We have nothing else to prove.

The MetAware Tier demonstrates the repetitive patterns as such:

Person Perspective	TIER: Object of Awareness	SOCIAL STYLE	LEARNING STYLE	STAGE NAME
6.0	MetAware	Individual	Receptive	Construct Aware
5.5	MetAware	Individual	Active	Transpersonal
6.0	MetAware	Collective	Reciprocal	Universal
6.5	MetAware	Collective	Interpenetrative	Illumined

O'Fallon, T., Barta, K. (2017) Essentials Course Manual, Stages International.

THE GOLDEN THREAD METAWARE TIER: WITNESS CREATES ADAPTABILITY & ACCEPTANCE

In this chapter, we are describing the stages of the MetAware Tier to identify how the Golden Thread may show up in each stage. These same repeating patterns also occur in the Concrete and Subtle Tiers, but with different objects of focus (i.e., Concrete objects, Subtle objects).

Very few adults make it to the MetAware Tier, with some estimates (O'Fallon, 2016) at less than 5 percent of the human population. As we make our way into this "awareness of awareness" stage (thus the "meta" designation), the ground literally shifts out from under us as we begin experiencing everything in our wide landscape from a witness stance. As we traverse into the MetAware Tier, rather than focusing on Concrete objects (we can see) or Subtle objects (which we experience or create, subtly), our focus is on the awareness of all things.

The MetAware perspective and its inherent capacity vary greatly by early and late stages as in the earlier two tiers. In general, people in the MetAware Tier are very easy to be around and don't generally bring up the same kinds of projections or agitation from earlier tiers because of their adaptability and acceptance.

In this tier, our perspective about life is so vast that it all becomes simple and ordinary, yet also rich and delightful, rather than provoking an emotional reaction.

As we move into the later stages of this tier, a common experience is that of pure love.

The MetAware Tier includes fifth- and sixth-person perspectives, and we begin again, focusing on MetAware objects, in the cyclical pattern of:

- creating a new identity in 5.0,
- taking on either/or choices at 5.5,
- integrating both/and perspectives at 6.0, and
- merging all ways of seeing at 6.5.

And, as with the Subtle Tier, not all adults who enter the MetAware Tier evolve to the later stages of the tier. As in the Concrete and Subtle Tiers, a person is "had by" their experiences of the newly discovered MetAware world in the early stages, and then later has a greater command and utility of those experiences.

The MetAware Tier requires practice and commitment to exploring the unknown territory of one's inner milieu, within the broader context of the Universe, but also a commitment to integrating the Universe into the contexts of our human lives.

We "merge" all aspects of our lives, inner and outer, including the Concrete and Subtle experiences. The experience is evolutionary and involutionary, simultaneously (see chapter 7).

Most of the unfinished tasks of the Concrete or Subtle Tiers will be completed before entering the MetAware Tier, though we almost always seem to have more layers of the onion to peel. This process usually occurs easily and swiftly relative to the previous tiers. Those of us in the MetAware Tier often have nuanced perspective on the healing to be done and greater capacity to resolve issues as they arise. In some cases, when shadow work hasn't been resolved adequately before this tier, the healing itself is quite challenging and can lead to a manipulative and narcissistic personality.

Several specific challenges of the MetAware Tier are worth noting. Living from an "awareness of awareness" in a Concrete and Subtle world can lead to isolation and aloneness (rather than loneliness), as so few others live at this level of awareness. While relationships are still possible, fewer resonate with the level of capacity we bring to the table. This experience is not one of being "better than" (though a level of arrogance does arise early in this tier with the "meta" seeing), but instead of seeing life in a way that may not make sense to most others.

With the loss of "normal" identity, those in this tier have less to "associate" with, so typical leisure activities and friend groups may fall away as the MetAware person tends to find solace with themselves or in nature, at least upon entering the tier. Most of my clients in this stage who live in parts of the globe without a community of "like-minded" (or similar stage) peers are very isolated and crave online connection to people like them. People also frequently move to new locations (as I did) to find others who can resonate with their fifth- to sixth-person perspectives.

The shift into the MetAware stages of practicing and acting from this open "awareness of awareness" experience is unlike anything we've ever experienced, and we have few mentors to count on to support the journey. As noted earlier, many spiritual teachers may assist in the "awakening" process, which is more transcendent and creates state experiences, yet they don't necessarily have the developmental capacity to promote a holistic evolution into and through this tier. More specific developmental coaching or therapy supports the development and integration in these later stages.

The following are the specific stages in the Subtle Tier, and all cases assume that someone has grasped most of the developmental tasks in the Concrete and Subtle Tiers.

Metaware Tier, Stage 5.0: Construct Aware Stage
CONSTRUCT AWARE: MEANING IS CONSTRUCTED;
PERCEPTION BECOMES FLUID

This stage is an upshift again from the 1.0 Impulsive and Expert 3.0 stage, and the new MetAware receptive self arises to face a challenging developmental transition into being identified with awareness, rather than the egoic self. Because we move into a discernment that life itself is socially and individually constructed and everything is an illusion, the Construct Aware sojourner may be completely disoriented.

All former guideposts and ways of being are interrupted. Awareness is beyond thinking, yet former concepts of the world interrupt our new simple awareness. Speech becomes erratic or difficult as we struggle with former definitions of all things that no longer hold meaning, and we look for ways to "settle down" in our new self. As was my story, people entering this stage (without a realization that this point is where they are at) tend to shed parts of their lives—jobs, relationships, homes—as they search for themselves in the vast landscape.

In the Construct Aware stage, leaving behind "reality" of what we once knew can be challenging, yet eventually we also find a new opening into limitlessness of possibility.

As we shift solidly into this stage, we experience a recognition that all the stories of our lives are "made up," distinct from the earlier 4.0 storytelling that is a means of getting to know others (swapping stories). Our perceptions of life become much more fluid, as we realize that our "mind-made" reality shifts easily depending on the context and our awareness. We see ourselves as both creators of and referent points for our stories.

We've constructed our lives to create those stories through words, definitions, boundaries, assumptions, and projections. What we began to perceive in the late Subtle stage now reveals itself to be "made up" and can spontaneously shift. We become very agile in our approach to life, to see things others can't because of their steadfast belief in "reality."

CONSTRUCT AWARE: INDIVIDUAL VS. SOCIAL
CONSTRUCTIONS OF REALITY

While people in the late Subtle stage question "reality" in a collective sense (*Who are we to each other?*), in the 5.0 stage we question, *Who am I?* relative to the construction of meaning as it occurs in my life (*What does anything mean in my life?*). We experience a new emptiness, and a recognition of when we project our meaning or interpretations onto others.

Some new skills are available here that make life in the "awareness of awareness" simpler. We become very facile at receiving feedback from others as we see our own mind's definitions and boundaries as impediments. As we become adept at perceiving the made-up nature of our fixed identities and inflexible structures of our lives (usually created with safety in mind), we also loosen the patterns that used to control us. We let go into a deconstructed state and find openness and expansiveness.

To avoid falling into the Construct Aware abyss of emptiness, the best practice is to hold the tension between the dawning awareness of no reality and the reality of the material world obligations. In other words, we shouldn't quit our days jobs just yet. By holding onto the Concrete and Subtle world structures, we are able to create a deep presence to life that allows us to expand our boundaries of the physical world and self-identity.

Life in this stage requires a trust (similar to the 1.0 birthing from the womb, and the 3.0 birthing from the Concrete tier) that our experience will defy logic and magically hold us. As we move out of this stage, we begin to interact with awareness more dynamically and coherently, and we experience states of awe, wonder, delight, and humility at being present in this wild stage beyond our conception.

These experiences are distinct from "states of oneness" often experienced during spiritual practices or encounters, as those are transient experiences and limited in duration. Though an experience of these kinds of spiritual states seems to be precursor to "living" in the Construct Aware stage, having regular state experiences doesn't necessarily imply that someone has completed the developmental tasks of earlier stages and evolved into Construct Aware.

CONSTRUCT AWARE: PURPOSE DECONSTRUCTED

Purpose in this stage may appear ill-defined or incoherent, as meaning is deconstructed in the shifting sands of reality. Or if we created stable structures to hold us in the transition into MetAware, purpose could look similarly to a 4.5 Strategist stage, but likely with a lot of questioning about why we're doing what we're doing. In this stage, we doubt everything we created before now, as we see the story in our own creations. This tendency can lead to positive transformation, both personally and in our work, and a new expression of purpose evolves here, waiting to be expressed in the world.

MetAware Tier, Stage 5.5: Transpersonal Stage
TRANSPERSONAL: RECONSTRUCTING SELF

This stage is an upshift of the 1.5 Egocentric and 3.5 Achiever stage that has the same active (practicing) individual stage where ownership arises, but now related to owning our unique and distinct creations devised from this deep space of awareness. In this stage, we can redefine, reconstruct, and shape connections between almost any life or work arena, creating new models and fields previously inconceivable.

As in the 3.5 stage where we had use of Subtle constructs, in the Transpersonal stage, we can see how we create our own constructed realities and codify them (or not). Here we are able to create initiatives for the benefit of humanity or the planet, in elegant and unique approaches that haven't been possible before now. And we start to have uber-paradoxical solutions to solve the "wicked" problems of humanity. Our capacity is expanded because we can readily see the volatility, uncertainty, complexity, and ambiguity, known as VUCA (Bennett and Lemoine, 2014), behind the issues on the planet, and we can devise unique approaches to solving them. At this stage, we are ready and willing to share the mature and facile wisdom that has emerged from moving through the stages.

As an individual stage, the Transpersonal pioneer is characterized by an either/or thinking and may not feel seen by others. While we can see the two sides of an argument or decision, we usually choose the one most familiar, yet can combine many facets of an idea to integrate or reconstruct newly. As we advance in this stage, we're likely to build meta-models to represent the compound systems that we can perceive (see chapter 8 for examples).

Paradoxically, in this stage we can witness life both happening in the moment and being a spiritual practice. But we can also offer our explosive energy arising from sharing our pure purpose in the world. The Transpersonal stage is a hugely welcome relief to the 5.0 Construct Aware chasm, as spontaneous play, creative innovations, and traveling in the multiverse are grounded in actionable tactics that span space and time.

TRANSPERSONAL: PURPOSE AS BROAD AND IMPACTFUL

As we shift into gear again in the 5.5 Transpersonal stage, our purpose-driven endeavors may take on steam and produce impactful and global offerings in the world. We may create broad platforms that take advantage of our awareness of socially constructed realities and construct them to be evolving and agile systems. If we are oriented to allow our greatest work, at this stage we become noble agents of change.

MetAware Tier, Stage 6.0: Universal Stage
UNIVERSAL: RECIPROCAL WITH THE UNIVERSE

At this time, evolving to this stage is an extraordinarily rare yet profoundly rewarding occurrence because we become reciprocal with the Universe. This upshift from the 4.0 Pluralist Subtle stage is where we become reciprocal with others and with our internal voices.

Early in the Universal stage, we have a sense of self in the Oneness, and later, as each individual is backgrounded, a sense of unity with the infinite arises, which creates a wholeness. Energetically, we may experience the whole Universe coming through us, as us, and begin to integrate emptiness and fullness, individual and collective. These signals of the collective Universe (or quantum field, God, source, Divine, whatever you may choose to call this force) can cause us to lose ourselves in time and space. It is among the most intimate spaces a human can experience. We surrender our unique individuality to become merged with the vast Universe. As we do so, we can alter our vibration, shift our thoughts, and recreate reality.

UNIVERSAL: SUBMISSION TO PURPOSE

Purpose in this stage is similar to the 5.5 Transpersonal stage but evidences a more coherent and yielding approach to creative forces. We submit to the Universal forces coming through us by abdicating our "mind-made" maps of how to do things, allowing the experience to be directed by the manifest presence already existing and waiting to be acknowledged. As we practice being reciprocal in this new collective, we may be led to create intricate and complex social structures that can reach millions of people with significant offers, or create simple structures that resolve entrenched issues in innovative ways.

MetAware Tier, Stage 6.5: Illumined Stage

ILLUMINED: NESTED WORLDS

This sixth-person perspective Illumined stage is the final Interpenetrative stage, merging the three tiers of Concrete, Subtle, and MetAware into one integrated holographic nest.

As an upshift from 2.5 and 4.5, the 6.5 stage has its own unique set of rules or parameters that define the unbounded experience. At 2.5, the Conformist moved beyond the peer pressures of the Concrete stage to form principles. At 4.5, the Strategist moved beyond the social conformity of political correctness to create prioritization of collective values. At 6.5, the Illumined moves beyond the "surrender" to the Oneness of the Universal awareness to understand the processes associated with that unification.

Emptiness and fullness mature and allow prioritization and categorization because we can see the nested worlds within the Universe. As an upshift of the 4.5 Strategist capacity to create systems of our internal and external worlds, the Illumined can create systems that integrate all of those "realities" and with the broader consciousness of the Universe; this place is where human awareness "ends" and the Universe "begins." This stage shifts into the next Unified Tier, and again the witness will "birth" and reflect upon reflection of the Universal experience.

Purpose in this stage is a wild expansion of the 6.0 Universal stage, as the ability to prioritize the Universal collective allows vast Meta Visions to be held and created in Concrete, Subtle, and MetAware form. We can dare suggest that purposeful interventions formed at this stage may indeed shift the world.

The meaning of life is to find your gift. The purpose of life is to give it away.

—PABLO PICASSO

METAWARE PURPOSE MOVES BEYOND "REALITY"

CHALLENGES OF THE METAWARE TIER

The initial stage of the MetAware Tier is one of the most challenging phases of life for many of us who endure it. Being birthed newly as a Universal being in a material world is confusing and many get lost or stuck here. With a loss of meaning, identity, time and space, or any sense of reality, and no real map to the other side, this phase is a rickety bridge to cross. This reality is true especially because the collective upon which this stage initially draws is the 4.5 Strategist Collective (as is true for 3.0 drawing upon the 2.5 Collective).

As an incomplete grasp of the unique experience of 5.0 within the Subtle Tier exists, few mentors, peers, or support systems who still reside in the Subtle Tier can help us through this stage. O'Fallon's research (O'Fallon, 2017) has suggested that some "spiritual" teachers have a Center of Gravity (the primary stage that one occupies and from which we orient) within the Subtle Tier, perhaps because their focus has been on spiritual ascension, rather than human development. Because moving into the MetAware Tier is less of a "spiritual" issue and more of a developmental issue, developmental coaching or mentorship (rather than more "spiritual awakening") is paramount in this stage, to facilitate an easeful awareness and transition.

Unfortunately, many support systems or professionals will see the collapse in the 5.0 stage as a "spiritual emergency," or a problem to be solved, rather than an evolutionary advancement into a stage that helps us rid ourselves of the illusions of the Concrete and Subtle worlds.

We always have more shadow work to be done here, which will facilitate a more efficient and organic transition. However, getting "stuck" in solving trauma too long in this stage may preclude other important developmental tasks being completed. Deepening our consciousness in this stage, like any other stage, requires patience, attention, and intention to replace our former conceptions of things through our mental capacities to arrive at pure awareness.

THE METAWARE PARADOX

A particularly distinct and paradoxical experience in this tier is worth grappling with—philosophically. In the MetAware Tier, we show up as our most unique version. Our expression in this tier is a much more nuanced and granular expression of our essential Soul Self because we've managed to dissolve the egoic constrictions of our personality and deconstruct the sense that the world can impose its reality on us. In this stage, we become "free to be" as that which is our birthright and responsibility.

Meanwhile, we also become a merged expression of ourselves in the Universal All, knowing that we are just a speck of stardust in the greater Cosmos. Our eternal evolution is also an involutionary process (see chapter 7), as we are the specks that hold the Universe and its stars within, simultaneously. This paradox is the greatest of all to grasp.

EXAMPLES OF PURPOSE IN THE METAWARE TIER

AGATHE DAAE-QVALE: CREATING INCLUSION IN A WORLD OF SEPARATION

CONCRETE: My former client Agathe, whose story is in chapter 1, had an early childhood craving to meet other people and explore new things, begging her mom to include outsiders and extended family in family dinners and events. She often stayed up late so she could hear the stories of visitors to her childhood home.

SUBTLE: Agathe traveled internationally early (at age sixteen, she went to New Zealand as an exchange student) to learn new languages and cultures, and she spent decades as an immigrant or traveling consultant. Her early subtle awareness created a desire to transform the "inside-outside" experience of distinctions into commonalities of experience. As Agathe immersed herself into her professional ventures, she always looked for opportunities to include those who were deemed outsiders. As we worked together, Agathe began to explore how this curiosity and intrigue could benefit the problem of immigrants in Norway (and internationally) and began exploring how to build a "hub" or network of support for potential entrepreneurial immigrants.

5.0 Construct Aware: Also during the time of our work together, Agathe began to experience the incongruence of her new self with her work as a tech consultant and developed a deep desire to create new systems that would support excluded populations. While exploring how to create a startup company, Agathe also sought to leave her current work situation, move out of Oslo, and let go of her self-construct of being "solo" in life. She quit her corporate career, continued with the startup phase of her new company, TinkerBlue, began a new relationship, and moved to a rural area of Norway. She began applying her new way of seeing reality to building a network that incorporated her advanced awareness aligned with her purpose.

5.5 Transpersonal: Agathe's early expressions in this stage landed her in a recent collaboration with several other entrepreneurs in an active startup to create support structures for immigrants. She's also recently become chair of the board for startup DoubleYou.

MIRA MEGS LATHROP: SPANNING INTERNAL AND EXTERNAL CONNECTIONS FOR GLOBAL CHANGE

CONCRETE: Mira Megs (formerly Megan) Lathrop, a former client whose story is in chapter 2, had the early experience of putting others first in order to feel safe in her connections with her family. In this process, she began to abandon herself and developed anxiety when in individual connections with others. This type of interaction, where she became extremely adept at creating external relationships to meet others' needs, became her "currency."

SUBTLE: Mira flourished in the external world because of her outward orientation in connecting with others, and the experience of "hosting" connections with others, though she didn't feel "nourished" by these relationships. She entered the world of financial systems, which connected her to others through systems of abundance and nourishment. She achieved a high profile of visibility and contribution through her own business, Finanseer, and through founding the Money Coaching Program to rectify the systemic perceptions of money as disconnected from our internal desires. As we worked together, Mira began to integrate the aspects of her childhood and a relationship that had kept her disconnected and not feeling fully nourished.

5.0- Mira explored questions about meaning, value, and connection during our work together, and shortly after decided to move to New York City to start anew. As she has become more connected to herself and her next expression of purpose in this context, she has started building networks to impact broader social issues, incorporating her advanced awareness, including hosting the "Women Power Our Planet" platform to help women disconnect from banks that fund climate-negative enterprise.

ME (HOLLY WOODS, PHD): RECONCILING TRUTH, POWER, AND LOVE

Because I have so few clients confirmed in the MetAware Tier, I will include my own journey in the description of this tier.

CONCRETE: Because of the poor attachments formed during my childhood, I had an early abandonment of self in the context of my family life, which created a false understanding about the truth of power and love. I became very inward-focused, dissociating early from my body. I began to question the truth of the world as seen through the context of my family, while maintaining a deep faith in God and spirituality.

SUBTLE: I had a very early subtle awareness (around ages three to four) and mystical experiences, including hearing voices saying I would do important work in the world (which was one of the only reasons I stayed on the planet, having had early and protracted suicidal ideation). I also had an early and extended "expert" phase (high school valedictorian, four college degrees, and a long migration through multiple careers of varying expertise, including my doctoral work and research career in human development) to learn about the "truth" of our human experience. I felt a keen awareness of others in my teens and began "healing" work (thirty years of therapy, many modalities), then became a "healer" myself. I began envisioning and building "systems" in my late twenties, first during one of my research careers, where I was notorious as an early scientist. Later, I built systems to build and scale businesses, nonprofit organizations, initiatives, and projects—including four of my own businesses. In many of these professional experiences, and in most intimate relationships, I struggled mightily with systems of power and influence, and became a professional mediator to attempt to reconcile these challenges with love and power (including mediating my own divorce). In the later Subtle Tier, I spent significant effort to integrate the fractured childhood parts to allow my more coherent self to emerge.

5.0 Construct Aware: My slow traverse into the 5.0 stage followed a "jumping off" into a new life after divorce as I moved to California from Colorado to shed the skin of my former life that had become meaningless. A soft landing in California was followed by a swift plummet into the chasm of 5.0 after leaving a job, ending a relationship, and having few support structures. Following this plummet, I experienced a long "dry" spell, as everything around me appeared to crumble, including financial and emotional stability. A deep insecurity related to childhood trauma emerged, and I was forced to integrate the shadow aspects of my remaining childhood wounds to enter the stage fully. From this new awareness, I reconstructed my identity and sense of the world as something that could hold me. This led me to redevelop my "faith" newly in the Universal laws of truth, power, and love so I could be of greater service.

5.5 Transpersonal: In this stage, my work became an active expression and integration of my entire lifetime of work, synthesizing over twenty careers from a more advanced perspective, creating complex and integrated systems that were inclusive of expanded self. I've learned that the whole Universe (including the Concrete and Subtle worlds) is merely a reflection of my internal experience. My work became a fuller expression of the purpose work I'd been doing for several decades and a process of integrating that into systems to support purpose-driven visionaries, innovators, and companies to launch and scale their meaningful work in the world.

6.0 Universal: Though I have not fully arrived in the 6.0 stage, I see early signs of this emergent stage as being held by the Universe, with a new faith I've not experienced before and a truthful expression of the unification of power and love that I know I am and it is.

NOTES FROM THE FIELD

Significant elements of the MetAware Tier make it both enticing and fear-inducing among those entering the territory. The most notorious of these is the destabilization that occurs in 5.0. As shared above in the case studies (perhaps most significantly my own), the loss of meaning and sense of reality creates significant disruption in our perceived safety nets. We begin to experience life and truth as relative, and life can become a chaotic jumble.

LOSS OF MEANING EQUATES WITH LACK OF COHERENCE
Another element of this 5.0 stage is the potential disillusionment and loss of energy that accompanies the loss of meaning. As the safety nets recede or disappear, one experiences a sense of having been "abandoned" by the Universe (the emptiness described earlier), and a loss of vitality as the

deconstruction phase begins. If we enter this stage having done most of our childhood reintegration work (and not having had overwhelming trauma), this experience may not be so traumatic. And those who are required to complete the integration of their childhood wounding in this tier will usually quickly fly forward in their evolutionary progression through the tier as they were required to become nimble to enter the tier at all.

I've come to see that the "loss of meaning" that occurs in this and all other evolutionary transitions we experience, moving from one stage to the next, simply reflects the lack of coherence of our purpose with the guiding elements of the stage from which we're emerging. In entering the MetAware Tier, we no longer completely resonate with the worldly systems and structures we are immersed in because we recognize the illusory quality of them. And yet we need a "holding" environment (of the material world) that can integrate the Universal experience simultaneously. Traditional structures now seem too rigid, restricted, and conformist; they seldom allow the fluidity or adaptability needed to respond to the emergent and "inspired" visions or innovations in this tier.

NEED FOR METAWARE COLLECTIVES

Another element of this tier is the early sense of aloneness or isolation, primarily because so few people have been in this tier. As the world wakes up and shifts into this tier, we will encounter more outlets for recreating ourselves among others like us. The 6.0-6.5 Collective Tier exists in very few spaces on the planet at this time, but they are beginning to form. Essential elements of these Collectives include fluidity, emergence, responsiveness, adaptability, and structures to promote evolutionary forces. As noted earlier, all MetaAware structures must include elements of earlier tiers, such that those evolved structures and innovations can be built on foundations that will thrive in the material world.

CLEANSING OF PERSONALITY

I find it fascinating to consider that many people who think of themselves "spiritual teachers" of some sort don't necessarily evolve to this tier. As one becomes a "guru" or "expert" at any stage, in any field, they have a tendency to lose sight of advancing their own development as the need for approval or accolades diminishes the inner inquiry required to do so. The egoic personality associated with that particular stage becomes more rigid or fixed, disallowing the personality to drop away. One of the blessings of the trauma or wounding we experience early in life is the continuous need (requirement) to resolve the associated deep pain. Most of us who make it to the later stages had significant inner trauma to overcome and thus have shed much of our egoic limitation upon arriving at MetAware.

Generally, people in this stage are delightful beings, and we are lucky to have any kind of relationship with them. People in the MetAware Tier have brilliant, creative, and facile approaches to life because of their access to mental constructions that are not "mind-made" but instead extract wisdom from the Universe itself.

For a New Beginning

In out-of-the-way places of the heart,
Where your thoughts never think to wander,
This beginning has been quietly forming,
Waiting until you were ready to emerge.
For a long time it has watched your desire,
Feeling the emptiness growing inside you,
Noticing how you willed yourself on,
Still unable to leave what you had outgrown.
It watched you play with the seduction of safety
And the gray promises that sameness whispered,
Heard the waves of turmoil rise and relent,
Wondered would you always live like this.
Then the delight, when your courage kindled,
And out you stepped onto new ground,
Your eyes young again with energy and dream,
A path of plenitude opening before you.
Though your destination is not yet clear
You can trust the promise of this opening;
Unfurl yourself into the grace of beginning
That is at one with your life's desire.
Awaken your spirit to adventure;
Hold nothing back, learn to find ease in risk;
Soon you will be home in a new rhythm,
For your soul senses the world that awaits you.

—JOHN O'DONOHUE

SELF-REFLECTION: WHAT DO YOU EXPERIENCE AS YOU WITNESS YOURSELF BECOMING RECIPROCAL WITH THE UNIVERSE IN THE METAWARE TIER?

Entry into and progression in the MetAware Tier require an awakening to the awareness of the illusory constructs of society and our individual meaning-making. We begin to stand as witness to ourselves in the universal, allowing an awareness of our awareness. First, we become somewhat "lost" as we deconstruct in the disorientation of the universal experience, then we realize the potential possibilities of life creating itself, emergently.

Many (or most) of us will not have arrived here and therefore may not be able to recall experiences in this tier. However, we can all imagine what it may be like to experience living within the Universal and having the Universal live within us.

EXERCISE AND QUESTIONS TO CONSIDER:
Take some time to settle into this exercise, to create a visual and sensory experience of being in the MetAware Tier.

I want you to visualize and imagine that you are inside of the living world, which has groups and communities, nations and systems, within the context of the planet and all life on the planet. Imagine the verdant green planet and its diverse life forms, plant and animal, with a wide diversity of species on land and water. Some estimate that about 8.7 million species* (Science Daily, 2011) live on this planet, roughly three-quarters on land and one-quarter in the oceans. Visualize the range and diversity of living beings just on this planet, human and non-human, animal and plant. Let those images float through your mind's eye. What experience do you have of that in your body? Where do you feel those sensations? What emotions do you associate with that?

And imagine that our planet Earth is also inside the galaxy, which is inside of many other constellations of galaxies, which are inside of the whole universe, inside of the whole cosmos. Visualize and imagine our small planet as it swirls and turns within these many other systems of planets and stars, that our planet is just one small speck of 8.7 million living species swirling around in the cosmic tapestry, with its potential other unknown millions or billions of living species.

And then imagine that you are an authentic person in a relationship with all other humans and living things on the planet, living inside all of the other systems. You see and experience all other beings and living things, and they see and experience you. You are a finite but significant part of the whole of the cosmos.

Just take a moment to experience that. Who are you in all of that? What is your experience being a significant being in the vastness? What is your role or authentic contribution? If you had to imagine your unique purpose in the context of being in the vastness of this expansive experience, what would it be?

Take a few minutes to steep in the vastness and complexity of living in such a cosmos as one individual being.

Now, in addition to visualizing and imagining that you are *in* all of that, playing a unique role in the cosmos, I also want you to visualize and imagine that all of that is inside of you. All of those living beings on this planet and all of that vast array of planets, galaxies, constellations of galaxies, inside the universe and the cosmos, are also inside of you. Just breathe that in, for it is true, even if you are not aware of it.

You are interpenetrating with all living things, with all of the planet and the whole cosmos, and now it is *inside* of you. Just imagine that for a moment: that the wholeness of the cosmos is inside of you. Let these images float through your mind's eye. What experience do you have of that in your body? Where do you feel those sensations? What emotions do you associate with that?

In this state, you are so aware of the moment, and awareness is your experience, who you are, that you are aware of awareness. Who are you now? What is your role or authentic contribution? What might be your unique purpose now, in the vastness of this experience?

This exercise provides just a brief taste of what living in the MetAware stage is like.

*These data are just a hypothesized number from data extraction and interpretation, rather than actual counts. Scientists also estimate that the Earth may lose 67% of its species (World Wildlife Fund, 2018) by the end of 2020, if all things remain the same. Not to take you out of the MetAware stage.

CONCLUSION: PREVIEW OF WHAT'S NEXT

This chapter begins to explore how the Golden Thread may arise in the MetAware Tier only to be deconstructed and then reemerge with even more nuance and authentic expression to guide significant multisystemic endeavors capable of resolving significant human dilemmas. And each person who enters the MetAware Tier does not have a guaranteed trajectory to be able to move through into a higher stage of contribution. However, given the prevalence of effective healing modalities, the acceptance that all of us have "baggage" to work on, and the recognition that our "inner state" of being is related to all external manifestations of us, I assume (and hope) that more and more of us who make it into MetAware will evolve through the stages.

As we begin to experience ourselves as Beings in a relationship with the Universe, we will have less attachment to tangible material world constructs. We will instead be interested in rewards that are more tangibly beneficent to the whole world and its 8.7 million species, rather than the egoistic version of us that wants what we want. We will have more impact because of our attention to the worldly and broader contextual forces that shape our experiences, and we'll submit to the life forces that move through us in purposeful ways.

In the MetAware Tier, our purpose may seem less "individualistic" and instead focus on the broader circumstances of life, even though we still bring our nuanced portrayal of purpose into the expression of even multinational endeavors. Our purpose will always have our own flavor.

I've demonstrated the early portrayals of purpose in the Concrete Tier through the case studies of Agathe and Mira Megs, and a few stories from my own life. In the next chapter we'll delve into a synthesis of chapters 4-6 and look at what this all means. We'll talk about the role of "flow," the evolutionary nature of being human, the personality related to purpose, and what limits our purposeful expression.

REFERENCES

Bennett, N. & Lemoine, GJ. (2014). What VUCA really means
for you. Harvard Business Review. Jan-Feb 2014. Retrieved
on January 1, 2020

O'Donohue, J. For a new beginning.

O'Fallon, T. (2016). Personal communication.

O'Fallon, T. (2017). Personal communication.

O'Fallon, T., and Barta, K. (2017) Essentials Course Manual, Stages
International.

Science Daily. (2011). Retrieved on January 9, 2020

Living Planet Index. (2018). World Wildlife Fund. Retrieved on
January 9, 2020

CHAPTER 7

WHAT IT ALL MEANS

———

PURPOSE AS EXPRESSION OF PRESENCE TO FLOW

When you're in the slipstream of purpose, it feels like magic. So says Bill Kern, now living into his dream of facilitating CEO peer groups. Or Carol, living into her vision of working in sustainable agriculture. Or Jane Sheppard, supporting parents in developmentally nurturing their children by working through their own trauma, just as she did.

The synchronicity of events that transpire when we have purpose pouring through us can feel as though we're in the middle of the vast ocean and the currents are all running in the right direction. And finding that place in our own slipstream of purpose doesn't require us to wander around in the desert (or anywhere else), as it's the unfolding nature of us that's a mix of inside-outside awareness.

Wandering, however, won't harm us—and may even be of benefit if it opens our eyes to the broader context of awareness that allows us to see more than what's in our own backyard.

As Emanuel Kuntzelman describes, wandering in other cultures lessons the "acculturation (that) strangles us." Whatever we can do to find a deeper way of accessing and being present with our true self is essential.

Getting quiet enough, and still enough, to listen-hear-witness who we really are in the world, and rid ourselves of all that we are not, is the essential task for unlocking the Golden Thread of our purpose.

This process is the gist of what happens when we allow the purpose GPS to pull us along in our lives, unfolding in the context of the story of what life brings us, both enlivening and challenging. If we remain flexible and adaptable to the circumstances and scenarios of our lives, recognizing that the "wrong turns" too are teachers, we swim back into the slipstream and pick up the current where we left off. It's only when we get stuck in the shame of the maladies of life that we stay outside of our own slipstream. The Golden Thread of purpose is indeed our lifeline.

And once we're in purposeful flow, usually everything else in life also tends to improve, including our career or business, relationship, financial abundance, health, and other random synchronicities that don't easily fit into categories (Russo-Netzer & Icekson, 2020). Refer back to chapter 2 to explore how scientific studies suggest that purpose stacks the odds in our favor!

Many of my clients are executives, entrepreneurs, innovators, founders, or soon-to-be entrepreneurs. These three steps lead us all into greater purposeful expression:

- Gaining clarity about our purpose,
- Getting rid of the doubt, fear, limiting beliefs, childhood wounding, shadow, and karma that holds us back, and
- Taking small bold steps onto our aligned path.

If we do this work, we are able to make big visions happen in an extraordinarily short time and with more ease than we ever imagined. My former client, Agathe, founded or co-founded three startups in the two years after we worked together, bringing her purpose and interests to a sector that sorely needed her technologic skills.

Along with the markedly improved career and entrepreneurial aspirations that my clients are able to fulfill, most of them also have improved relationship status. In the five years prior to this book, 92 percent of my clients have had either improved intimate, family, and collegial relationships, ended those that weren't working, or started new love relationships. One of my former clients credits our work together for leading her to new love and marriage!

And, once in alignment, they begin to experience the flow of financial abundance in our lives. Many of my clients' business revenue has doubled or tripled, they end jobs that no longer align with them, start new careers (as many of these case studies demonstrate), or they find their way to improve their own awareness about how they're sabotaging their work. One of my clients was a former Google manager who left to start her own company, which floundered under the weight of her self-doubt. At the end of our work together, she had an extremely viable business model and had embarked in new product creation aligned with her purpose.

The effects of alignment also include an improvement in health outcomes, and/or a recognition that mindset and self-awareness affect our physical and mental health conditions. One of my clients had insomnia, anxiety, depression, fatigue, and stress-induced disorders, which resolved during or shortly after our work together and led to her youthful expression in her new business.

In finding purpose, synchronicities abound, and opportunities arise that would have seemed inconceivable a few months earlier.

The issues that seemed like sticky wickets may suddenly resolve. The energetic vibration and frequency of our lives improves such that we become available to all that is transpiring within and around us—that we may have pushed away before.

PURPOSE IS NOT PERSONALITY

In the quietness of our evolving expanded perspective, we realize that our personality derived from our childhood beliefs about our "personal reality." The mental constructions arising in childhood about "how things are" served us in the early stages as we had to survive within the contexts of our family of origin and we needed food, shelter, and safety (which may not have been there).

We came to know reality as what was offered to us through the belief systems of our ancestral lineage, our culture, and whatever social-historical-environmental contexts were occurring at the time (including all forms of violence and injustice). You may recall how Brandon Peele acquiesced to the gender-biased normative expectations of the male culture in which he was embedded, which prevented his full expression for decades.

The point of knowing this truth—that we become what was offered us in the context of our lives—is the coiled spring against which we must resist to find ourselves again.

The most significant job of our lives is to become ourselves newly, continuously, to find our way back home after being lost in the cauldron of the early disruption of our authentic childhood self.

We do that at each stage of our development, and especially in the transition points that represent the major points of individuation, or where we cross the bridge into a new tier of consciousness. Birth to infancy, Concrete to Subtle, and Subtle to MetAware: these are the major inflection points at which we must commit to reconstructing ourselves again as we head back into the individual stages of identity.

The more rigidly we hold onto the identity of our prior expression, the greater the challenge of crossing into the new version of us. While Jane Sheppard's story of not being of value looked different at different stages of her life, each stage at which she enhanced her experience of her own value increased her ability to contribute more significantly to her family and her career offerings.

Living into purpose is not only following the Golden Thread of your essence; it is also about losing and loosening your identity, just as it seems to be coalescing.

As you become practiced in each stage of development, you'll organically let go and become the next version of you.

PURPOSE ACROSS THE DEVELOPMENTAL STAGES

And yet, we live across a range of developmental stages at any time. Thus, our expression of purpose may include a combination of strategies, conceptions, and visions rather than the somewhat linear versions presented in earlier chapters. If we develop skillfully, we transcend and include all former stages and have great facility to express the wondrous capacities of each. If we embrace each stage of life gracefully, we can simultaneously:

- Playfully express childhood wonderment (Concrete Tier Egocentric),
- Be imbued with the enthusiastic kinship of an adolescent (Concrete Tier Rule-Oriented),
- Build loyal connections to support common interests (Concrete Tier Conformist),
- Walk courageously with the aspirations of young adult knowledge (Subtle Tier Expert),
- Make bold strategic moves with the confidence of adulthood (Subtle Tier Achiever),
- Compassionately embrace our diverse interests through adult mutuality (Subtle Tier Pluralist),

- Intertwine divergent distinctions as thoughtful adult wisdom (Subtle Tier Strategist),
- Reconstruct our identities newly with deep compassion (MetAware Tier Construct Aware),
- Create broad and agile platforms for change that represent meta-models to guide action (MetAware Tier Transpersonal),
- And so on into the later stages of the MetAware Tier and beyond.

In fact, another tier exists beyond MetAware in this framework, but with so few people and so little data about it, I chose not to discuss it here.

Each stage brings its own unique gifts and challenges. Our task is to move solidly into each stage, and then choose to embrace the inklings of the next stage so that we don't get stuck in the limited perspective of a hat worn too long. Certainly our ability to move into the next stage of our developmental journey will hinge on the "readiness" or resistance to letting go and allowing a new identity—and a long list of cognitive, affective, and behavioral processes required to be "ready" to tackle the next stage (Prochaska, DeClemente, Norcross, 1992; Prochaska, Prochaska, Redding, & Evers, 2002.)

For instance, as Jacqui Webb was able to evoke more self-intimacy and nourish herself, she began to recognize her gifts of purpose enough to express them when the opportunity arose at AfrikaBurn. Stage-specific interventions and approaches can support us to develop depth and breadth in each stage, so that our experience is grounded in the relevant developmental tasks and we organically unfold into our next expressions of purpose (O'Fallon & Barta, 2018; Noar, Benac, & Harris, 2007).

And rather than aspiring to make a mad dash to the next stage of consciousness, the perfection comes in allowing ourselves to fully embody the current stage. As we enjoy the fruits of our labor at each stage, we create an optimal scenario for healthy and organic development. If we continually seek the next stage prematurely, we'll likely preempt or "bypass" some important tasks and create a developmental gap that we'll have to reintegrate before going into later stages.

Some of the recent touted methods for creating "flow states" (Kotler & Wheal, 2018) or other spiritual techniques that encourage state-level transcendence (without stage-specific embodiment) create a lightning rod for bypassing important tasks, resulting in imbalanced development and narcissistic or other wounded behaviors. Jeffrey Smith learned to accept his own fallibilities as a human in order to be nourished enough to allow his next stage of world-changing transformation to emerge.

Wherever we are and whatever our purpose is expressing in that moment are perfect.

"If you are really interested in being yourself, that interest begins with the awareness of where you are at this very moment. Being who you are can only arise from the love of being where you are."

—ALMAAS, AH (2008).

And that also includes not getting stuck at any particular stage because the rewards or recognition are so great that we refuse to acknowledge and integrate life's grand lessons. We often become enamored of the decorations of the Concrete (e.g., material possessions, financial incentives) and Subtle world (e.g., power of influence, accolades, and distinctions). Bill Kern had to recognize the shadow elements of his power and influence before he could more fully benefit those he desired to serve. Our quest for expertise, success, or enlightenment can stymie our spiritual adeptness and developmental progression.

THE EVOLUTIONARY (AND INVOLUTIONARY) NATURE OF OUR SOUL'S PURPOSE

The Stages of Consciousness, and other human development models, represent an evolutionary framework. We are evolutionary beings—always birthing another version of our essential beingness. In this way, we are also always birthing another version of our purpose—one that is more expressive and integrates all of us or that transcends and includes all that came before. Purposeful expression is not static any more than our human development, the Earth and natural world, or manifest consciousness is.

Purpose and our own development are a process of not only Evolution but also of Involution. Simply put, our Soul Purpose inwardly unfolds and then outwardly expresses itself over and over throughout our lifetime. In Allan Combs' (2013) synthesis of the "transcend and include" theories of Ken Wilber (2010), he describes the idea that "spirit projects or steps itself downward, permeating and finally losing itself in the various levels of being [involution] . . . and evolution is a reversal of this course, one in which spirit progressively manifests and discovers itself again." Here Combs [and Wilber (1980, 1981), and the works of Sri Aurobindo (1990) and others] is describing the evolutionary nature of Spirit [or God, the Divine, or whatever name you give to a higher power] to expand its awareness of self, and then the involutionary nature of spirit to deconstruct itself to near nothingness.

I suggest that the soul and its purpose follow the same trajectory. As Soul is the individuated Spirit made manifest in our worldly journey, our soul's trajectory follows the stream of consciousness within our spiritual and egoic development, both evolving and "involving" itself.

Our soul's journey into purpose is thus a holographic experience, repeatedly transcending its former self and reforming into something grander, more expressive, more evolved.

The act of "manifesting" our soul's purpose, then, is to envision and allow what is wanting to unfold within us, without worrying about the "how." The fractal nature of reality, both within and without (external and internal to our human self) will drive the evolutionary (and involutionary) impulses of our existence to the frequency that can hold where we are at any given time. As this organic process interfaces with our stage of development, we begin to live in the energy of possibility, rather than limitation.

WHAT LIMITS OUR DEVELOPMENT AND PURPOSEFUL EXPRESSION

Very little in a human life or on the planet, even in the current vulnerable, uncertain, complex, ambiguous conditions of the world (Bennet & Lemoine, 2014), should preclude this normal evolutionary and involutionary process. It is the natural order of things, just as the roots of trees grow downward and the limbs grow skyward. If you are alive, you should unfold through organic evolution and involution. However, the wounding and trauma that persist (and have persisted for millennia) in the human zeitgeist can prevent these natural processes from occurring among a significant sector of the human population, preventing our purposeful expression.

Trauma comes in many forms and can persist throughout life, usually representing the original trauma of childhood, repeated over and over as a fractal version of itself. My own life journey was such an experiment of hitting my head against the veritable wall enough times until I found solutions, one small bit by bit. Extensive trauma is a violent disruption to our human systems (e.g., biologic, emotional, mental, psychic) and creates an egoic mandate to stay safe at all costs.

As our ego fights to be safe at any stage of development, it creates a fractured sense of self, disrupted by the triune brain's response system, which then sets us up to demonstrate the egoic personality trapped by the bonds of violence.

Trauma and violence can include childhood abuse, neglect, or physical injury. We can be traumatized by catastrophic weather events, relocation or dislocation, loss of important people, or loss of our native culture and language. We are most certainly traumatized by forms of social injustice, including racism, gender inequity, economic injustice or disparity, and many other forms of bias, bigotry, or injustice on the planet.

While some of these forms of trauma or violence can be overcome with the proper resources, we don't all have access to the same type or level of resources to do so. In addition, some of us bear our ancestral wounds so deeply within our psyches and bodies that we are trapped within the bondage of whatever injustices and violence were carried out centuries before.

When we are unable to move past the constrictions generated by individual or collective trauma or violence, we carry with us the attachment to an identity of being a victim, prohibiting us from living into the normal progression of developmental stages without losing parts of ourselves in the process.

The ultimate integration of trauma and violence is forgiveness, yet until we can first release the bonds within our bodies, minds, and spirits, we remain malnourished and unable to complete important developmental tasks.

The lack of integration stunts our evolution and involution, and thus our soul's journey of expressing purpose.

It's never too late to start heading in the right direction.
—SETH GODIN

NOTES FROM THE FIELD

Most of my clients move well past their wounding during (and after) our work together so they can get to the fullest (next) expression of purpose, appropriate for their developmental stage. Yet a small number manage to evade the truth of how their battle scars (or their successes) are affecting them.

Generally, when our identity has become so entrenched that we can't imagine any other "way of being," we have to look carefully to see what is limiting the next version of our life. One of my former clients very clearly saw how her way set back her next career move and her relationships with her husband and children. She desperately wanted to live up to the talents she had been preparing for her whole life. Yet she had trouble giving up the intrinsic rewards of being stuck in the "old way." The identity of being a victim to her life circumstances was too powerful and had formed all kinds of peculiar rewards to keep her from taking the next steps. Because of the internal violence she was still perpetrating upon herself, she would have to repeat the cycle of trauma and disconnection to herself once again before moving forward.

Sometimes this journey takes longer than we wish. Sometimes we must be patient to be "ready" enough to have the courage and resolution to find our "new way" into purpose. Exposing ourselves to others who have made the journey into their purposeful expression can inspire us to take the leap and let go into the wild machinations of our imagination.

SCIENTIFIC VALIDATION

While I have offered several hypotheses to ponder, this book is obviously not an experimental study using the linear scientific method to explore how purpose shows up across the stages of consciousness. Having conducted quantitative research in several domains of study as a scientist for more than two decades, I came to know that these methods can limit our awareness of the broader contextual factors at play. Early in my research career, I was called to begin eliciting a deeper understanding of human dynamics and became adept in the area of grounded theory, partly because I had an expanded perspective and could see these many contextual factors.

This type of inquiry intends to create new potential models of understanding based in observation of human behavior, rooted in qualitative methods and an anthropologic approach.

This book was intended to provide some validation about the proposed hypotheses, and the importance of these questions in our becoming more self-aware and intentional in our lives. I have observed these patterns in working with several hundred clients and a few dozen organizations over a period of a decade, and in my own life, using both observational and more empirical methods.

In addition, given that the data I've presented "fit" well into the existing models and validated measures of human development, I am suggesting that they help to clarify that the hypotheses are indeed valid. Further exploration using similar methodologies or other forms of study may be useful to continue to explore answers to important questions of our time.

SELF-REFLECTION: WHERE DO YOU FIND PURPOSE LIVING IN THE STAGES OF YOUR OWN LIFE?

As you've traversed the stories of people across the stages of consciousness, and witnessed the range of expressions that naturally occur in the Concrete, Subtle, and MetAware Tiers, you've likely had some sense of how your own life compares to that of case studies described in this book. You may have found some similarities—and probably many differences in your own story. You likely reflected upon experiences—good or bad, life-affirming or challenging—that propelled your own life in ways similar to the people here.

We are all, always, living on purpose, more or less. Our souls pull us along a trajectory that is intended to help us live as ourselves in the most potent expression of us. And then stuff happens, and life can get in the way. These obstacles are also normal and are sometimes the best scenario you could have imagined for yourself, though it may be uncomfortable.

Almost always, the way out of a challenging situation is the way through.

QUESTIONS TO CONSIDER:

As you were reading the case studies and the explanations of the various stages, what did you see in your own life that would have made it difficult to live a purposeful life or prevented you from doing so?

How did you see yourself expressing the various stages of purpose? Do you express various forms of purpose in your life simultaneously now?

Do you have specific ways of being in the world that represent your personality and shadow, rather than your purpose?

CONCLUSION: PREVIEW OF WHAT'S NEXT

In this chapter, I've discussed how purposeful expression leads to the almost magical flow and synchronicity that happen when we align with our most authentic selves. The enhanced "outcomes" available at every stage of life when we are living purposefully are depicted in the stories of real peoples' lives, and in the scientific data (chapter 2) that suggests purpose positively affects many areas of life.

We also demonstrated that purpose is not personality, even though many of us have interests or passions that stem from personality and can look like purpose. We become our true selves by resisting the temptation to live solely into our egoic needs and desires. Holding onto our identity and moving past the many types of traumas we experience in life are the biggest hurdles to overcome in order to live purposefully.

And each stage of development has important gifts to offer us as whole beings. Including each of these gifts as we traverse the developmental trajectory is critical to becoming a whole human who can live fully into the next purposeful expression. If we don't accomplish the developmental tasks of the last stage and attempt to evolve too quickly, we bypass foundational capacities that may be critical for executing our next endeavor.

In the next chapter, I provide an overview of what is needed now, given we have a vision of how significant the evolution of human development and consciousness are for living our grandest purposeful expressions. This burning desire to become ourselves can be expressed with specific purpose-related developmental tasks at each stage in the framework. I make additional recommendations for how to accomplish these from a cultural and social perspective, in addition to the individual tasks that we must each undertake.

REFERENCES

Almaas, A.H. (2008). The unfolding now: Realizing your true nature through the practice of presence. Boston: Shambhala.

Aurobindo, S. (1990). The life divine. Wilmot, WI: Lotus Light.

Bennett, N. & Lemoine, GJ. (2014). What VUCA really means for you. Harvard Business Review. Jan-Feb 2014. Retrieved on January 1, 2020.

Combs, A. (2013). Transcend and Include: Ken Wilber's contribution to transpersonal psychology. In Friedman, H.L., & Hartelius, G. (Eds.). (2013). The Wiley-Blackwell handbook of transpersonal psychology. West Sussex, U.K: John Wiley & Sons, Ltd

Kotler, S & Wheal, J. (2018). Stealing fire: How Silicon Valley, the Navy SEALS and maverick scientists are revolutionizing the way we live and work. New York: Dey Publications.

Noar, S.M., Benac, C.N., & Harris, M.S. (2007). Does tailoring matter? Meta-analytic review of tailored print health behavior change interventions. Psychological Bulletin, 4: 673-693

O'Fallon & Barta, K. (2018). STAGES Certification for Coaching, Counseling and Psychotherapy Courses, Stages International. www.stagesinternational.com.

Prochaska, J.O., DiClemente, C.C., & Norcross, J.C. (1992). In search of how people change: Applications to the addictive behaviors. American Psychologist, 47, 1102-1114. PMID: 1329589.

Prochaska, J.O., Redding, C.A., & Evers, K. (2002). The transtheoretical model and stages of Change. In K. Glanz, B.K. Rimer & Lewis, F.M. (Eds.) Health behavior and health education: theory, research, and practice (3rd Ed.). San Francisco, CA: Jossey-Bass.

Russo-Netzer, P, Icekson, T. (2020). Engaging with life: Synchronicity experiences as a pathway to meaning and personal growth. Current Psychology Retrieved on 1/10/20.

Whyte, D. (1996) All the true vows, The House of Belonging. Langley, WA: Many Rivers Press, p. 24.

Wilber, K. (1980). The Atman project: A transpersonal view of human development. Wheaton, IL: Quest Publications.

Wilber, K. (1981). Up from Eden: A transpersonal view of human evolution. Wheaton, IL: Quest Publications.

CHAPTER 8

WHAT WE NEED NOW

BURNING DESIRE TO BECOME OURSELVES

At some points in our lives, we are compelled to become our true selves more than ever before. These inflection points coincide with moving into an expanded perspective of being able to see ourselves and the world newly. As we explore a new form of identity, either individually or in a new social group, doing so can feel like we're standing in a different part of the room or seeing through a window that wasn't there before.

With these important expansions of perspective, we also take on more important roles and tasks and grow into a new identity (for instance, as we move from childhood into adolescence), then an awareness of our new identity, and ultimately an awareness of awareness itself. At each step we claim an expanded version of ourselves and our role in life, individually and collectively.

Claiming a "new" version of us has not been commonplace in society, with the morass of social and cultural expectations. In my childhood, where few options for self-expression existed and the collective culture didn't embrace personal evolution and development of self, we equated these inflection points of individuation as the terrible twos, teenage or young adult rebellion, or a midlife crisis. Even though we all go through a version of these events (ranging from slight to extreme), these transitional stages are viewed as temporarily radicalized moments, or aberrations, and we assume that the "rebels" will settle back down into their normal lives soon enough. We now see that these radical expressions are (often) healthy deviations from systems of oppression that kept us from being ourselves.

EVEN WHEN LIFE IS GOOD, THERE IS MORE

Especially if life is going well, we tend to think we have reached some "pinnacle" of success or peak, or at least a comfortable place, and decide we want to stay there. And while in the material world the comforts may be tempting, our souls are always drawing us into another version of us—so the next expression can be released. We are always more than we think we are. Another evolutionary-involutionary turn of the wheel exists, ready for us to take it out for a spin.

And as I've demonstrated here, our Golden Thread more naturally (or distinctly) shows up at later stages, and not everyone gets there, especially if we've not expressed our true self in earlier stages. When we deny the next expression of our purpose and shut down the pull or call to be that next version, typically some constriction or constraint draws us into a crisis, which may look like trauma or disease. At any time in life, and especially as we move into the elder years, if we've not fully expressed our soul's calling, our physical form may manifest a discomfort too great to ignore. While I hesitate to suggest that all disease or trauma is related to the non-expression of our fullest purpose, certainly both scientific data (see chapter 3) and thousands of case studies (a few hundred within my own practice) suggest this plausible hypothesis. We have much we don't yet know about the cause and effect of a purposeful expression on the dimensions of life.

To step into the next expression of our purpose, or any expression at all, we need to both identify the missing Golden Thread and tend to the developmental tasks of our Stage of Consciousness, wherever we are. For each of us, our job is to gain the skills, capacity, or adeptness to see ourselves and resolve our wounding. Taking these steps will support our evolutionary and involutionary processes with greater awareness and agility to live into the depth and breadth of self.

WHAT IS NEEDED AT EACH STAGE: THE DEVELOPMENTAL TASKS TO ACHIEVE PURPOSE

In chapters 3-6, I identified the specific tasks needed at each stage, unique to the object of focus for each of the Concrete, Subtle, and MetAware Tiers. How well we are able to accomplish these tasks will predict whether we express our purpose in these different stages of life. Who we are is unique to the one-of-a-kind nuanced version of our purpose and also the stage of life in which we are situated.

In the following tables, I present a synthesis of the developmental tasks (discussed in chapters 4-6) required of each stage, the elements needed to deepen in that stage, and what purposeful expression might look like in the stage. While we need to accomplish the generic developmental tasks outlined for each stage, the purposeful tasks will be more specific, related to the one-of-a-kind nuanced expression that is our purpose.

For instance, the purposeful expression in the 2.0 Rule-Oriented stage (generally adolescents or young adults) are the "nuanced curiosities, interests and passions within relationships and groups." This stage might look like a teenager who is able to choose what extracurricular activities she engages with, what topics she may elect to research or study as a part of school projects, what curiosities drive her internet searches or reading or cause her to "light up" or be motivated to pursue further.

The focus of these activities would be indications of her purpose. At this stage, the teenager or young adult is also pursuing these interests as part of a group or network, so that the interests become more defined in the context of peers and peer pressure. A parent or adult or even a peer may be able to point out the commonalities of these areas of interest and encourage an even deeper exploration and engagement with the topic as a means of furthering their expression.

And, to be clear, the "topic" itself is not her purpose, but what is foundationally underneath the why and how she would engage with the topic is more related to the purpose. You'll notice that in the tables below, I am sharing the "indicators" of purposeful expression, not purpose itself. Purpose itself can be found through deep inquiry and exploration, using direct and indirect methods (see chapter 9).

The Stages of Consciousness framework hypothesized and studied with rigor by Terri O'Fallon and her team at Stages International has significantly deepened my own understanding of human development and evolution of consciousness. In these charts, the Developmental Tasks, Elements Needed to Deepen, and Purposeful Expression are derived from my own thirty-year study and practice of human development and purpose-based coaching, mentoring, and coaching.

CONCRETE TIER				
Social Style	**Individual**		**Collective**	
Learning Style	Receptive	Active	Reciprocal	Interpene-trative
Stage	1.0 Impulsive	1.5 Egocen-tric	2.0 Rule-Ori-ented	2.5 Conform-ist
Typical Age	Infant	Toddler-Child	Adolescent-Adult	Adult
Develop-mental Tasks Required of Stage	Learn to receive information through the senses. Formation of physical identity. All about me.	Developing concrete thoughts. Expressing self through action.	Developing friendships. Seeing feelings and thoughts. Start of peer pressure, romance.	Standing in principles. Develop sta-ble relation-ships. Create structures for safety and stability.
Elements Needed to Deepen in the Stage	Learning to trust each sense organ, including movement. Trusting the new world outside of the body.	Using action to gain pow-er. Applying power to a broader array of life circumstanc-es.	Learning to engage in positive relationship dynamics in a broad array of circum-stances. Learning self in relation to other.	Applying principles to broad array of life settings and scenarios to expand stability and sense of community.
Purposeful Expression in the Stage	Curiosity, seeking personal fulfillment.	Curiosities explored, interests ex-pressed and practiced in unique ways.	Early expression of nuanced curiosities, interests, and passions within rela-tionships and groups.	Early choices of avocation/vocation related to curiosities, interests within social expectations of collective (may need to rebel from childhood collective to achieve).

SUBTLE TIER				
Social Style	Individual		Collective	
Learning Style	Receptive	Active	Reciprocal	Interpene-trative
Stage	3.0 Expert	3.5 Achiever	4.0 Pluralist	4.5 Strategist
Typical Age	Adult	Adult	Adult	Adult
Develop-mental Tasks Required of Stage	Developing interior subtle experiences, including thoughts and feelings, visualization and imagina-tion. Expand-ing mental depth.	Using active thinking and feeling, and the building blocks of mind cre-ations, inno-vations, and sophisticat-ed planning.	Developing deeper sub-tle intimacy with others, as well as an interior intimacy with ego states.	Developing systems for interior con-text and ex-terior world, including social and contextual feedback loops.
Elements Needed to Deepen in the Stage	Exposing self to new experiences, which allows discovery of new unique aspects of self outside of the norm.	Applying expand-ed Subtle awareness to improve life functioning, including us-ing thoughts, feelings, and managing the brain successfully.	Expanding awareness of the inner and outer Subtle conceptions about self and others.	Integrating, exploring, and seeing the inter-connected system dynamics in a broader array of life circumstanc-es. Integrat-ing inner ego states.
Purposeful Expression in the Stage	Explor-ing new traits and capacities, especially perfect-ing Subtle skills and professional mastery.	Masterful use of Subtle skills, power-ful nuanced expression, manifest-ing from individual orientations/ visions.	Collective Subtle awareness and inner voices dig-nify human rights, social justice, inclu-siveness, and co-creation as important aspects; Purpose becomes extremely nuanced.	Nuanced Pur-pose begins to "fit" within the internal and external systems of life and within multi-dimensional contexts.

METAWARE TIER				
Social Style	Individual		Collective	
Learning Style	Receptive	Active	Reciprocal	Interpenetrative
Stage	5.0 Construct Aware	5.5 Transpersonal	6.0 Universal	6.5 Illumined
Typical Age	Adult	Adult	Adult	Adult
Developmental Tasks Required of Stage	Developing awareness, actively creating awareness newly through thoughts and feelings. Redefining capacities and creativity. Developing early sense of timeless and boundless.	Developing a deeper intimacy and interconnection between the timeless local and nonlocal fields of awareness and infinity. Manifesting from the interconnected whole.	Integrating into the Oneness, lessening of time-space reference.	Maturing of emptiness and fullness, allowing prioritization and categorization of integration with Universal forces.
Elements Needed to Deepen in the Stage	Adapting to life in the moment with efficient speed of awareness. Replacing thought as a primary source of information-gathering.	Submitting the MetAware ego to the MetAware Collective, creating a greater intimacy with the interconnected whole.	Surrendering unique individuality to merge with Universal quantum field, recreate reality.	Integrating all systems of "reality" within broader context of Universal field.
Purposeful Expression in the Stage	New expressions of Purpose based on evolving liberation and questioning of meaning.	Creative and spontaneous innovations span socially constructed reality to be agile and evolving.	Surrendering to the forces of the Universe, create intricate and complex social structures, solve complex problems in innovative ways.	Prioritizing the Universal collective, creating "meta" visions and systems

The Framework for the tiers and stages is derived from O'Fallon's Stages of Consciousness (O'Fallon, Stages International).

LIVING PURPOSEFULLY IN THE
DEVELOPMENTAL TRAJECTORIES

EMPHASIZING EARLY-STAGE DEVELOPMENT

I've shown here what needs to happen in each stage for purpose to come alive. And, evidently, an emphasis on early
childhood development and the accompanying developmental tasks is critical to our individuated expression and expansion. While the tasks for each stage are critical for continued
evolution, we don't even get to the Subtle Tier if we haven't
accomplished the early childhood tasks. Or if we happen to
advance to the Subtle Tier without integrating our childhood
parts, our personality looks like the fractured parts we didn't
integrate, rather than a "whole" version of us that will walk
seamlessly into our next stage.

When we act from our personality, which comprises our fractured and wounded sub-psychic parts (and look like "children in the basement"), rather than a mature version of us,
we won't advance to the later stages of the Subtle Tier (where
the Subtle Collective can support us) and become a mature
contributor in the human Collective. Thus, we remain the
impulsive and egocentric versions of ourselves that consume
and destroy the contexts around us as we attempt to satisfy
our egoic desires. No wonder we have arrived at a critical
stage in the climate crisis, as the early-stage focus on possessing Concrete objects is leading us to the "end game."

DEEMPHASIZING MATERIAL WORLD CONSTRUCTS

As we move out of the Concrete Tier and into the Subtle, we
begin to experience life beyond the material. We gain access

to thoughts, emotions, and a meta-cognitive experience (e.g., thinking about thinking, thinking about feeling) and a more nuanced and richer version of life and ourselves. We recognize that life encompasses more than possessing "things" and that meaning and fulfillment lie beyond that which we can see and touch. We begin to see that the world around us has abundance that lies in the "natural order" of things, rather than that which we manipulate.

We have placed an extreme emphasis on Concrete or material objects in our world to date, primarily because earlier generations didn't have access to personal or spiritual development to overcome the restrictive constraints of our developed world. Evolving beyond a prescribed identity wasn't an option, or at least wasn't the norm, for the early baby boomer generation and generations prior. This reality changed as the late baby boomers came into their youth and early adulthood during two important sociocultural movements.

First, the science and practice of human development emerged within the academic realm, leading to the Human Potential movement and an awareness that we do evolve as humans. Secondly, and perhaps even more importantly, spirituality and philosophical practices from the "East" (e.g., primarily Buddhism and Hinduism from Tibet, Nepal, China, India) migrated to the "West" as spiritual seekers who went far afield to discover themselves (moving into the MetAware stage?) brought back their discoveries and developed large followings. Thus, the "radical" 1960s movement was birthed.

As younger generations are now able to take advantage of sixty expansive years of human and spiritual development, and make use of traditional and alternative modalities for healing, the youngest boomers, Gen X, millennials (Gen Y), and Gen Z cohorts have begun to rapidly (and earlier) move into the Subtle Tier and live from the Subtle Tier Collective. The massive shift to the later Subtle Tier among these generations has been responsible for the myriad activist uprisings and focus on broad humanitarian and planetary issues of racial, economic, gender, and environmental justice and many other issues related to a sense of equity among all human, animal, and planetary beings.

While older or more "established" generations (which rely on the Concrete Tier Collective principles) may consider these activist factions as rebellious and nonproductive, the movements are in fact collective evolutionary shifts rising up in our midst. We must encourage, support, and provide guidance to these movements to ensure they don't "flame out," as has occurred in previous generations of wise youth speaking out to their more entrenched elders. To paraphrase what I hear millennials and Gen Z members saying: "We didn't create this mess. We just inherited it. Get off the couch and help us fix it!"

FOCUS ON INNER WORK TO ACCOMPANY OUTER LIFE
At this time in human evolution, our dominant culture encourages us to see each other from the outside in. Our communication channels revolve around youthful expression, material image, and physical beauty or prowess (early individual/adolescent stage of the Concrete Tier). This fact creates in us a desire to live up to others' expectations and "be like the cool ones" (the collective norms of the late Concrete

Tier.) And we are taught to attain power, money, and influence (individual orientation of the early Subtle Tier.) Currently, our world is designed to focus us on the earliest stages of evolution. In traditional media channels, and through the halls of power, we are collectively encouraged and oriented to seek to "be" someone who is relatively undeveloped, non-individuated, and unprepared for the complex world that we live in. This path won't take us where we need to go to live intentional and purposeful lives that can create a different scenario on the planet.

Only one strategy makes sense and is scientifically well-substantiated in many fields (health and mental health, business, education, finance), attested to in the various fields of human and personal development, and substantiated in every spiritual lineage and practice of millennia.

The only strategy that will give us an opportunity to collectively reshape humanity is to enhance our awareness about who we truly are, to live a life of alignment and sovereignty, and to focus our resources on creating equity among all humans who don't have resources to do so themselves.

Also, to live according to our deep inner knowing covered over by millennia of human violence and trauma. To focus on the inner work that will promote the rebirthing into each new tier of consciousness and allow us to become that which we truly are.

As we do this work, the only work actually required of us as humans, we allow our essential selves, our souls, to:

- Receive the next version of us, to be birthed into what is emerging in us,
- Practice this new way of being, trying it on and claiming what it offers,
- Interact with others in this new way, so we can be in relationship with ourselves and all others, and
- Merge what we've learned into the inherent systems of our lives.

RESOLVING PERSONAL AND COLLECTIVE TRAUMA

We each can and should do our part to resolve the personal trauma of our childhood or later wounding so we are able to uncover our purpose and that which is ours to do. But just as importantly, we need to resolve the collective trauma in broader society. This collective trauma has been created by generations of bias (i.e., racial, gender, economic, cultural), forced migration and other systemic injustices and inequities. We should recognize that the epigenetic (generational) effects of each of these traumas (Youssef et al., 2018) have had recurring insidious effects on the human potential of already oppressed social groups. The profound effect of these generational traumas has led to at least some of the current dilemmas we face in our species' development.

If we as a society do not choose to repair these injustices and the resulting collective trauma, we also won't be able to resolve the "lag" in maturation, as the human species is currently primarily adolescent in its development. If we do not choose to repair the collective trauma, we also will fall short of moving our species to the vastly increased perspective of the late-stage Subtle Tier and early MetAware Tier needed to resolve the complex problems of our times. Current social movements to rectify injustice and inequity and provide reparations to oppressed groups should be at the forefront of collective social efforts to rectify disparity in solutions to human potential.

Unfortunately, we as a global society cannot even "see" these issues until we get to the later stages of the Subtle Tier, and only a small proportion of the human population has any interest in resolving them. We are all fortunate that some portion of the younger generations among us are "woke" to these issues because they are migrating into the Subtle Tier at much younger ages than the middle-aged and older populations. And, of course, this awareness of social issues is entirely dependent on the contexts in which children and youth are raised and their opportunities to develop appropriately in each stage.

Young wisdom soon will far surpass what is available among the elder generations. Our attention to and intention to support these young movements to rectify vast social problems will likely prove to be more astute, inclusive, and multidimensional than many solutions put forth by our current political leaders and elders (many of whom are stuck in late Concrete and early Subtle Tiers).

EVOLVING: BACK TO THE EARTH

According to at least one important Soulcentric expert, Bill Plotkin (2019), we also must come to grips with the need to return our focus to the planet itself, the "more than human world."

As we return to a focus on nature, we also come to know ourselves as "belonging" to this broader world, which loosens our egoic grip on our human identity.

This "loosening" must occur early enough to have an effect on the mangling that occurs in our forced cultural obeyance to the unconscious mean (or the Oasis stage in Plotkin's conceptual model, or the late Concrete stages in O'Fallon's model). I believe that Plotkin's notion of "belonging" to the natural world is critical not only for our further evolution, but also for our survival on the planet. As we expose ourselves (and especially our children) to this "more than human" world around us, two things happen.

First, our children can grasp broader principles and larger contexts at work beyond their family, peer, and social groups, which expands their perspective and facilitates their "seeing beyond" the prescribed roles of those conformist collectives. As they have a vision of what is beyond themselves, they migrate more easily into the Subtle Tier. Secondly, the "natural" world of plants, animals, and other beings, large and small, exposes them to the fractal world of ecosystems, migration patterns, oceanic and atmospheric tides, and many other natural systems of the earth.

When we experience the vastness of these intrinsic systems of the earth, we gain an appreciation of the imperceptible qualities of the planet. These "invisible" or energetic qualities of the Subtle Tier can be felt viscerally and appreciated psycho-spiritually by almost anyone—and especially by children.

Through exposure to the "more than human world," our children are more likely to grow up with a "knowing" that reality exists beyond the material objects they see, and they will begin to look for those patterns in their own lives and in the contexts in which they live. This Subtle perception enhances their own perspective-taking and thus their advanced development. In other words, we can accomplish developmental tasks more effectively when we can see the broader natural world around us. In my own life and work with clients, I observed that those of us who spent a good deal of time in nature in childhood had a swifter transition to the Subtle Tier, which gave us access to capacities and resources more likely to support an interest in and longing for purpose.

SUPPORT SYSTEMS TO LIVE PURPOSEFUL LIVES

So what are the systems that would support people to live these purposeful lives? What kinds of resources would promote the exploration of purpose and the inner work required to find it, so they can offer their most evolved contributions? The following are a few broad suggestions for elements of support and systems that would benefit humanity at this critical juncture.

The recommendations below are categorized by the hallmark "stages" depicted primarily by our physical growth. I'm using these more conventional stages because we don't currently have sufficient markers or indicators—beyond a Stages assessment (Stages International) or work with a Stages of Consciousness or other developmental practitioner—to accurately assess where we are developmentally.

Children

- Early childhood development in schools and other natural/common settings.
- Childhood educator/coach/leader training re: purpose and child development.
- Access to the "natural" world and the "more than human" earth community.
- Mindfulness and other practices to create acceptance and evolved awareness.

Teens/Youth

- Educator/coach/leader training re: purpose and youth development.
- Access to the "natural" world and the "more than human" earth community.
- Mindfulness and other practices to create acceptance and evolved awareness.
- Support to tweens and teens to uncover early expressions of purposeful threads to expand exploration of interests and orient to future study or purposeful work and contribution.

Young Adults/College Students

- Support to young adults/college students to uncover purposeful threads to focus their attention and career objectives on meaningful work and contribution.
- Educator/coach/leader training re: purpose and youth development, specifically related to vocational and avocational choices.
- Access to the "natural" world and the "more than human" earth community, especially for avocational offerings and contributions.

- Mindfulness and other practices to create acceptance and evolved awareness.

Mid-Adults/Mature Adults
- Education/training to reorient their lives for a second career or more meaningful contribution and fulfillment as a part of their career plan by orienting them to their Golden Thread of purpose.
- Mentoring collaborative with youth/young adults for career mentoring.
- Access to the "natural" world and the "more than human" earth community, especially for avocational offerings and contributions.
- Mindfulness and other practices to create acceptance and evolved awareness.
- Participation in offering wisdom and guidance to broader systemic networks.

Elder Adults
- Education/training to "Re-Purpose" their lives for meaningful contribution and fulfillment as a part of their retirement plan by orienting them to their Golden Thread of Purpose.
- Mentoring collaborative with youth/young adults for career exposure.
- Access to the "natural" world and the "more than human" earth community, especially for avocational offerings and contributions.
- Mindfulness and other practices to create acceptance and evolved awareness.
- Participation in offering wisdom and guidance to broader systemic networks.

Parents

- Parent education and mentoring for appropriate at-home childhood, tween, and teen developmental tasks and purpose orientation.
- Education/training to orient their lives for meaningful contribution and fulfillment as a part of "beyond parenthood" plan by orienting them to their Golden Thread of purpose.
- Mindfulness and other practices to create acceptance and evolved awareness.

Organizations/Businesses

- Consult/train leaders of corporate, nonprofit, and entrepreneurial enterprises to:
  - Identify founder's (and executive team's) purpose and create alignment in all systems, culture, and training programs, and
  - Assess stages of development of their employees to reorient their systems to meet them where they are and to promote developmental tasks.

- Consult/train leaders of corporate, NGO, and entrepreneurial enterprises to:
  - Assess stages of development of their customers and other external audiences to reorient their systems and products to meet them where they are and promote developmental tasks.

Educational Systems

- Retool/reframe formal educational systems to focus on developmental tasks and exploration of innate interests of students, rather than (or in addition to) traditional or contemporary standards.

Communities (Local, Global), Incl. Networks

- Access to online resources for disenfranchised communities to rectify the digital divide in support of providing adequate resources for human development.
- Generative communities focused on exploring purpose among all its inhabitants to create a multidimensional "web" of contributors.
- Resources for disenfranchised or unengaged communities or populations who don't have resources to undertake these tasks for themselves and their constituents.
- Networks (local, global) to resolve interconnected and intractable human dilemmas integrating a multitude of perspectives.

GLOBAL PURPOSE LEADERS NETWORK

The Global Purpose Leaders (GPL) is a worldwide membership organization and community of practice formed in 2018, composed of a diverse group of practitioners who help individuals, groups, and organizations discover and align themselves with their unique purpose in life. GPL was founded by several of my colleagues, including two featured as case studies here (Susan Lucci and Brandon Peele). GPL members have written many books on the subject of purpose, convened several gatherings and summits, and debated countless issues related to the practice of our craft.

In 2019, members of GPL wrote a paper on "Purpose: What Is It?" responding to the plethora of new purpose-related offerings in the market and the debate in an effort to create some alignment around "What is purpose?" and recommendations about how to find purpose through practices steeped with integrity. This paper gives the general public, and even practitioners or scholars, an overview of what some of the "experts" in the field imagine purpose to be (as I provided input to this paper, its recommendations are consistent with what is offered in this book). I have stepped into a leadership role for GPL in 2020 as the community and programs guardian.

Download a copy of "Purpose: What Is It?" at http://bit.ly/GPLpurposepaper, and learn more about GPL at https://www.globalpurposeleaders.org.

Also, in collaboration with the Global Purpose Leaders, I created a list of resources you can view that includes examples of businesses, programs, initiatives, and organizations providing some of these types of programs in the world:

http://bit.ly/PurposeResources

NOTES FROM THE FIELD

I've noted throughout this book that the awareness, desire, and ability to live into or execute on purpose are enhanced as we gain broader perspective across the stages of our lives as our consciousness expands. The ability to witness the world outside of ourselves affects the ways in which we can become a more integral, and contributing, part of our world.

In the later stages of development, we have an expanded awareness that we can actually shape our own experience, for ourselves, other humans and species, and the planet itself.

Until we see ourselves in the role of shaping our lives (as we evolve), we have little noble desire to make greater contributions unless the responsibility is imposed on us by external sociocultural forces. In traditional cultures, religion has assumed an important role in creating these expectations to contribute broadly to humanity.** The moralistic doctrine of "contribution and goodness" was cemented in most global cultures by religion, well beyond the dominant forces of politics or economics. In some cultures, these forces were intertwined, but in most they were separated.

As religious participation has declined worldwide, and most political and economic systems have not picked up the concern with contribution and goodness (that was sanctioned by the church or religion), we have seen a loss of societal representation of these values. As we have evolved as a species, the need to integrate these values into our everyday lives (in political or economic systems, or even education or other social health/welfare structures) has been a hard sell, given the long-standing separation.

This shift is somewhat related to a global evolution to the early Subtle Tier, where economic influences are greater than the collective influences of "tribe" (where religion also had a greater role). While all in all this shift is a good thing, it has also created two challenges.

First, with the lessened influence of religion and its doctrine, formal sociocultural structures that promote contribution and goodness are less predominant or influential in Concrete and early Subtle Tiers. Thus, "mass media," politics, and economic forces become the dominant voices among rule-bound (Concrete) and individual-oriented (early Subtle) stages.

Second, as society shifts to the economically driven early Subtle stages, societal patterns, laws, and governing bodies also then focus on the economic-driven values, leaving behind the aspirational frame of contribution and goodness within social infrastructure.

We can see emerging trends and movements in the late Subtle stages, especially among millennials and younger cohorts, to promote values of systemic equity, justice, and contribution (because of their expanded perspective-taking). However, these movements have not become formalized adequately to evoke a sense of contribution and goodness (or purpose) among the broader society.

We can envision and imagine that, as humanity evolves into the latter Subtle stages, we will also reclaim values even more consonant with a just and equitable world as we begin to see our intrinsic connections to all others. We will move out of the frame of our comfortable, complacent and rule-bound lives into more aspirational visions of our collective future.

For many of us now, as we evolve and focus on the inner work to resolve the outer challenges, and resolve our own (and collective?) traumas, we can truly begin to ask the question,

Who can I imagine becoming?—which is more consistent with our Soul Purpose than ever before.

****I am not arguing for or against religion here, only suggesting that the current dominant social structures of the late Concrete and early Subtle stages have not fulfilled the need for external reinforcement of collective life-affirming values.*

REFERENCES

Plotkin, B. (2019). Personal Interview.

Youssef, N.A., Lockwood, L., Su, S., Hao, G., & Rutten B.P.F. (2018). The effects of trauma, with or without PTSD, on the transgenerational DNA methylation alterations in human offspring. (2018). Brain Science 8(5): 83. Retrieved December 12, 2019.

CHAPTER 9

WHY YOUR "WHY" MATTERS

———

I'll admit that I never had the "luxury" of not wondering about my "Why." I suggest that I would've found it a luxury to not care because the overwhelming impulse of my life was to figure it out, and it drove a near-manic search for meaning, leading to an abundance of careers, skills, and a nomadic lifestyle.

Oddly, I came into this life knowing that I was supposed to find my purpose, and the longing only intensified over time. So that the desire to find what "I couldn't not do" became an imperative for staying on the planet. This motive was my Golden Thread in its purest form. To apply my own facets of purpose to my life, speak my powerful truths so I could shine love onto and liberate my shadows and gifts, and unify the love and power that lived within me. Ultimately, I figured that out and have organically unfolded into each stage to yield my life to my purposeful greater expressions.

This chapter is intended to help you explore why you need a "Why", to encourage you to explore your unique one-of-a-kind purpose. This chapter is *not* intended to take you all the way there, but to give you some insight into some of the steps along the way to uncover and create your Live On Purpose life.

I work with many types of people to help them uncover their purpose, including groups, online programs, and individuals. Later in this chapter, I'll provide an overview of the *Purpose to Impact Roadmap*™ that guides my work inspiring and activating people to live into their purposeful lives.

You can download the *Purpose to Impact Roadmap*™:

http://bit.ly/PurposeImpactRoadmap

Explore and learn more about my coaching/mentoring and consulting work, in addition to gaining access to courses, group programs, workshops and speaking opportunities:

http://hollywoodscoaching.com

The *Purpose to Impact Roadmap*™ includes the following elements, inspired and validated from my thirty-five-plus years of human development research and practice:

Awareness of your own ways of being and the broader world around you.

Alignment with your true and inconceivable purpose, in all aspects of life.

Agility with your new identity and actions over the stages of your life.

Amplify your impact and influence, to affect your own life and the broader society and planet.

IMAGINE A VERSION OF YOU LIVING INTO YOUR POTENT POWERFUL PURPOSE

Imagine a world where more of us are Living On Purpose. The kind of purpose that's more than a passion or interests, and instead the version of you that you "can't not be."

Purpose is *not* a career or job or product, but an essential part of you that begs to be fully lived each moment of every day.

What if everyone you knew was living according to their own personal unique one-of-a-kind Golden Thread? What if all your friends, family, coworkers and peers, neighbors, the person who delivers your mail or packages, the bus driver, your yoga teacher, the people in your gym or dance studio or biking club, the retail clerks and grocery store checkers, the people in your classes or courses or poker nights or book clubs . . . what if they all knew exactly *why* they are here and had begun to contribute their unique version of purpose? What if even your children were beginning to know why they're here?

Maybe they haven't figured out exactly how to express their purpose fully in the world, but they're moving in the right direction, beginning to see shifts in their lives and excited to finally have meaning and direction. Can you just imagine how that could make a difference? How might we all be together in this journey to make this planet hum?

In case you can't imagine a version of you that's totally and completely Living On Purpose, below I offer a Guided Visualization that may help you to take yourself to a place where you too can make your biggest contribution in this lifetime.

A SHORT VISUALIZATION TO ACCELERATE YOUR HIGHER CALLING

This short visualization will help you begin to imagine who you are when you're living into your highest calling, or your most potent purposeful and powerful life. By imagining this powerful being, you can start to energetically and psychically accelerate your own evolution. In this way, you can begin to have more impact and contribution, and potentially help solve some of the most urgent problems on the planet.

You may be asking: *why do I need a visualization to help me do that?*

If you're like I have been in this lifetime, you may walk around with a mask that says, "I've got it all figured out." I may have looked and played the part because I didn't necessarily want the world to know where I was at any given moment.

We all wear these masks.

But inside, most of us still have fear or doubt, or we stay awake at night worrying about stuff. And we ask ourselves, *Why can't I figure this out?*

Like me, you've probably been to graduate school in the life of hard knocks, and even though you did the work and got your diploma, you still have days when you feel that you're really not cut out for the challenges you're now facing.

And the voices of fear and doubt limit or defeat us—the inner critic, the saboteur, the doubter, the shamer, the hider, the one who has no faith that it can be different . . . you know what I'm talking about.

What are your fears? What are the voices that speak to you?

Just for a few seconds, as you listen to these voices we all have, I want you to think about who you can be from this place. What do you imagine is possible in your life when you're considering all these worries and doubts and fears? Who can you possibly become?

Close your eyes and take a few deep breaths. And, for just ten seconds, imagine what's possible for your life when you're living from these fears.

So, what was that like? What did you think was possible for yourself when coming from this place of living in fear?

Most of us try to manifest our purpose from this place. And when we do, we look one of two ways. We either look like a

- faded, burned-out, overwhelmed, and disillusioned version of self,

or an

- amped-up, efforting, manipulative, and egoistic version of self.

That's how most people in the world imagine their lives, their futures, their possibilities. Their conception is constricted, constrained, and dominated by egoic fears that want to keep them safe and small.

When you're in that place of fear, doubt, and constriction, you'll find it hard to figure out what is *of* you, and what is *not* of you.

And yet, even amid this dilemma, you are so much more than that. You are a powerful being. In fact, you came here to be a magnificent, expanded, heroic Being.

In all truth, we are perfectly designed for being here on the planet, living into our true power and potential, even if the world provides triggers to make us hugely uncomfortable.

So I invite you to join me and begin to imagine what it's like to call in your magnificent, expanded, and heroic Being.

Download the audio here: http://bit.ly/HigherPurposeAudio

Find something more important than you are and dedicate your life to it.

—DANIEL DENNETT

THE SECRET TRUTH OF PURPOSE: FULFILLMENT AND HAPPINESS

We can come up with many compelling reasons to find purpose: improved health and well-being; personal financial success and business optimization; healing personal or collective trauma; the magic of synchronicity and more ease and flow in your life; resolving the crises on the planet at this time of volatile, uncertain, complex, and ambiguous times—to name a few. Each of those would be an adequate reason to justify spending time figuring out our purpose and living into it.

Yet none of those reasons sustain us when we're on the razor's edge of transition into a new identity. These longer-term outcomes won't make us feel seen as we leave behind the uniforms and facade of the home and neighborhood from which we emerged. They won't prepare us as we walk into the demands of our new chosen profession.

Anticipating the longer-term effects of a Life On Purpose won't comfort us as we face the insults hurled by those who expect us to conform. Those reasons won't prepare us for the startlingly bright lights of our new expression, or the darkness behind the curtain that inevitably shows up when the lights go down and our shadow emerges.

Nothing truly prepares us for these potential pitfalls of a Life On Purpose with its new identity and unfamiliar territory. But…

What sustains us is the moment-to-moment inspiration of being fulfilled by living our real life. Of coming home to that which we had lost. Of sharing the most intrinsic part of us that we "can't not do."

It's like shouting the deepest secret that exists into a cosmic Grand Canyon, knowing that the reverberation will create a wave of familiar and comforting vibration and frequency that will beg us to be met by the synchronistic ripples of deep happiness at being ourselves.

The only reason to live a life of purpose, truly, is to become the best self we came to be and to offer our ultimate gift to the planet from that place. And, from that place, we can find fulfillment and happiness.

We seem to have been debating how to create "happiness" as long as time itself. Maria Popova, founder of Brain Pickings, shared a synthesis of the reasons we should attempt to find eudemonia, or an objective flourishing across a lifetime that seems to create happiness and well-being (Popova, 2010). Purpose can help you achieve these things by bringing you home to the deep satisfaction that you are living your best life and launching your greatest contributions into the world.

PURPOSE AS SINCERE COMMITMENT

As I helped my friend Steve see that his Golden Thread was not his career, but some facet of what he most naturally does, he shared a profound truth for most people as they are able to express that which they "can't not do":

"I can take on anything, and have fun doing it! I always have fun when I'm bringing people together and creating common connection."

And Steve does that in a particular way that demonstrates his own nuanced expression of his purpose. It guides our every move, unconsciously or consciously.

And our soul requests a sincere commitment from us to make that greatest contribution. As we begin to experience living on purpose, it generates in us a stick-to-it-ness that will sustain us wherever we are, no matter the stage we're in or the travails we're experiencing.

From his research at Stanford, William Damon (2009) suggests that people exhibit four patterns that determine whether we are able to express our "ultimate concern" or purpose. The Dreamers have aspirations but are not grounded. The Disengaged are primarily seeking enjoyment. The Dabblers jump from interest to interest.

But the Purposeful, because we are intentional and have a sustained commitment to sharing our important gifts with the world, find ways of being resilient in challenging times, which lead to deep joy, fulfillment, and happiness. For the

Purposeful, everything in life serves this instrumental goal. The effort of living purposefully can be sustained over extended periods of time because purpose is the compass that guides us through life.

Finding a life and work we love requires an independence from the opinions of others and typical markers of success. Even Paul Graham, entrepreneur, venture capitalist, and co-founder of the influential startup accelerator and seed capital firm, YCombinator, writes in an open letter to prospective partners (2006) about finding work we love:

"What you should not do, I think, is worry about the opinion of anyone beyond your friends. You shouldn't worry about prestige. Prestige is the opinion of the rest of the world."

The failure rate of startup ventures would likely be reduced, employees would be more engaged, and profits would soar if founders were guided by the seeds of purpose, rather than just revenue projections or exit strategies. Similarly, governments of the world would be more effective if they were oriented to the collective purpose of their people. And what about families, or schools, or NGOs, or any other collective of people?

A sincere commitment to our own purposeful work also means being guided by our own passions. Alain de Boton, founder of London's The School of Life, writes in *The Pleasures and Sorrows of Work* (2010) that:

"We should focus in on our ideas and make sure that we own them, that we're truly the authors of our own ambitions."

Even the late Steve Jobs, founder of Apple, who dropped out of college, was fired from his own company, and eventually found his way back there because of his love for the work, shared in a 2005 commencement address at Stanford:

"If I had never dropped out, I would have never dropped in on this calligraphy class, and personal computers might not have the wonderful typography that they do. Of course, it was impossible to connect the dots looking forward when I was in college. But it was very, very clear looking backwards ten years later. . . . You can't connect the dots looking forward; you can only connect them looking backwards. So you have to trust that the dots will somehow connect in your future. . . . This approach has never let me down, and it has made all the difference in my life.

"Your work is going to fill a large part of your life, and the only way to be truly satisfied is to do what you believe is great work. And the only way to do great work is to love what you do. If you haven't found it yet, keep looking. Don't settle.

Your time is limited, so don't waste it living someone else's life. Don't let the noise of others' opinions drown out your own inner voice. . . . Have the courage to follow your heart and intuition. They somehow already know what you truly want to become."

BECOMING WHO WE REALLY ARE

And so the goal, after all, is primarily about becoming who we really are. Of finding our way to the truth of our existence on this earthly plane.

As depicted by the late Alan Watts (1966):

"We suffer from a hallucination, from a false and distorted sensation of our own existence as living organisms. Most of us have the sensation that 'I myself' is a separate center of feeling and action, living inside and bounded by the physical body—a center which 'confronts' an 'external' world of people and things, making contact through the senses with a universe both alien and strange."

"This feeling of being lonely and very temporary visitors in the universe is in flat contradiction to everything known about man (and all other living organisms) in the sciences. We do not 'come into' this world; we come out of it, as leaves from a tree. As the ocean 'waves,' the universe 'peoples.' Every individual is an expression of the whole realm of nature, a unique action of the total universe."

Watts was very likely speaking from a MetAware perspective and knew that, ultimately, as we evolve into more aware beings, we come to perceive that we are all part of mega-systems that transcend all perceived limits of reality.

ACCOMPLISHING DEVELOPMENTAL
TASKS, EARLY AND CONTINUOUSLY

However, because we are humans, our own purposeful tra-jectory depends on whether we accomplish specific tasks in each stage of life. The practical nature of our task as humans is to be directed and intentional so that we can impact the very real milieu we live in. If we somehow miss or skip steps, we fall into the cracks where the shadow covers the gift of purpose. Often, we get stuck there until we can uncover that which is hidden, which in itself is purposeful. To be the authentic version of us who is capable of offering what is in the "right timing" at the space-time of our existence, we should make an authentic commitment to emerge as best we can, taking strides to explore and inquire into who we really are so we can be driven by the pull of purpose.

THE PRESENT MOMENT
And in each moment lie opportunities to do the best we can, aligned with purpose or not, because this point is where we gain the capacities we need. We don't need to change ourselves—or wait until the future arrives—to live a good life. We can do that in each and every moment, every task, every word.

Who we truly are will arise in each moment more gracefully, more deliberately, if we allow ourselves to be here in the pres-ent moment. A.H. Almaas, founder of the Ridhwan School and the Diamond Heart spiritual approach, speaks about each moment we spend "fixing" ourselves, or disallowing some part of us to be present:

"[W]e become something different than what we are, we leave our place of abiding. In some sense, we abandon our self, our nature, to become this active entity that is always trying to change itself" (Almaas, 2008).

The good life is finding things we love and doing them. At work, home, in leisure time or as a volunteer. Do more of that, until we find the thing we "can't not do." Stand outside ourselves and witness what we love most.

Whether you think you can, or whether you think you can't, you're right.

—HENRY FORD

FOUR GUIDING PRINCIPLES TO FIND YOUR PURPOSE AND DO WHAT MATTERS MOST

Ultimately, here's the question:

How would you live your life if nothing stood in the way of your ultimate fulfillment and your grandest gesture?

Rather than searching for money, fame, prestige, or external rewards, what would you do if money was no object?

You can watch Alan Watts here, in his inimitable cheeky way, https://vimeo.com/63961985. Or he sums it up, in the proverbial nutshell:

"If you say that money is the most important thing, you'll spend your life completely wasting your time. You'll be doing things you don't like doing in order to go on living, that is, in order to go on doing things you don't like doing."

And why on God's green earth would we do that, other than we don't know how to find the thing we "can't not do"?

In my more than thirty-five years of helping hundreds of clients live into their true potential and purpose, and assisting visionaries, entrepreneurs, and innovators in building and scaling their businesses or projects aligned with purpose, I've discovered four principles to guide people into living their purpose. These principles make up your *Purpose to Impact Roadmap*™, the foundation for my work with individuals, groups, and businesses or organizations.

You can download the *Purpose to Impact Roadmap*™ here:

http://bit.ly/PurposeImpactRoadmap

GUIDING PRINCIPLE ONE: AWARENESS

Awareness—of self, of other, of our community of humans and the "more than human world" around us—is by far the most significant, pressing, and compelling precept of our time. If we cannot truly know ourselves and each other, we cannot solve this mess. And, of course, awareness, as I've demonstrated here, requires a maturity of perspective that occurs as we evolve beyond ourselves to come to know the other (and all others).

We must get right to this.

In Texas, where I grew up, when we were contemplating an action, we'd say, "I'm fixin' to..." which means "I'm not ready to do that now, or perhaps ever." We gotta stop "fixin' to" grow up, clean up, and wake up. We gotta do it now.

One means of gaining awareness is to begin a contemplative practice of Mindfulness meditation. Mindfulness moves us beyond the everyday stressors of our lives to something that transcends our current experience. The global Mindfulness movement is creating more awareness of what is present right here and now in our daily lives. Mindfulness creates enhanced:

- self-awareness,
- stress resilience,
- emotional regulation,
- focusing capacity,
- witnessing capacity for thoughts and feelings without judgment,
- mental health outcomes, including depression and anxiety.

Research on Mindfulness-based therapies, interventions, trainings, and programs have produced more than adequate data (American Medical Research Association, 2019) to justify each of us taking on a meditation or Mindfulness practice to deconstruct and reconstruct our narrow view of ourselves. Now. No "fixin' to."

And here's how it works, in simple non-medical terms: Mindfulness is a practice that creates an internal "space" or safe container through which we can witness ourselves, allow our current way of being, and support the next version of us to emerge without repression or judgment. Feelings of "stuckness," anxiety, and the Fear of the Unknown, or FOTU, (Carleton, 2016) appear when we are less than satisfied with where we are. We won't live into purpose if our primary mode of operation is to judge ourselves, in whatever stage we live. Thousands of Mindfulness apps and programs support you in gaining access to this way of being.

And yet Mindfulness is just one aspect of the space-holding container needed for us to evolve as "present and available" for what wants to emerge.

Other practices that facilitate the slowing-down and space we need to be present to who we are and what's emerging include:

- A Gratitude Practice that can change the neurotransmitters in your brain to create an "upward spiral" in your life,
- Brain entrainment practices and tools that can help you develop advanced brainwave state function, exercising your brain much like you exercise your body in a gym,
- Neuropsychological shifts in your neural pathways to help you reframe and re-story your life, and
- Grasping the developmental tasks of your current stage, or the capacities that are needed right where you are, to help you gain depth and breadth in your current evolutionary stage so you can continue to organically evolve.

Increasing your level of awareness and/or the space-holding container will also open you up to receive all the other forms of information or "data" that exist in the larger quantum field (or "unified field"). While they might be called intuition or psychic power (including clairvoyance, clairsentience, clairaudience, etc.), these data are always here for each of us (if only we were open to them) and provide additional insight and guidance to support our purpose discovery process.

GUIDING PRINCIPLE TWO: ALIGNMENT

The second principle is where the rubber meets the road for uncovering and living into your purpose. Alignment consists of three elements. First, you need clarity about who you are, which includes the essence of your purpose. This quality allows you to make your greatest purposeful contribution at this stage of your life (your current expression) to have your biggest impact.

Second, gaining confidence is foundational for who you really are, as opposed to living from who you are not. Over time, you'll learn to witness the patterns that keep you shackled to a status quo life (including the limiting beliefs, fears, doubts, self-judgment, criticism, distractions, bad habits, fractured ego parts, and misguided or sloppy intentions about your life) and to live a life of possibility.

And lastly, you'll learn specifically about your contribution, that which you are meant to do, your primary driver or burning desire. You'll gain a draft of your purpose statement and learn how to live "as if" you are on purpose and in a state of flow, which is a direct expression of being on purpose (though only if you have more clarity and fewer constrictions).

In my work with clients, I use a mix of tools and methodologies for gaining clarity about purpose, including direct methods where we listen to and connect with your soul or essential nature (for example: guided visualizations, active imagination journaling, dream interpretation, wilderness journeys, soul quests).

I also use indirect methods that inquire into how your purpose shows up in the world (for example: feedback systems, story dissection, archetypal analysis) and which are useful for clarifying the expression of your purpose over your lifetime. Quite a few tools are available for each of these tasks—gaining clarity and confidence, and gaining awareness and practice of your greatest contribution.

FINDING CLARITY
Exploring Stories to Find Your Golden Thread
The "stories" we create for ourselves about our lives serve as justifications for what we haven't accomplished or what we haven't yet tried. We retell these stories countless times as a means of hiding from ourselves what lies within, repressed and unbidden. Most of us refuse to live into our purposeful lives, or as Henry David Thoreau noted in *Walden, we are:*

"The mass of men [who] lead lives of quiet desperation" (1854).

Generally, this desperation occurs for two reasons: Conformity and Fear.

CONFORMITY:

We are in a perpetual quest to live like our neighbors—or even worse, the upper-crust or famous—which prevents us from seeking a life beyond what we see or can imagine. As Thoreau writes (1854):

"If a man does not keep pace with his companions, perhaps it is because he hears a different drummer. Let him step to the music which he hears, however measured or far away."

When we do "step to the music" of a drum that's different from that of our families or forebears, we generally find greater happiness and self-fulfillment. And yet, as I described in the collective Conformist stage of the Concrete Tier, the "principles" devised to create order and cohesion also construct rigid boundaries that trap us inside the commonalities of this stage. When we march to the beat of our tribe, we seldom deviate from the road they've traveled.

FEAR:

Moving beyond our given station or stage in life, and all that is known to us there, and into a stage for which we have no reference point other than those around us (who may not be any further ahead) keeps us from doing the work required to grow past our current stage or expression. In fact, Fear of the Unknown (FOTU) is a "fundamental fear":

"The oldest and strongest emotion of mankind is fear, and the oldest and strongest kind of fear is fear of the unknown" (Joshi & Schultz, 2001, referencing early work by HP Lovecraft, 1927).

This recent research suggests that FOTU is, in fact, "fundamental fear" related to anxiety and psychopathology, emotions, and decision-making, and likely to many other disorders, including depression, somatic and eating disorders, and possibly chronic diseases. The significance of this distinction is that:

Fear of the Unknown will be more likely if we don't have a good sense of direction, or GPS, to guide us into our future, and don't have good measuring devices or feedback loops to assess our next steps.

Fear is also produced when we don't have a sense of how our life has been unfolding in the stories of our lives.

Story Maps Yield Puzzle Pieces

One of the most significant means of uncovering our Golden Thread of purpose is to create a "map" of our life history, specifically as seen through the "story" we tell ourselves, or what's been told to us. As you can see from some of the case studies earlier in this book, most of my clients and colleagues had "stories" about their lives, which were usually justification for their own misery or suffering. In fact:

Our stories are the puzzle seeking its pieces.

A retrospective timeline can help to uncover the "missing pieces" to gain insight about what we've been attempting to accomplish in a lifetime. As we dissect the stories, they elicit both elements of the purposeful gifts and the shadowed wounding. I use a simple version of creating a story map or timeline to help you find the puzzle pieces that will provide insight about your Purpose and the wounding that hides it across the different stages of your life. You might review the questions at the end of each chapter in this book to begin to unravel your story map.

Choosing an Expression for Your Purpose

While finding the Golden Thread of your Purpose is a significant step toward Living On Purpose, you'll also begin to explore how you want to best express your purpose in this stage of life. As you read through chapters 3-6, you'll begin to explore where you may "live" in the stages of human development. Notice some of the developmental tasks needed to develop your capacities wherever you are. Remembering that you express your unique purpose in many forms throughout your lifetime as you evolve, and that choosing one key expression now will help you step into and claim your unique and essential way of being in this lifetime. You might review the questions at the end of each chapter to begin to unravel your purposeful expression at this time.

GAINING CONFIDENCE IN WHO YOU ARE
Moving Beyond Your Status Quo

As I discussed throughout this book, to live into your purposeful expression, you must move past the early (or subsequent) wounding of your life to uncover who you really are. It is not possible to access your Soul Purpose (or even an earlier expression of your purpose) if you're trapped by the false and constrained identity that originated in the Conformist structures you grew up in. Anything we call a "purpose" that comes out of your egoic understanding of who you are will likely be uninspired and short-lived.

As background to why we need to do this work—to liberate the wounding, the shadow, and move beyond the status quo—let's review what happens in childhood. Living up to the standards of your family, peer group, or social network may have created pressure to conform in ways that weren't optimal for your own individuation and development. These pressures to conform created a set of limiting beliefs, habits, and distractions that emerged from your childhood context and created a version of you that may not have truly represented who you were (and are). The restrictive conformity of childhood also reinforced the wounding that you likely developed early in childhood and kept you repressed or limited in your full expression.

Therefore, to be yourself fully absolutely requires that you begin to reduce the limiting beliefs, distractions, and roles that may be inhibiting your purposeful expression. You might revisit the earlier chapters and examine what elements of your life may need to be "de-cluttered" by removing the distractions or limitations.

Witness Capacity

Living into your higher expression of purpose also requires that you begin to integrate the repressed elements of your personality or your "sub-psychic parts" that live in the shadows of your personality.

They're called "shadows" because they are parts of you of which you are unaware, not because they are bad or wrong.

These "parts" became fractured elements of your psyche in childhood because they weren't welcome in your childhood context. As long as these "parts" of you that were split and repressed in childhood remain unearthed and lie dormant as shadow, your essence will remain covered up, and your purpose will remain somewhat elusive. Doing the deep work (which doesn't have to be painful if done well!) will liberate your purposeful expression.

Psychic "parts" or inner child work is not new, though it has evolved significantly in the last few years due to the Stages International team of Terri O'Fallon and Kim Barta. Much credit should be given to the initiators of Voice Dialogue methodologies, Hal and Sidra Stone (Voice Dialogue International), and their elucidation of a means to gain access to our inner voices. Recent psychotherapeutic advances have demonstrated that we are able to access several different types of inner voices or "parts," and that distinguishing the "type" is important as we attempt to repair the fractures of childhood.

Kim Barta's work as a psychotherapist in integrating the developmental aspects of the Stages framework into the day-to-day expression of shadow (Barta, Stages International) has led me to understand that the types of "parts" include projections, introjections, and split-ego states. A therapeutic-type interview, both discerning the Stage of Consciousness and the type of split, is needed to gauge the type of repair work or intervention that would best serve the individual desiring wholeness. This work has been profound to create a new story in my own life and in serving my clients. While I do shadow work as a part of my individual coaching and mentoring, it is also part of my group programs.

CLAIMING YOUR CONTRIBUTION

And, of course, determining the specific contribution you are here to make (at least next) is crucial to moving forward into a Life On Purpose. We gain access to an even deeper awareness of the expression of your purpose through exercises designed to elicit the thing you "can't not do" in various settings and create a purpose statement to guide your potential expressions. The specific career or business possibilities emerge from the articulation of your purpose and an awareness of your Golden Thread.

GUIDING PRINCIPLE THREE: AGILITY

When we think of Agility in our personal lives, we think of the quick moves required of graceful dancers on a stage, or basketball players on a court, or even of a parent who juggles several children while balancing coffee and the steering wheel (or at least I remember this type of agility in my own life!). Agility requires physical grace and speed, and mental processing skills that are faster than our typical daily routines. Additionally, agility allows us to respond to numerous swiftly moving pieces and requires us to be "nimble" or flexible.

Agility also allows us to respond uniquely to shifts occurring in our world, the kinds that are typical when our lives and work evolve quickly. As we engage in purposeful pursuits, the need to adapt our actions and identity to the incoming feedback is best approached through an agile and responsive action and mindset.

CREATING AN AGILE PURPOSEFUL EXPRESSION
The Role of Agility

The key to being agile in creating a Life On Purpose is to notice how you may see the world from a fixed and rigid frame or perspective, and then allow things to shift and be fluid and changing. Living a purposeful life is most easily attained by responding emergently to challenges or scenarios as they arise, not holding expectations about what may occur next. If you consider your life and career (or business) to be a series of "pivots," you're more likely to give yourself permission to explore options that really matter to you.

Jenny Blake describes in her book, *Pivot: The Only Move That Matters Is Your Next One* (2016), that:

"the fears that ride in on the coattails of an invigorating vision are a good sign. They signal that you are approaching something meaty enough to challenge you, and that you are squarely in your stretch zone."

This situation would be the case if you're deciding on a new relationship, different career direction, or making a strategic decision related to execution of a new business or product. Being agile enough to respond to new circumstances allows you to take advantage of synchronistic circumstances when they arise, rather than stepping back from opportunity because it's different than you anticipated. Blake describes "impacters" as people who respond with agility by seeking continuous "momentum and expansion," by first turning to their inward desire for growth, then seeking problems they can tackle.

The evolution of innovative entrepreneurialism itself has instilled the notion of agility into every square inch of guidance for business startups. The wildly viral "agile" and "lean" startup culture in the technology industry (Ries, 2011; Furr & Ahlstrom, 2011; Olsen, 2015; Harnish, 2014) spawned a decade of business culture and operational innovation that bled into most other industries. The extent of the sweep into corporate culture has allowed the business environment in general to become nimbler and more responsive to changing feedback and data inputs and customer demand, shrinking the gaps between consumer needs and product responsiveness.

However, despite the shift into corporate culture, most of us are still reluctant to approach our lives with the agility required to respond to life's changing circumstances. Just as a sailor must navigate across the open water by continuously assessing the wind speed and direction and trim the sails to take advantage of the wind, we must also evaluate the scenarios we face to "trim the sails" of our shifting circumstances.

Each time we sense the wind shifting direction, we must take small, bold steps to respond swiftly and decisively, and then shift again when the time calls for it. Sailors wear heavy gloves for a reason: because the shifting winds require lots of "hauling" of lines to change directions. Our ability to respond with agility also requires us to have mechanisms in place to both monitor and discern the shifting weather systems, but also a mindset that can withstand those shifting patterns and create resilience to get to the next calm weather pattern.

Each of these types of "pivots" creates for us a new identity, a new story, a healthier individuation of our more expressed selves, and allows us to live into that Life on Purpose.

A POSSIBILITY MINDSET FINE-TUNES OUR NAVIGATION SYSTEM
Using a Possibility Mindset™ to Reframe & Re-Story

As we've come to know that "thoughts become things" in our everyday lives, based on science of energetic potential and resonance, we must reframe our beliefs and re-story our lives and work so that we can remove the blockages and chart a new course to navigate our lives.

I use many methods to create a Possibility Mindset™ to liberate my clients from their constraints, including energy medicine, neurolinguistic and other mindset methods, brain entrainment, heart coherence, visualizations, reframing, re-story-ing, and other just-in-time capacity-building activities for human development. This new mindset creates an opening to allow you to live into what you "can't not do."

Creativity Supports Purposeful Expression

Are you familiar with the term BHAG? It refers to a Big Hairy Audacious Goal, defined as a single medium- to long-term goal that is audacious, likely to be externally questionable, but not internally regarded as impossible.

Living On Purpose requires you to imagine possibility and opportunity. Living On Purpose requires letting go of the "limits" or preconceived notions of who you are, what's "right" or "wrong," and any beliefs about yourself and your capacity to Live On Purpose. And to some extent, that's pretty audacious, right? To imagine that you can "let go" of all (or much) of who you've been, to live into something that others may question, if not believe to be impossible. But you know that it's possible, because it comes from your inner core, the deepest place in you, where you are at home within yourself.

So Living On Purpose is like a BHAG. It's not going to settle well with the Joneses. Or perhaps your parents. Or the braggart friends from high school. Or maybe your typical companions that might include buddies or sisters from whatever clubs or groups you belong to.

We have to get past the stories we tell ourselves about how the world works and about our lives. These stories, or "heuristic narratives," that we create are based in the preset patterns of thinking from our childhood synaptic circuit (brain) connections, and they generally limit the way we can generate new ideas or innovate. Our stories create a status quo bias.

While these narratives are useful for being efficient in the world (think about how challenging life would be if you had to relearn to use a fork everyday), they also limit the possibility of new ways of thinking or acting in our lives. Our stories are the nemesis of BHAGs. A leap of creative imagination, and letting go of beliefs and assumptions, is required to allow an inconceivable vision for your life.

Letting go requires you to reconfigure your brain's shortcuts—nothing short of opening your mind and turning off everything you believe to be true. The goal is to play, produce wild and random ideas, and stop worrying about doing it "right." Letting go cancels the heuristic narratives and status quo biases by encouraging you to make mind-bending associations and consider problems or opportunities in a fresh way.

I use many methods to help people develop their BHAGs in our work together, including practices like those in the book *Think Wrong* (Bielenberg et al., 2016) or *Let Me Out* (Himmelman, 2016.) Other methods to learn to "let go" include: taking an improv class of any kind, playing with children of any age, playing childlike games with your friends, visiting "typical" childhood haunts—such as playgrounds, amusement parks, the circus, story time at the library (yes, seriously) —and spending time in nature with no predetermined outcome (because hiking to the top of a mountain won't cut it!). Think out of the box about how you can invite your childlike nature back into your life!

PROFITING FROM THE ARTICULATION OF PURPOSE
We can only profit from knowing our purpose if we have the ability to navigate successfully in living it in as many moments of our lives as possible. Profit includes not only financial abundance, but also the reciprocal exchange systems of the natural, material, Subtle (and later Universal) worlds. Knowing and sustaining the delivery of your purpose requires tuning into feedback systems, planning experiments, and learning the persistence required to make routine pivots.

Using Feedback to Align Your Purpose in the World around You
In every area of our lives, we experience feedback loops that provide data about "what's working" or not. Many of these

feedback loops we barely notice as they govern our lives (e.g., traffic lights tell us when to stop or go; pangs of hunger tell us when to eat). Other systems of feedback are unconscious to us, as we have a Subtle or unconscious experience of them (e.g., recoiling from someone's hostile energy, avoiding areas of your town that feel unsafe). As our lives become more complex, we have more refined and unconscious metrics to guide us.

In our journey to become more purposeful and intentional, we can choose to make conscious those feedback systems that automatically generate data but which we may not heed. If our purpose serves as a GPS, then we can use our built-in guidance systems to navigate our future and limit the amount of Fear of the Unknown (Carleton, 2016) that we know is our greatest angst and source of "stuckness."

These feedback loops can also be developed and honed through attention and practice.

Much like the principles of Action Inquiry that guided early organizational development work (Argyris, 1990; Torbert, 2004), we each can establish methods for collecting and using data to refine our personal actions and organizational behaviors. I routinely mentor clients and businesses to establish feedback loops that take advantage of not only concrete world metrics, but also the inherent somatic, emotional, intuitive, energetic, and psychic feedback systems that can guide us if we're listening.

Being in Flow with Your Purpose

Your soul begs you to live "as if" you are already living a life of coherence with the most potentiated or expressed version of you, even if you do not know what that is. Sometimes we have a "sniff" of who we are and can then imagine some version of us beyond our everyday reality. To be in alignment requires us to "be" in alignment, which is some version of "flow" in an everyday state, not just in a sitting meditation or other contemplative practice.

When we create "flow" from a non-aligned place, it's less oriented to support us in living into our highest potential. If you only ever create flow from specific activities or practices, but don't begin to integrate that into an aligned life, it won't have the same kind of impact as imagining that you are living " as if" you are in alignment and in flow. My work with clients taps into the natural flow state derived from living into your deepest essence, like the natural "slipstream" effect discussed earlier.

GUIDING PRINCIPLE FOUR: AMPLIFY

The first three steps, or Guiding Principles, to uncover and live into your purpose create a solid foundation for a life of increased focus and direction, fulfillment and meaning, joy and abundance, greater contribution and bigger impact. A greater level of AWARENESS allows you to see the world from a calmer, neurologically and emotionally regulated place. This calmness lets you be in life without reacting to life circumstances with stress and anxiety. It creates a spacious container, which then generates the potential for you to imagine possibility from a wider perspective.

Finding Clarity, Building Confidence, and Defining Your Contribution allow you to live from an ALIGNMENT with the deep core of who you are: your inner wisdom, insight, and internal compass that represent your purpose or essence. Deconstructing the stories of your identity and embracing the feedback you get from your everyday milieu can allow you to be open to some new version of you. This Alignment then is the Golden Thread around which you develop your purposeful expression, gain a Possibility Mindset and begin to profit internally and externally as you take the small bold steps to respond with AGILITY.

Once these foundational steps for living into purpose are solid, your purpose begins to AMPLIFY almost of its own accord through a series of small, then growing, synchronistic events. These occurrences may seem like magic at first, as people appear out of nowhere to contribute solutions to your everyday dilemmas, or to connect you with someone who knows just the right someone who has an important piece to your puzzle. Time and space almost seem nonexistent when you get to this stage. As these forms of synchronicity begin to happen, the time has definitely come to claim your purpose, because you've found your current expression as magically as one can find it.

BEING INSPIRED TO CLAIM YOUR PURPOSE

The inspiration that emerges from the amplification of purpose doesn't mean that you get to sit back and watch it happen, but quite the opposite. When you begin to experience that your purpose has come "alive" in most vectors of your life, you have to claim your purpose through a statement or manifesto that will announce to others what you're about, and you should invite people in to work with you who resonate with your own purpose.

For instance, my own purpose of "I speak powerful truths to shine love onto shadow, to liberate soul's potential and reunite love and power" very clearly outlines that anyone who works with me will likely have a catalytic and transformative experience, reveal their shadow (both the hidden gift *and* wounding), release their inhibitions to living their purpose fully, and feel more powerful and in love with their life.

I often say Buyer Beware: if you're not ready to move into a more advanced version of yourself, where you can liberate the parts of you that have kept you stuck, best to avoid being in my presence! In fact, when you begin to claim your purpose loudly and with sincerity, people have difficulty not being affected by your very presence! You too can have the same magnetic and catalytic effect on others, when you are Living On Purpose fully.

So while you may not be ready to claim your purpose fully yet, or to create a Manifesto about who you are and what you're ready to contribute to the world, you'll be ready to imagine and re-envision who you can be in the next—or the next few—expression(s) of you in the world.

And just because I love this Manifesto so much, I'm also including the Holstee Manifesto here: https://www.holstee. com/pages/manifesto.

INFLUENCE INSPIRED BY AND DERIVED FROM PURPOSE

As you make your way into a more purposeful expression, you will also be amazed at the amount of influence that you begin to have and are inspired to both receive and give to others. New support systems will emerge, new partners and collaborative networks will form (depending on the stage that you're in), and you will begin to broadcast your purpose, anchored in your inconceivable vision, and speak with influence "as if" you are already living from that place.

From this place, whether you are in alignment and integrity with your true purpose becomes obvious. You will notice when you are in the world in integrity, and when you are not speaking or living from a place of sincerity. And you will also begin to notice others are or aren't in alignment, as the Golden Thread of purpose is a pure and sincere impulse that cannot be mistaken for efforting or faking it.

INSPIRED IMPACT ORIGINATES FROM PURPOSE
Careers, Businesses, and Systems:
Expressing Purpose Now
And, of course, we have to move into implementation and execution to bring our purposeful vision into the world. Through this work you may decide that you want to more fully Live On Purpose through any of the following:

- Reorienting your existing job or career,
- Finding a new job or career,
- Expressing your purpose in a relationship,
- Starting a new project to express your purpose,
- Taking on a volunteer role to express your purpose,

- Launching a new business,
- Creating a new product in an existing business, and/or
- Scaling an existing business.

The options for expressing your purpose are endless and can be accomplished in myriad ways by following some of the principles here and stepping one foot at a time into your purposeful future!

Because you've taken the time before now to become aligned with your purpose,

The potential frustration and anxiety that come from not having direction or focus are alleviated by your intrinsic awareness of who you are and who you intend to be.

Decisions such as job, career, product, and business become much easier as you pivot, step by step, into your new future, or reorient your new way of being to your existing life.

Sometimes a decision to stay in all of your current life scenarios is the most optimal, as you've done a great job setting up systems that work for your purpose. If you are lucky enough to have that scenario, refine your current life plans and ensure that you are gifting yourself with your purpose, and that is fully expressed within every facet of your life.

In my work with clients and groups, we take the time to orient fully to your purpose at each step of the way so you can experiment, try on for size, and pivot into various options for expressing purpose in your life and work. No right or wrong way to experiment here exists, and some tried-and-true tools can assist you in re-envisioning your life.

Purposeful Product Development or Career Redesign

Many of my clients find me as they're surveying their many career successes and capacities and wondering how to "tie it all together." Purpose work is practical and ideal for these scenarios—as for these people, their soul has been pulling them along but they haven't found the Golden Thread that ties it together.

In these cases, identifying the thread and arriving at a career or product to create emerges as we gain clarity about purpose, identify the existing capacities in alignment with the purpose, and explore the market needs related to purpose and capacity. In all cases, I support people to Live On Purpose in ways that are financially realistic and sustainable, and which call upon their greatest gifts. And really, we don't see final expressions of purpose, as it unfolds over time into more and more nuanced expression.

Business Development: Building and Scaling Products and Systems

If building a product or business is the desired outcome for a Life On Purpose, all systems and infrastructure of the business should emerge from (or be re-engineered with) the purpose and vision of the founder and the company's teams. I have worked as a consultant and intrapreneur for many businesses and organizations, helping build systems to calibrate with the organization's purpose.

A true systems alignment must originate with the founder's purpose, be translated into vision, then wend its way into the leadership team, product development, branding and marketing, divisional alliance, and all other systems (e.g., financial, distribution, people/HR, R&D). I have numerous systems and products to aid a founder, business, or organization (or community or network) with this type of Purpose and Vision Alignment process.

Support Systems for Living on Purpose

You'll likely encounter some bumps along the road as you begin Living On Purpose. Having a support system for your purposeful life will create accountability, tactical support, and consistent encouragement and inspiration for moving through the challenges and celebrating your successes. A support system might include family, friends, or colleagues who encourage you to remain inspired or to tackle the internal challenges on your journey into Living On Purpose (and you may even convince them to join you on the journey!). A peer group like a Mastermind may provide you practical advice, engage you in strategic decision-making, or bring friendly business experience to support you. In your community, you may find like-minded networks, meetups, or business groups in which people are inspired to live their own purposeful journeys alongside you. Having friends, colleagues, and supporters on this intentional journey into our most meaningful life really helps!

RESOURCES

You can download the *Purpose to Impact Roadmap*™:

http://bit.ly/PurposeImpactRoadmap

Explore and learn more about my coaching/mentoring and consulting work, in addition to gaining access to courses, group programs, workshops and speaking opportunities:

http://hollywoodscoaching.com

In collaboration with the Global Purpose Leaders, I have created a list of resources for facilitating moving into a life with greater alignment.

http://bit.ly/PurposeResources

CONCLUSION

This chapter outlined the foundational reasons why you need to find your Golden Thread of Purpose. In becoming who you really are, you come home to yourself and make a sincere commitment to live a life of truth. In doing so, you also unlock the secrets to living into your greatest joys and happiness, and potentially your boldest impact in the world.

REFERENCES

Almaas, A.H. (2008). The unfolding now: Realizing your true nature through the practice of presence. Boston: Shambhala Publications.

Argyris, C. 1990. Overcoming organizational defenses: Facilitating organizational learning. Englewood Cliffs, NJ: Prentice-Hall.

Barta, K. Stages International.https://www.stagesinternational.com/shadow-patterns/

Bielenberg, J., Burn, M., Galle, G., & Evitts Dickinson, E. (2016). Think wrong: How to conquer the status quo and do work that matters. San Francisco: Instigator Press.

Blake, J. 2016. Pivot: The only move that matters is your next one. Great Britain: Random House.

Carleton, N. 2016. Fear of the unknown: One fear to rule them all? Journal of Anxiety Disorders Volume 41, June 2016, Pages 5-21.

Damon, W. (2009) Path to Purpose: How young people find their calling in life. Free Press; Reprint edition (April 7, 2009)

De Boton, A. 2010. The pleasures and sorrows of work. Vintage International.

Graham, P. (2006) Finding work you love. http://www.paulgraham.com/love.html

Harnish, V, 2014. Scaling up: How a few companies make it... and why the rest don't. Gazelles, Inc.

Himmelman, P. (2016). Let me out: Unlock your creative mind and bring your ideas to life. New York: TarcherPerigee.

Jobs, S. (2005). Stanford Report, June 14, 2005. Commencement address at Stanford.

Joshi, S.T., & Schultz, D.E. (2001). H.P. Lovecraft encyclopedia. Westport, CT: Greenwood Press.

Furr, N., & Ahlstrom, P. (2011). Nail it then scale it: The entrepreneur's guide to creating and managing breakthrough innovation. Lexington, KY.

Olsen, D. (2015). The lean product playbook: How to innovate with minimum viable products and rapid customer feedback. Hoboken, NJ: John Wiley & Sons.

Popova, M. (2010). Brain Picking. https://www.brainpickings.org/2010/12/01/tedify-happiness/

Ries, E. (2011). The lean startup: How today's entrepreneurs use continuous innovation to create radically successful businesses. New York: Crown Business.

Stone, H. & Stone, S. https://voicedialogueinternational.com/index.html

Thoreau, H.D. (1854). Walden and Civil Disobedience. Boston: Ticknor and Fields.

Torbert, B. (2004). Action inquiry: The secret of timely and transforming leadership. San Francisco: Berrett-Koehler Publishers.

Watts, A. (1966). The book: On the taboo against knowing who you are. New York; Vintage Books.

Watts, A. What would you do if money was no object? https://vimeo.com/63961985.

HOLLY'S STORY & PURPOSE STATEMENT

When I hear people talking about their "dark night" of the soul, I laugh (and cry). I think, *How did they get so lucky to have just one?* I don't know many people who've experienced as much trauma as I have, though I also realize I've lived in an affluent part of the world and have had relative creature comforts compared to many. But for much of my life, I wished I'd been born into a different life than the one I chose.

It dawned on me at some point how lucky I've been, really, to have had so much to combat, or survive. That's a hard truth to stomach for most, and I hope to explain my thoughts through a few short stories.

After my older sister committed suicide, my grief was profound. But mostly I was grateful. You can imagine most of my friends and family were astonished, wondering what in the hell was I thinking: "You just lost a sister; how can you be grateful?"

But her passing was a total wakeup call to me. I'd been depressed and suicidal on and off for thirty-something years and I didn't know if I'd ever kick it. My sister's alcoholism and inability to cope with the repercussions of our childhood abuse were the end of the line for her. After some fairly traumatizing decisions that lost her custody of her own daughter, she'd had enough. She was done. And I could certainly resonate with that feeling. I'd reached that exclamation point at other times, and while I was significantly more stable than in other parts of my life, I still felt some iffy-ness about how it was going to turn out.

At some point, I realized that the time had come to either call it quits or to activate and amplify what I came to do. And, as I'd chosen in many other points in my life, I chose the latter, catalyzed by my sister's death.

I've come to know, through my own life, through my parenting and other significant relationships, and in my nearly forty years of working as a practitioner and a scientist in the field of developing human potential, that:

The key to Living on Purpose is to look squarely in the face of your greatest sorrows and greatest joys, find the connection between them over time, and understand that they are flip sides of the same coin. Joy is the expression of light; sorrow is the expression of the dark. Neither are right or wrong, and both illuminate who you really are.

As one who "speaks powerful truths to shine love onto shadow in order to liberate soul's potential and reunite love and power" (my purpose statement), you'd imagine that I've had to overcome a lot of stuff to be resilient, courageous, and skilled enough to live into that purpose gracefully and have impact. In hindsight, I see that my marching orders were cut out for me, and the life I chose would produce a great end result, if I could just survive it.

I believe that I came "awake." Much as a Bodhisattva devotes their life to supporting others, I came back to help us find our way to the next stage of humanity, which is in fact an updated purpose statement. Except I had to figure out how to do that for myself first. I chose a helluva training program to figure it out. I'm delighted to say that I've (mostly) found my way home again. I always have another layer of the onion to peel, and I've gotten down to the juicy core.

I experienced many, many wrong turns, foiled attempts, setbacks, and failures. More than most. Shame was a foundational fissure in my core for a while, keeping me from being grounded and glad to be human. But in each of those wrong turns I learned a lesson, gained new skills and tools, and picked myself up again. I'm proud to say I'm strangely resilient, vulnerable, and delighted to still be here.

Those multiple iterations of traumas in my life, and even the multiple "dark nights," created efficiencies in recovering from each catastrophe or trauma.

When your tire gets flat a lot, you learn to fix it quickly (and to avoid the nails in the road).

In childhood, I broke a lot of bones in my right arm; as a result, I learned to write left-handed. I spent a lot of my childhood and teen years alone, being different than most kids my age; in that time, I not only absorbed more knowledge and insight but also refined my internal navigation system. Grace exists in every curse.

As a child, my soul spoke to me. I knew I was here to do important things. And that voice kept calling, year after year. Each time I'd get settled into something, I'd hear another call and realize it was time to move to the next thing: job, career, geographic location, relationship. After twenty-one careers and thirty residential moves since age eighteen, I do hope that I'm nearing a slower pace.

After the first purpose-oriented book I read in my thirties (Gregg Levoy, *Callings*, 1997), just after I'd started my doctorate, my adulthood became both more focused and evolving. I learned how to listen to my soul. The clarity and invitation to heed the calling was so profound that I switched the direction of my doctorate and my existing research career to focus on what mattered most to me. I was pregnant with my second child, well into my doctoral program focusing on health and human behavior, and working as an evaluation officer at a Colorado foundation focused on statewide health issues. I realized that a) I didn't have a clue how to raise the child growing in my belly, and b) I wanted to learn more about how people develop over time to reduce my own suffering—and that of those around me.

Before that, I thought I knew where I was headed. The road had been long, but I was on a good, solid career track with a stable family life, something I'd never had until then. As I picked up the gauntlet and decided to make the changes suggested by Gregg's *Callings* book, some of my preconceived notions about "how life should be" began to unravel. I ventured into a new job as a research scientist for a statewide study on youth development, refocused my doctoral studies in human development, and found a new home with my family, closer to support systems. These changes all should have portended an easier life, not harder.

But very quickly, I watched the knots of my personality unwind in these systems, and I could no longer sit back and watch life happen to me. I became very vocal in every area of my life, asking (or demanding) for things that I'd never stood up for before. From my mother's notes in my baby book where she writes in eloquent cursive about me at age eighteen months: "Holly is quite grown up she thinks, and will get right in with older children. She is still a most cuddly little thing, but has really developed a mind of her own"—it seems I had a strong will as a child. But since then, I'd mostly gone along with or accommodated every other situation in my life. I was beginning to stand up for what I wanted and needed, but my approach was very messy and unproductive. Both the job and the marriage ended, and I was left questioning why following your own path had to be so hard.

In hindsight, I see that this situation was a delayed individuation that didn't go well in my childhood (my mother very quickly repressed that "mind of my own" with abusive patterns). It also should've happened in my teens but didn't because the repression had entrained my desire to please others above myself. But deciding that I would follow my own dreams certainly did "loosen the constrictions" of my outwardly "tidy" life.

In my forties, after completing my doctorate and undertaking about three decades of therapy and a long haul of personal and spiritual development work, I became fairly adept at listening to the whispers of my soul. Each year would bring more stability, more loosening, more liberation. When I finally was able to hear my soul whisper its purpose to me, I realized I'd been living it all along but had not been able to fully hear it (or actualize it) because of the "dark side of the coin" shutting down the light. My non-integrated, fractured, and wounded parts from childhood had kept me living a default life, so common in the cultures of our developed world. The wounding, or lack of adequate individuation and integration, had kept me from hearing the powerful truths that were my own to share.

As I looked back over my lifeline, I realized that several aspects of my purpose had been poking through all along, both the shiny and not-so-shiny parts of me. For the sake of transparency and to explicate how this works, I'll share some brief stories and examples of how the light/dark aspects of purpose were evident in my life's story.

My purpose statement, "speak powerful truths to shine love onto shadow in order to liberate soul's potential and reunite love and power," was a hefty order for a baby who came in with a loving disposition and was "laughing out loud" at three months. Fortunately, I've kept the laughter. I've learned to shine love rather than judgment onto shadow. And my power now holds mostly love. But it wasn't always that way.

SPEAK POWERFUL TRUTHS

As noted, I was an extremely headstrong and vocal child to a young and frazzled mother who had little sense of parenting. Because of her undiagnosed mental illness, she was often out of control and abusive. As a middle child, I became the calm and deliberate voice that would attempt to remedy horrific situations (when I wasn't hiding from the abuse). I learned how to mediate to "fix" things, which later translated into a career as a professional mediator and an end to an irreparable marriage.

I stood up for the less fortunate as a child: those who didn't have friends or didn't belong because they needed a voice, and I had one. I became a social justice and political activist as a young adult and like to think I was a model for both my children who became activists. I became a powerful voice for those whose voices needed to be heard and also learned to speak truths that people needed to hear. This virtue has been significant in my work with clients and in my own life to help people see themselves as they are, rather than just what they can see of themselves. This shadow work is a significant part of my own purpose methodology.

But it wasn't always pretty. As I was learning to use my voice in adolescence and adulthood from a traumatized place, I engaged in more talking than listening, and my truths were narrow perspectives formed from the hyperalert state of my childhood trauma response. This approach created more conflict than was necessary, and I seldom felt seen or heard even when I was. For much of my young adulthood, I kept hitting my head against the wall until I learned new trauma recovery and communication techniques and tools to heal myself and be a more powerful truthteller.

SHINE LOVE ONTO SHADOW

I recall as a young girl being called "little angel" routinely, as people received my true nature of unconditional love from very early on. I was very affectionate and well-loved by my larger community, which included extended family and a large church body. I was a very happy child—often giggling and laughing—who loved nature and animals and trees and anything sweet. I have always loved people easily and deeply, seeing the potential in everyone, at times to my own detriment. Over time, I learned to share love more easily, without fear for my own safety, though this matter is still a fine line I walk. And while I see the potential in every soul, I also see the shadow easily and quickly and can access the origin and essential gift of the pattern to support people moving into a higher level of integration.

And the challenge in this facet of my purpose (mostly in the past) has been in illuminating shadow in less than productive ways, where the sentiment is hard for the other to hear, or my words create a sense of rejection because they come from a place of judgment. I am an Enneatype 1, the Perfectionist, and I organically see the "gaps" in life, a quality that appears as judgment. This pattern kept my life "churning," moving in and out of relationships, because of this default tendency.

LIBERATE SOUL'S POTENTIAL

The third facet of my purpose statement is the core element that drives me to support people in finding purpose. My soul wants your soul to be free from the constraints, so that you can live into your potential, much as I have and continue to do. No end exists to the journey for how this feat occurs, and I am always the tour guide to help my clients (and my blessed children and various friends and partners!) unwrap the next version of themselves.

Coming into this part of my purpose required me to overcome my repressed sense of self, created in childhood, so that I could gain a more accurate sense of who I was—my identity. This level of individuation occurred at many points in life, but inadequately in my childhood, therefore requiring me to integrate my fractured parts left behind in childhood. And, as I've demonstrated here, our identity continually changes.

My soul was always calling me into its next version of me to liberate some new potential that I had yet to express. I've also come to see that each stage of life is a new, more subtle form of individuation, stretching from the earlier identity into a new version of us. Having accomplished these tasks for myself (and always on the path for the next level), I learned many modalities, skills, and capacities that I bring to my work with clients and companies.

And, as you can imagine from this continual self-assessment and process of evolving, at times my life has felt like a treadmill, requiring me to heal just one more thing or clear one more trauma or attempt to overcome one last limiting belief.

Perhaps, I had more karma than most to liberate, or you could imagine that under other circumstances people like me wouldn't have survived (as my sister didn't) or would've lived with much less meaning or joy.

This constant churning of my own life kept me in a pattern of assuming that others had the same challenges or need to "overcome" their own lives, while this thought was just a projection I was making from my own experience. I no longer have that expectation; I accept that we're all on the perfect journey wherever we are, allow people to speak their own desires to achieve liberation (or not), and support whatever part of the healing or emancipation journey they're ready for.

REUNITE LOVE AND POWER

This element of my purpose surely brings me the most joy (and laughter). When I am on my game, aligned and in flow, people can hear my powerful laughter and excitement for life across a very large room. Most days now I'm so delighted to be alive and free from the burden of my own life (and also free from perceiving that all of life itself is a burden) that my joy is infectious.

Learning to love and appreciate myself, because of and despite my boatload of mistakes and faults, and to forgive all those ways that I may have harmed others in this lifetime, I am able to have deep compassion and commitment to others attempting to become their best version of human. And, having integrated so many fractured and disparate parts in my life brought in the powerful energy of those formerly dissociated parts of me, I feel almost superhuman, able to move things forward easily, decisively, and with loads of enthusiasm. I call this "True Power"—when the impulse of your purpose drives your every cellular and subtle response and all wind seems to be behind your back as you are driven by the alignment of purpose.

I am still coming to terms with the actual power of my purpose, and the need to genuinely tend it as a gift and to support it responsibly so that it (and I) may come into the fullest fruits of expression.

The shadow of this facet of my purpose has been in wrongly using either love or power to influence, manipulate, or seek willful power. While I was unconscious to how any of these dynamics played out, over time and looking back, I came to see how my unique ability to love deeply and use power were not always in integrity. This, perhaps, has been among my greatest sorrows in life: to witness the ways in which the sacred gift of my purpose may have been misused or genuinely expressed fruitfully.

IN SUM

I do feel to be among the most blessed humans on planet Earth. I have been given so many opportunities to liberate my own soul and purpose in this lifetime, with so many resources available to me to learn and grow just how to do this. I am pressed to imagine that I would ever have chosen another life that would not have had so many blessings bestowed upon me.

APPENDIX B

REFERENCES

—

Introduction

Baumeister, R.F. & Vohs, K.D. (2001). The pursuit of meaningful-ness in life. In Snyder, C.R. and Lopez, S.J. (Eds), Handbook of positive psychology, 608-618. New York: Oxford University Press.

Dispenza, J. (2019). Becoming Supernatural: How Common People are Doing the Uncommon. How common people are doing the uncommon. Carlsbad, CA: Hay House.

Encyclopedia of World Biography. Oprah Winfrey biography, accessed September 5, 2019, https://www.notablebiographies. com/We-Z/Winfrey-Oprah.html).

Frankl, V.E. (2006). Man's Search for Meaning. Boston: Beacon Press.

Keyes, C.L.M. (2011). Authentic purpose: The spiritual infrastruc-ture of life. Journal of Management, Spirituality & Religion, 8 (4): 281–297.

Levit, A. and Licina, S. (2011). "How the Recession Shaped Millen-nial and HIring Manager Attitudes about Millennials' Future Careers." Commissioned by the Career Advisory Board: DeVry University. Accessed on October 10, 2019 http://www.careeradvisoryboard.org/public/uploads/2011/10/Future-of-Millennial-Careers-Report.pdf

Maddi, S.R. (1970). The Search for Meaning, in M. Page (Ed), The search for meaning. Nebraska symposium on motivation, 137-186. Lincoln, NE: University of Nebraska Press.

Maslow, A. (1947). A theory of human motivation. Psychological Review 50(4): 370-396.

Meade, M. (2010). Fate and destiny: The two agreements of the soul. Housatonic, MA: Greenfire Press.

Net Impact. (2012). Talent report: What workers want in 2012. Accessed on October 11, 2019 www.netimpact.org/whatworkerswant.

Park, N., Park, M., and Peterson, C. (2010). When is the search for meaning related to life satisfaction?" Applied Psychology: Health and Well-Being, 2(1):1-13.

Rainey, L. (2014). The search for purpose in life: An exploration of Purpose, the search process, and purpose anxiety. Master's thesis Philadelphia: University of Pennsylvania. http://repository.upenn.edu/mapp_capstone/60

Seligman, M.E.P. (2011). Flourish: A visionary new understanding of Happiness and well-being. Miami: Atria Paperback.

Swanson, C. The torsion field and the aura. Subtle Energies & Energy Medicine 19(3): 43. http://journals.sfu.ca/seemj/index.php/seemj/article/view/425

Winfrey, O. (2019). The path made clear: Discovering your life's direction and purpose. New York: Flatiron Books.

Chapter 1

Hill, P.L., Burrow, A.L., & Sumner, R. (2016). Sense of Purpose and Parent-Child Relationships in Emerging Adulthood. Emerging Adulthood: 4(6). Accessed December 10, 2019 https://doi.org/10.1177/2167696816640134.

Jacoby, J. (1942). The psychology of C.G. Jung: An introduction with illustration. Abingdon-on-Thames, U.K.: Routledge and Kegan Paul Publishers.

Kelley, Tim. (2013). Personal communication.

Kelly, Tim. (2009). True purpose: 12 strategies for discovering the difference you are meant to make. Berkeley: Transcendent Solutions Press.

Kins, E., Byers, W., and Soenens, B. (2012). When the separation-individuation process goes awry: Distinguishing between functional dependence and dysfunctional independence. International Journal of Behavioral Development. 37(1):1-12. DOI: 10.1177/0165025412454027v.

Mahler, M.S., Pine, F., & Bergman, A. (2008). The psychological birth of the human infant: Symbiosis and individuation. New York: Basic Books.

Muehsam, D. & Ventura, C. (2014). Life rhythms as a series of oscillatory patterns: Electromagnetic energy and sound vibration modules gene expression for biological signaling and healing. Global Advances in Health Medicine, 3(2): 40–55.

Peele, Brandon. (2018). Planet on purpose: Your guide to genuine prosperity, authentic leadership and a better world. Balboa Press, 2018.

Ross, C.L. (2019). Energy medicine: Current status and future perspectives. Global Advances in Health and Medicine. 8: 2164956119831221. doi: 10.1177/2164956119831221

Steele, C. (2017). Psychological interventions for working with trauma and distressing voices: The future is in the past. Frontiers in Psychology, 7: 2035. Accessed on November 10, 2019 doi: 10.3389/fpsyg.2016.02035.

Chapter 2

Animas Valley Institute. https://animas.org.

BetterUp. (2018). Meaning and purpose at work. San Francisco, CA: BetterUp.

Boye, P., Buchman, R., Wilson, R., Yu, L., Schneider, J., and Benett D. (2012). Effect of purpose in life on the relation between Alzheimer Disease pathologic changes on cognitive function in advanced age. Archives of General Psychiatry, 69(5): 499-506.

Brown, W. (2019). Unified physics and the entanglement nexus of awareness. NeuroQuantology, 17(7): 40-52.

Burrow, A., & Spreng, R. (2016). Waiting with purpose: A reliable but small association between purpose in life and impulsivity. Personality And Individual Differences, 90, 187-189. doi: 10.1016/j.

Collins, J., Porras, J. (1994). Built to last: Successful habits of visionary companies. Harper Business.

Crosby, D. (2016). The laws of wealth: Psychology and the secret to investing. Harriman House.

Deloitte. (2013). Culture of purpose: A business imperative. 2013 core beliefs & culture survey. https://www2.deloitte.com/content/dam/Deloitte/us/Documents/about-deloitte/us-leadership-2013-core-beliefs-culture-survey-051613.pdf.

Deloitte. (2014). Culture of purpose- building business confidence; driving growth. 2014 core beliefs & culture survey. https://www2.deloitte.com/content/dam/Deloitte/us/Documents/about-deloitte/us-leadership-2014-core-beliefs-culture-survey-040414.pdf.

Ernst & Young, (2016). The business case for purpose. Harvard Business Review. https://www.ey.com/Publication/vwLUAssets/ey-the-business-case-for-purpose/$FILE/ey-the-business-case-for-purpose.pdf.

Fredrickson, B.L., Grewen, K.M., Coffee, K.A., Algoe, S.B., Firestine, A.M., Arevalo, J.M., Ma, J. & Cole, S.W. (2013). Proc Natl Acad Sci USA 110(33): 13684-9. doi: 10.1073/pnas.1305419110.

Frankl, V.E. (2006). Man's Search for Meaning. Boston: Beacon Press.

Friedman, E., Hayney, M., Love, G., Singer, B., & Ryff, C. (2007). Plasma interleukin-6 and soluble IL-6 receptors are associated with psychological well-being in aging women. Health Psychology, 26(3), 305-313.

Gallup & Healthways. (2014). State of global well-being: Results of the Gallup-Healthways Global Well-Being Index. Gallup, Inc. & Healthways.

Gartenberg, C., Prat, A., & Serafeim, G. (2016). Corporate purpose and financial performance. Harvard Business School Working Paper No. 17-023, September 2016. Retrieved September 30, 2017. http://nrs.harvard.edu/urn-3:HUL.InstRepos:30903237.

Gladwell, M. (2002). The tipping point: How little things can make a big difference. New York: Back Bay Books.

Global Purpose Movement. https://www.globalpurposemovement.org.

Levoy, G. https://www.gregglevoy.com.

Gustin, J. (2019). Personal interview.

Happiness Research Institute & Nordic Council of Ministers. (2018). In the shadow of happiness. Analysis 01/2018. Denmark: Nordic Council of Ministers. http://norden.diva-portal.org/smash/get/diva2:1236906/FULLTEXT02.pdf.

Haramein, N. (2012). Quantum gravity and the holographic mass. Physical Review & Research International ISSN: 2231-1815, 2013, 270-292.

Hedburg, P., Gustafson, Y., Alex, L., & Brulin, C. (2010). Depression in relation to purpose in life among a very old population: A five-year follow-up study. Aging and Mental Health, 14(6), 757-763.

Hill, P.L., Burrow, A.L., & Bronk, K.C. (2014). Persevering with positivity and purpose: An examination of purpose commitment and positive affect as predictors of grit. Journal of Happiness Studies, 17(1): 267-269. DOI 10.1007/s10902-014-9593-5.

Hill, P.L., Turiano, N.A., Mroczek, D.K., & Burrow, A.L. (2016). The value of a purposeful life: Sense of purpose predicts greater income and net worth. Journal of Research in Personality, 65, 38-42. doi: 10.1016/j.jrp.2016.07.003.

Hillman, J. (1996). The soul's code: In search of character and calling. New York: Warner Books.

Imperative, LinkedIn. (2016). Purpose at work: The largest global study on the role of purpose in the workforce. 2016 Purpose Workforce Index. https://cdn.imperative.com/media/public/Global_Purpose_Index_2016.pdf.

Kang, Y., Strecher, V.J., Kim, E., & Falk, E.B. (2019). Purpose in life and conflict-related neural responses during health decision-making. Health Psychology. DOI: 10.1037/hea0000729).

Kaplan, A and Anzaldi, L. (2015). New movement in neuroscience: A purpose-driven life. Cerebrum: The Dana Forum on Brain Science, 2015: 7. https://www.ncbi.nlm.nih.gov/pmc/articles/PMC4564234/.

Kashdan, T.B. (2015). What do scientists know about finding a purpose in life? The psychology of ultimate concerns. Psychology Today 2/24/2015. https://www.psychologytoday.com/us/blog/curious/201502/what-do-scientists-know-about-finding-purpose-in-life.

Kelly, T. (2009). True Purpose: 12 strategies for discovering the difference you are meant to make. Berkeley: Transcendent Solutions Press.

Kelly, T. (2019). Personal interview.

Keyes, C.L.M. (2011). Authentic purpose: The spiritual infrastructure of life. Journal of Management, Spirituality & Religion, 8(4), 281–297.

Kim, E.S., Strecher, V. & Ryff, C.D. (2014). Purpose in life and use in preventive health care services. www.pnas.org/cgi/doi/10.1073/pnas.1414826111.

Kim E., Sun, J., Park, N., & Peterson C. (2013a). Purpose in life and reduced incidence of stroke in older adults: The Health and Retirement Study." Journal of Psychosomatic Research. 74: 427-432.

Kim, E., Sun, J., Park, N., Kubzansky, L., Peterson, C. (2013b). Purpose in life and reduced risk of Myocardial Infarction among older US adults with Coronary Heart Disease: A two year followup." Journal of Behavioral Medicine 36, 124-133.

Korn Ferry. (2016). Purpose powered success. Korn Ferry Institute. https://www.kornferry.com/institute/purpose-powered-success

Kotter, J.P., & Heskett, J.L. (2011). Corporate culture and performance. New York: Free Press.

Kuntzelman, E, & DiPerna, D. (editors). (2017). Purpose rising: A global movement of transformation and meaning. Occidental, CA: Bright Alliance.

Kuntzelman, E.(2019). Personal interview.

Laszlo, E. (2017). Intelligence of the cosmos: Why are we here? New answers from the frontiers of science. Rochester, VT: Inner Traditions.

Lewis, N., Turiano, N., Payne, B., & Hill, P. (2017). Purpose in life and cognitive functioning in adulthood. Aging, Neuropsychology, and Cognition. 24(6). https://doi.org/10.1080/138255 85.2016.1251549

Levoy, G. (1998). Callings: Finding and following an authentic life. New York: Harmony Publishers.

Levoy, G. (2015). Vital signs: The nature and nurture of passion. New York: TarcherPerigee Publishers.

Levoy, G, 2019. Personal interview.

Madrozo, V.L. (2014). Identity, purpose and well-being among emerging adult Hispanic women. Florida International University Digital commons. DOI: 10.25148/etd.FI14071157

Malin, H., Morton, E., Nadal, M., & Smith, K.A. (2019). Purpose and coping with adversity: A repeated measures, mixed-methods study with young adolescents. Journal of Adolescence 76, 1-11.

McLeod, L.E. (2012). Selling with noble purpose: How to drive revenue and do work that makes you proud. San Francisco: Wiley Publishers.

McKnight, P.E. & Kashdan, T.B. (2009). Purpose in life as a system that creates and sustains health and well-being: An integrative, testable theory. Review of General Psychology, 13, 242-251.

Peele, Brandon. (2018). Planet on purpose: Your guide to genuine prosperity, authentic leadership and a better world. Balboa Press, 2018.

Plotkin, B. (2003). Soulcraft: Crossing into the mysteries of nature and psyche. Novato, CA: New World Library.

Plotkin, B (2008). Nature and the human soul: Cultivating wholeness and community in a fragmented world. Novato, CA: New World Library.

Plotkin, B. (2013). Wild mind: A Field guide to the human psyche. Novato, CA: New World Library.

Plotkin, B. (2017). The realm of purpose least realized: But most essential in our time of radical, global change. In E. Kuntzelman and D. DiPerna (eds), Purpose rising: A global movement of transformation and meaning. Occidental, CA: Bright Alliance.

Plotkin B. (2019). Personal interview.

Prairie, B.C., Scheier, M.F., Matthews, K.A., Chang, C.C. & Hess, F. (2011). A higher sense of purpose in life is associated with sexual enjoyment in midlife women. Menopause, 18(8), 839-44. doi:10.1097/gme.0b013e31820befca.

Progoff, I. (1980). At a journal workshop: Writing to access the power of the unconscious and evoke creative ability. New York: TarcherPerigee.

Purpose Guides Institute. https://www.purposeguides.org.

Rainey, L. (2014) The search for purpose in life: An exploration of purpose, the search process, and purpose anxiety." Master's thesis. Philadelphia: University of Pennsylvania. http://repository.upenn.edu/mapp_capstone/60

Rockind, C.L. (2011). Living on purpose: Why purpose matters and how to find it. Unpublished masters thesis. Masters of Applied Positive Psychology Program. Philadelphia: The University of Pennsylvania.

Ryff, C.D. (1989). Beyond Ponce de Leon and life satisfaction: New directions in quest of successful ageing. International Journal of Behavioral Development, 12 (1), 35-55.

Sarafeim, G. & Gartenberg, C. (2016). The type of purpose that makes companies more profitable. Brighton, MA: Harvard Business Review. Retrieved on October 21, 2018. https://hbr.org/2016/10/the-type-of-purpose-that-makes-companies-more-profitable.

Singer, J., Cummings, C., Moody, S.A., & Benuto, L. (2019). Reducing burnout, vicarious trauma, and secondary traumatic stress through investigating purpose in life in social workers. Journal of Social Work. Retrieved on November 12, 2019, https://doi.org/10.1177/1468017319853057.

Sone, T., Nakaya, N., Ohmori, K., Shimazu, T., Higashiguchi, M., Kakizaki, M., Kikuchi, N., Kuriyama, S., & Tsuji, I. (2008). Psychosomatic Medicine. 70(6): 709-715. doi: 10.1097/PSY.0b013e31817e7e64.

Steger, M.F. (2009). Meaning in life. In C. R. Snyder & S. J. Lopez (Eds.), Oxford handbook of positive psychology (2nd Ed.) (pp. 679-687). New York: Oxford University Press.

Steger, M.F. (2012). Experiencing meaning in life: Optimal functioning at the nexus of well

being, psychopathology, and spirituality. In P.T. Wong (Ed.), The human quest for meaning: Theories, research, and applications (2nd ed.) (pp. 165-184). New York: Routledge.

Stengel, J. (2011). Grow: How ideals power growth and profit at the world's greatest companies. New York: Crown Business.

Smith J. (2006). Seeds of deception. Portland, ME: Yes! Books.

Smith J. (2019). Personal Interview.

Smith, B.W., Tooley, E.M., Montague, E.Q., Robinson, A.E., Cosper, C.J., & Mullins P.G. (2008). The role of resilience and purpose in life in habituation to heat and cold pain. Journal of Pain 10(5): 493-500. doi: 10.1016

Stillman, T.F., Lambert, N.M., Fincham, F.D., & Baumeister, R. (2010). Meaning as magnetic force: Evidence that meaning in life promotes interpersonal appeal, Social Psychological & Personality Science. https://doi.org/10.1177/1948550610378382.

Telzer, E., Fuligni, A., Liberman, M., & Galvan, A. (2014). Neural sensitivity to eudaimonic and hedonic rewards differentially predict adolescent depressive symptoms over time." Proceedings of the National Academy of Sciences. 111(8): 6600-6605).

True Purpose Institute. http://www.truepurposeinstitute.com.

Wilber, K. (2000). Integral psychology: Consciousness, spirit, psychology, therapy. Boulder, CO: Shambhala Publications.

Windsor, T.D., Curtis R.G., & Luszcz, M.A. (2015). Sense of purpose as a psychological resource for aging well. Dev Psychol. 51(7): 975-86. doi: 10.1037/dev0000023.

Chapter 3

Cook-Greuter, S.R. (1999). Postautonomous ego development: A study of its nature and measurement. (habits of mind, transpersonal psychology, Worldview). Dissertation Abstracts International: Section B: The Sciences and Engineering, 60(6-B), 3000.

Cook-Greuter, S.R. (2013). Ego development: Nine levels of increasing embrace in ego development. A full spectrum theory of vertical growth and meaning making. www.cook-greuter.com.

Csikszentmihalyi, M. (1990). Flow: The psychology of optimal experience. New York: Harper & Row.

Damon, W., Menon J., Bronk, K.C. (2003). The development of purpose during adolescence. Applied Developmental Science, 7(3): 119-128.

Dethmer, J. & Chapman, D. 4 ways of leading. San Francisco: Conscious Leadership Group. https://conscious.is.

Erickson, E.H. (1968). Identity; youth and crisis. New York: Norton Books.

Gebser, J. (1985). The ever-present origin. Athens, OH: Ohio University Press.

Graves, C. (2002). Claire W Graves: Levels of human existence. Santa Barbara: ECLET Publishing.

Kegan, R.L. (1994). In over our heads: The mental demands of modern life. Cambridge, MA: Harvard University Press.

Kelley, T. (2019). Personal Interview.

Kuntzelman, E. (2019). Personal communication, interview.

Loevinger, J. (1976). Ego development: Conceptions and theories. San Francisco: Jossey-Bass.

Loevinger, J. (1998). Technical foundations for measuring ego development: The Washington University Sentence Completion test. Mahwah, NJ: Laurence Erlbaum Associates.

Murray, T. (2017). Sentence completion assessments for ego development, meaning-making, and wisdom maturity, including STAGES. Integral Leadership Review. August-November. www.integralleadershipreview.com.

O'Fallon, T. Stages International. www.stagesinternational.com.

O'Fallon, T. (2013). The senses: Demystifying awakening. Sonoma, CA: Integral Theory Conference. www.terriofallon.com.

O'Fallon, T. (2015). Stages: Growing up is waking up—interpenetrating quadrants, states and structures. Retrieved on August 20, 2017 www.terriofallon.com.

Plotkin, B. (2008). Nature and the human soul: Cultivating wholeness and community in a fragmented world. Novato CA: New World Library.

Plotkin, B. (2017). The realm of purpose least realized: But most essential in our time of radical, global change. In Kuntzelman & DiPerna, D. (eds), Purpose rising: A global movement of transformation and meaning. Occidental, CA: Bright Alliance.

Plotkin, B. (2019). Personal interview.

Ronstadt, L. (2019). Quote from The Sound of My Voice. Greenwich Entertainment. Filmmakers: Rob Epstein and Jeffrey Friedman.

Seligman, M.E.P. (2002). Authentic happiness: Using the new positive psychology to realize your potential for lasting fulfillment. New York: Free Press.

Seligman, M.E.P. (2011). Flourish: A visionary new understanding of happiness and well-being. New York: Atria.

Wilber, K. (2001). A theory of everything: An integral vision for business, politics, science and spirituality. Boston: Shambhala.

Wilber, K. (2006). Integral spirituality: A startling new role for religion in the modern and postmodern world. Boston: Shambhala.

Chapter 4

American Academy of Child & Adolescent Psychiatry (2014). Attachment Disorders, No. 85. https://www.aacap.org/AACAP/Families_and_Youth/Facts_for_Families/FFF-Guide/Attachment-Disorders-085.aspx.

O'Fallon, T. Stages International. www.stagesinternational.com.

O'Fallon, T. Barta K (2017) Essentials Course Manual, Stages International. www.stagesinternational.com.

O'Fallon, T. & Barta, K. (2019). Stages Certification for Coaching, Counseling & Psychotherapy Diagnostics Manual. Stages International. www.stagesinternational.com.

Worldometers (2020). Retrieved from https://www.worldometers.info/demographics/world-demographics/ on 12/30/19.

Chapter 5

Beck, D.E. & Cowan, C.C. (1995). Spiral dynamics: Mastering values, leadership and change: Exploring the new science of memetics. Maiden, MA: Blackwell Publications.

Bennett, N. & Lemoine, GJ. (2014). What VUCA really means for you. Harvard Business Review. Jan-Feb 2014. Retrieved on January 1, 2020 https://hbr.org/2014/01/what-vuca-really-means-for-you.

O'Fallon, T. & Barta, K. (2017). Essentials Course Manual, Stages International. www.stagesinternational.com.

Maslow, A.H. (1943). A theory of human motivation. Psychological Review, 50(4): 370-96.

Chapter 6

Bennett, N. & Lemoine, GJ. (2014). What VUCA really means for you. Harvard Business Review. Jan-Feb 2014. Retrieved on January 1, 2020 https://hbr.org/2014/01/what-vuca-really-means-for-you.

O'Donohue, J. For a new beginning. http://www.poetry-chaikhana. com/O/ODonohueJohn/

O'Fallon, T. (2016). Personal communication.

O'Fallon, T. (2017). Personal communication.

O'Fallon, T. and Barta K (2017) Essentials Course Manual, Stages International. www.stagesinternational.com.

Science Daily. (2011). Retrieved on January 9, 2020 https://www. sciencedaily.com/releases/2011/08/110823180459.htm.

Living Planet Index. (2018). World Wildlife Fund. Retrieved on January 9, 2020 http://www.livingplanetindex.org/home/index.

Chapter 7

Almaas, A.H. (2008). The unfolding now: Realizing your true nature through the practice of presence. Boston: Shambhala.

Aurobindo, S. (1990). The life divine. Wilmot, WI: Lotus Light.

Bennett, N. & Lemoine, GJ. (2014). What VUCA really means for you. Harvard Business Review. Jan-Feb 2014. Retrieved on January 1, 2020 https://hbr.org/2014/01/what-vuca-really-means-for-you.

Combs, A. (2013). Transcend and Include: Ken Wilber's contribution to transpersonal psychology. In Friedman, H.L., & Hartelius, G. (Eds.). (2013). The Wiley- Blackwell handbook of transpersonal psychology. West Sussex, U.K: John Wiley & Sons, Ltd

Kotler, S. & Wheal, J. (2018). Stealing fire: How Silicon Valley, the Navy SEALS and maverick scientists are revolutionizing the way we live and work. New York: Dey Publications.

Noar, S.M., Benac, C.N., & Harris, M.S. (2007). Does tailoring matter? Meta-analytic review of tailored print health behavior change interventions. Psychological Bulletin, 4: 673-693.

O'Fallon & Barta, K. (2018). STAGES Certification for Coaching, Counseling and Psychotherapy Courses, Stages International. www.stagesinternational.com.

Prochaska, J.O., DiClemente, C.C., & Norcross, J.C. (1992). In search of how people change: Applications to the addictive behaviors. American Psychologist, 47, 1102-1114. PMID: 1329589.

Prochaska, J.O., Redding, C.A., & Evers, K. (2002). The transtheoretical model and stages of Change. In K. Glanz, B.K. Rimer & Lewis, F.M. (Eds.) Health behavior and health education: theory, research, and practice (3rd Ed.). San Francisco, CA: Jossey-Bass.

Russo-Netzer, P. & Icekson, T. (2020). Engaging with life: Synchronicity experiences as a pathway to meaning and personal growth. Current Psychology Retrieved on 1/10/20 from https://link.springer.com/article/10.1007/s12144-019-00595-1?fbclid=IwAR2Z3bYHEDDhUF9O7_TnAPbC2t9tI1mQOjAIXpx-RCVG9YdMmwx9Dadi3e-c.

Whyte, D. (1996) All the true vows, The House of Belonging. Langley, WA: Many Rivers Press, p. 24.

Wilber, K. (1980). The Atman project: A transpersonal view of human development. Wheaton, IL: Quest Publications.

Wilber, K. (1981). Up from Eden: A transpersonal view of human evolution. Wheaton, IL: Quest Publications.

Chapter 8

Plotkin, B. (2019). Personal Interview.

Youssef, N.A., Lockwood, L., Su, S., Hao, G., & Rutten, B.P.F. (2018). The effects of trauma, with or without PTSD, on the transgenerational DNA methylation alterations in human offsprings. (2018). Brain Science 8(5): 83. Retrieved December 12, 2019, doi: 10.3390/brainsci8050083 https://www.ncbi.nlm.nih.gov/pmc/articles/PMC5977074/

Chapter 9

Almaas, A.H. (2008). The unfolding now: Realizing your true nature through the practice of presence. Boston: Shambhala Publications.

Argyris, C. 1990. Overcoming organizational defenses: Facilitating organizational learning. Englewood Cliffs, NJ: Prentice-Hall.

Barta, K. Stages International.https://www.stagesinternational.com/shadow-patterns/.

Bielenberg, J., Burn, M., Galle, G., & Evitts Dickinson, E. (2016). Think wrong: How to conquer the status quo and do work that matters. San Francisco: Instigator Press.

Blake, J. 2016. Pivot: The only move that matters is your next one. Great Britain: Random House.

Carleton, N. 2016. Fear of the unknown: One fear to rule them all? Journal of Anxiety Disorders Volume 41, June 2016, Pages 5-21 https://doi.org/10.1016/j.janxdis.2016.03.011

Damon, W. (2009) Path to Purpose: How young people find their calling in life. Free Press; Reprint edition (April 7, 2009).

De Boton, A. 2010. The pleasures and sorrows of work. Vintage International.

Graham, P. (2006) Finding work you love. http://www.paulgraham.com/love.html

Harnish, V, 2014. Scaling up: How a few companies make it… and why the rest don't. Gazelles, Inc.

Himmelman, P. (2016). Let me out: Unlock your creative mind and bring your ideas to life. New York: TarcherPerigee.

Jobs, S. (2005). Stanford Report, June 14, 2005. Commencement address at Stanford.

Joshi, S.T., & Schultz, D.E. (2001). H.P. Lovecraft encyclopedia. Westport, CT: Greenwood Press.

Furr, N., & Ahlstrom, P. (2011). Nail it then scale it: The entrepreneur's guide to creating and managing breakthrough innovation. Lexington, KY.

Olsen, D. (2015). The lean product playbook: How to innovate with minimum viable products and rapid customer feedback. Hoboken, NJ: John Wiley & Sons.

Popova, M. (2010). Brain Picking. https://www.brainpickings.org/2010/12/01/tedify-happiness/

Ries, E. (2011). The lean startup: How today's entrepreneurs use continuous innovation to create radically successful businesses. New York: Crown Business.

Stone, H. & Stone, S. https://voicedialogueinternational.com/index.html.

Thoreau, H.D. (1854). Walden and Civil Disobedience. Boston: Ticknor and Fields.

Torbert, B. (2004). Action inquiry: The secret of timely and transforming leadership. San Francisco: Berrett-Koehler Publishers.

Watts, A. (1966). The book: On the taboo against knowing who you are. New York; Vintage Books.

Watts, A. What would you do if money was no object? https://vimeo.com/63961985.

Printed in Great Britain
by Amazon